BRINGING
IN THE
SHEAVES

BRINGING
IN THE
SHEAVES

Transforming Poverty
into Productivity

Revised and Expanded Edition

George Grant

Wolgemuth & Hyatt, Publishers, Inc.
Brentwood, Tennessee

Wolgemuth & Hyatt, Publishers, Inc. is a commercial information packager whose mission is to publish and distribute books that lead individuals toward:

- A personal faith in the one true God: Father, Son, and Holy Spirit;
- A lifestyle of practical discipleship; and
- A worldview that is consistent with the historic, Christian faith.

Moreover, the company endeavors to accomplish this mission at a reasonable profit and in a manner which glorifies God and serves His Kingdom.

American Vision is a Christian educational and communications organization devoted to the restoration of America's Biblical foundation. American Vision's purpose is to provide the educational material necessary to help God's people develop and implement a Biblical World View, that is, to apply all of God's Word to all of life.

American Vision's work includes studies on the family, church, education, law, ethics, art, medicine, journalism, science, economics, business, war and peace issues, welfare reform, foreign affairs, and civil government. For more information about American Vision's work and a free subscription to "The Biblical World View" perspective newsletter, write: American Vision, Post Office Box 720515, Atlanta, GA 30328.

Unless otherwise noted, all Scripture quotations are either the author's own translations or are from the New King James Version of the Bible, copyrighted 1984 by Thomas Nelson, Inc., Nashville, Tennessee.

The Villars Statement on Relief and Development, copyrighted 1987 by the Villars Committee on Relief and Development, Office of Communications, Philadelphia, Pennsylvania, is reprinted by permission.

Wolgemuth & Hyatt, Publishers, Inc., P.O. Box 1941, Brentwood, Tennessee 37027.

Printed in the United States of America.

Library of Congress Cataloging-in-Publication Data

Grant, George, 1954-
    Bringing in the sheaves.

Bibliography: p.
Includes indexes.
    1. Charity organization.   2. Charity organization — United States.
    3. Poor — United States.   4. Social service — Religious aspects —
    Christianity.   I. Title.

HV40.G68   1988   362.5'57'0973   88-27662
ISBN 0-943497-34-5

To Don Martin,
who daily gathers sheaves,
and
To Karen Grant,
my beloved, of course.

CONTENTS

AUTHOR'S NOTE

All the stories and vignettes in this book are true. In some, names have been changed; in others, editorial liberties have been taken to combine certain events for purposes of clarity or illustration. But in all instances, the events and conversations accurately reflect factual situations.

Many thanks are due to the hundreds of men, women, and children with whom I have talked and whom I interviewed over the years. I owe a special debt of gratitude to the clients and staff of HELP Services Women's Center. These stories are their stories.

ACKNOWLEDGMENTS

To call this book mine is both true and false. It is true in that the labor of committing words and phrases to paper was mine alone. It is false in that the labor would have been utterly impossible apart from the graciousness of many others. "There is no new thing upon the earth," wrote Francis Bacon, "so that all knowledge is but remembrance, and thus Solomon giveth the sentence, that all novelty is but oblivion."

When the idea for the first edition of this book was little more than wishful thinking, Gary DeMar, Bob Dwelle, George Getschow, David Chilton, Franky Schaeffer, James Jordan, and Gary North all spent precious time patiently instructing, guiding and coaching me in my work with the poor.

When I had actually begun the task of writing, the faithful people of Believers Fellowship and ChristChurch—the people who actually pioneered the principles of Biblical charity in Houston throughout the decade of the eighties—supported me, prayed for me, and encouraged me. Mike and Theresa Powdrill, Kelly and Karen Hartman, Mike and Karen Chakerian, Doug and Debbie DeGeus, Harley and Becky Belew, Brian and Lanita Martin, Kemper and Bekah Crabb, Dave and Marlin Marshall, J.D. and Helene McWilliams, Ray and Karen Plevyak, Frank and Mary Marshall, and Don and Suzanne Martin were especially helpful, taking up many of my duties in the ministry and enthusiastically cheering me on. And Kathe Salazar, Penny Kemp, and Dot Massey gave of their time, energy, and resources to make it all happen. Any measure of thanks is surely inadequate.

Once the first edition—which actually was never released to the bookstore marketplace—was published, a number of people worked selflessly to see that it received wide circulation among

journalists, churchworkers, relief workers, politicians, econo-
mists, teachers, and businesspersons: Rob Martin of the Fieldstead
Institute, Walt and Phil Hibbard of Great Christian Books, Howard
and Roberta Ahmanson of Phil Four-Twelve, Doug Foster of
Impact Foundation, and Larry Pratt of the Committee to Protect
the Family, as well as Herb Schlossberg, Bill and Connie Marshner,
Marvin Olasky, Gordon Walker, Tom Thompson, Gary Metz,
David Thoburn, David Dunham, Bruce Tippery, Greg Badgett,
Bill and Mary Pride, and Michael Hyatt. In fact, were it not for
their valiant efforts to promote the book, I'm sure I never would
have had the chance to prepare this fully revised second edition
for the general bookstore marketplace. To all these friends, co-
workers, and counselors I am again extremely thankful. Together
they have bestowed upon me the gracious gifts of faith, hope,
and love.

Finally, I am grateful to my wife, Karen, and to our children,
Joel, Joanna, and Jesse: "grow strong, my love and my life, that
you may stand unshaken when I fall, that I may know that the
shattered fragments of my song will come at last to finer melody
in you."

Feast of Dominic and Lide
Fort Worth, Texas

FOREWORD

In the seventies and eighties there grew to great intensity a debate within the evangelical world concerning the relative importance of evangelism and social action, the latter of which was understood principally as the helping of the poor. For most of those in the fray on both sides, evangelism meant the preaching of the Gospel to bring people to a saving faith in Christ. The social action side carried a meaning that was somewhat more vague — for some, it meant personal charitable activity; for others, it meant primarily supporting humanitarian activity by the State.

This debate was evidence of a terrible weakness in the Church, in both its theology and its practice. Evangelicals were united in their insistence on the Bible as the rule of faith and practice, and yet were unable to realize that the debate was being conducted on grounds that were foreign to Biblical thinking. The Law, the Prophets, the Gospels, and the Epistles are devoid of any idea that there is a contradiction between the communication of God's grace on the one hand and the doing of good works on the other. Indeed, it was in the midst of his missionary journeys that Paul organized the collection of funds for the Christians in Jerusalem who were living in privation. That ministry was the prime example of the unity between believing rightly and doing good.

Throughout the New Testament, love is described as the identifying mark of the Christian community to its pagan neighbors, its authenticating feature, that which proves that God's life is in its midst. James's statement that "faith without works is dead" is of one piece with the entire Biblical witness that the separation of the inner life from the exterior one makes no sense. Similarly, works without faith is of no religious significance except as a continuing testimony of the futility of trying to save ourselves. The task remains for each generation of Christians to ascertain how it can live an integrated life, fully exemplifying the inner and outer dimensions in the wholeness that only Biblical faith makes possible.

Once this is agreed upon, we're ready to address the thorniest issue of those debates: whether our responsibilities to the poor are to be discharged primarily by personal charitable action or through supporting the humanitarian policies of the State. There may have been some excuse to debate that issue ten years ago, but there is none today. Now that the "war on poverty" has entered its third decade, its record of abysmal failure is becoming increasingly clear. The substitution by officers of the state of humanitarian "good works" for Christian charity has been a disaster almost without precedent.

We now have presented for us in bone-chilling detail by such writers as P. T. Bauer, George Gilder, and Charles Murray how poor people, in our own country and abroad, have been transformed by humanitarian policy into helpless wards of the State, completely dehumanized by the programs that were supposed to be motivated by compassion. The bitterest denunciations of the State welfare system come from the pens of black economists Thomas Sowell and Walter Williams, fed up with seeing their people destroyed by the policies of "compassion."

It's a shame that we have to keep on going over that ground to convince people that State welfare is not the means for being obedient to the Biblical commands to help the poor. Yet, the battle has been largely won on the intellectual front, and we have only a mopping up operation to conduct, as well as the political task of making that victory operational.

But something is missing. If the welfare system is the wrong method for helping the poor, are we sure we want to find the right method? The political left has not been bashful about ascribing opposition to welfare to a callous disregard for the well-being of the poor. There may be something self-serving in that ascription, but there is also some truth in it. A friend of mine, who headed up one of the Reagan administration's poverty agencies, recently told me of his experiences after taking over the agency from the preceding administration. He found that the political left fought him every step of the way, as he expected. But he also discovered that conservatives opposed him in his quest to see that the legitimate cause of justice for the poor was served. He concluded that many conservatives are not interested in the poor.

Christians should not be in the position of choosing between those opposing pagan ideals. The State is not our savior and we do not look to it for earthly redemption, nor is it the conduit through which we advance our own interests at the expense of our fellow citizens.

That brings us to the questions of how Christians are to obey the Biblical mandate to serve the poor after they have identified the State welfare system for what it is. How can we recognize who we are to help and who we are to avoid helping? How can we accomplish the task through the communal actors and activities that the Biblical commands place at the center of our loyalties: family and Church? How can we ensure that poor people become productive and join us in assisting the helpless, rather than becoming our wards and dependents? How can we translate the prescriptions that worked in pastoral settings three thousand years ago into terms that make them effective in doing God's work in the late twentieth century? Above all, how can we comprehend our responsibility to help the poor in such a way that it is integrated with a Biblical understanding of the lordship of Christ over the whole cosmos, so that we don't isolate this work from the rest of life, thus idolizing it and turning it into something evil?

We're indebted to George Grant for helping us see our way through this complex of issues. Rather than continuing to beat the dead carcass of the welfare system, he leaves the putrefying mess and heads for fresh air. He shows us our real responsibilities, quoting the same Biblical passages as the defenders of public welfare. But he does it without the sense of helplessness and guilt that are the identifying features of humanist preachments, including those erroneously advanced by Christians.

Moreover, he presents the problem to us in its proper historical context. We don't face unprecedented problems; the poor have been with us from the beginning, and the Christian Church has always been doing something about it. C. H. Spurgeon's orphanages in nineteenth-century London were not as famous as his pulpit, but they were as fully a part of his ministry. We're not isolated in either time or space, Grant shows us, but are part of a community of vigorous service to the poor as far back as the ancients and as near as our families and neighbors. The body of Christ is the ministering agent that accomplishes God's commandments, and that includes the ministry to the poor.

But Grant intends this book to be a manual for service as well as a tool for understanding our true role in helping poor people. We learn in it how to make visible the hidden poor; how to gather and distribute food; how to find lodging for the homeless; how to minister spiritually as we help physically; how to anticipate and protect against legal challenges; how to work together as families and communities, thus avoiding defeat by the insidious atomization that is wreaking so much havoc on the larger society.

I have not read anything else so useful in helping us move away from the necessary but limited task of criticism and toward practical accomplishment in this vital area. Grant has based his work on solid analysis and solid experience. But it's not the last word. If we're able to put what he has told us into practice, we should be able to build up a solid body of knowledge that will make the next manual that much more useful. This process is called standing on the shoulders of our predecessors. I think George Grant will be happy to have his shoulders stood upon.

Herbert Schlossberg

INTRODUCTION

The more things change, the more they stay the same.

Although that "quoheleth" truism may not have universal application, it certainly holds true when it comes to poverty in America.

When I began to research and write the first edition of this book, we were in the midst of the longest and deepest period of sustained economic decline in American peacetime history.[1] The combination of runaway inflation and entrenched recession had crippled industry and subverted the established economic wisdom of the day.[2] Poverty was rampant.[3]

By the time I began the task of revising and restructuring the text for this second edition, we were in the midst of the longest and deepest period of sustained economic growth in American peacetime history.[4] The combination of steady recovery and confident entrepreneurism had rejuvenated industry and established an all new economic wisdom.[5] But poverty was still rampant.[6]

Indeed, the more things change, the more they stay the same.

So, despite the fact that the structural economy seems to be dramatically different today than it was just a decade ago, the need for a viable plan to transform poverty into productivity — to bring in the sheaves — is just as urgent today as it was then.

That has made revising this text much easier than I had originally envisioned. Apart from a few structural changes here and there — updating the statistics, copy editing earlier snafus, and heightening the clarity of the prose — I have actually done very little new work. Chapter Two is completely new, as are the Appendixes. And Chapters Three, Four, and Five have had extensive overhauls. But the rest of the book remains pretty well intact from the limited-circulation first edition.

Thus, as before, *Bringing in the Sheaves* is essentially a practical primer for families, Churches, and private enterprises who wish to begin erecting effective models of Biblical charity all over the country. As such, it is not primarily theory. It is primarily practice.

What can be done to help the homeless?

What can be done to ease the unemployment crunch?

How can we effectively get food to the hungry, clothes to the naked, and protection to the vulnerable?

And how do we do these things without adding fuel to the fires of ingratitude, sloth, negligence, and irresponsibility?

Bringing in the Sheaves outlines some of the Scriptural answers to these questions, and then hammers out practical applications. But, be apprised: these are but a beginning. No single book can possibly exhaust the compassionate alternatives open to faithful followers of Christ who willingly work with the poor and afflicted.[7] *Bringing in the Sheaves* is not an attempt to be a comprehensive manual.[8]

It is simply a start, an introduction, a catalyst. Neither does the book attempt to answer all the questions of wealth, property, and statecraft that seem to arise naturally in Christian circles when the subject of poverty is broached. Beside the fact that such questions are beyond the scope of this book, the excellent works of P. T. Bauer,[9] Stuart Butler,[10] Anna Kontratas,[11] Charles Murray,[12] Lawrence Mead,[13] John Jefferson Davis,[14] George Gilder,[15] Ronald Nash,[16] Walter Williams,[17] Michael Novak,[18] Henry Hazlitt,[19] Warren Brookes,[20] Gary North,[21] Herbert Schlossberg,[22] Thomas Sowell,[23] and David Chilton[24] have adequately answered them. *Bringing in the Sheaves* is a book of action alternatives, not of philosophical theorems and treatises.

In Part I, the dimensions of poverty are sketched in broad strokes. If we are to deal successfully with the dark denizens of deprivation, then we'll need to know what we're up against. Sun Tzu once said, "If we know neither ourselves nor our enemy, then in a hundred battles we will suffer a hundred defeats."[25] As Christians, we are called to victory. Hence, it would behoove us to prepare for victory rather than for defeat.

In Part II, the Scriptural solutions to poverty are introduced. And *what* solutions! Contrary to our current cosmopolitan concept of things, systemic urban poverty is nothing new. The ghetto did not take God by surprise. The Bible has answers.

In Part III, the strategy for implementing Scriptural solutions to poverty is mapped out. Throughout history, God has moved individuals and groups to accomplish great feats of compassion on behalf of the impoverished or the afflicted. Christian history is marked by the founding of hospitals, orphanages, almshouses, soup kitchens, etc. Slowly, as the state has assumed more and more responsibilities, the private initiative function in charity has diminished greatly in importance. The strategy for implementing Scriptural solutions to poverty involves reasserting the place and importance of families, Churches, and private enterprises in the work of compassion.

In Part IV, specific steps of action, steps that have been tested on the anvil of experience, are detailed. Cornelius Van Til has written, "The Bible is authoritative on everything of which it speaks. And it speaks of everything."[26] Thus, we can be assured that the Bible not only explains the whos, whats, whens, and wheres of compassion, it enumerates authoritative hows as well. In these chapters, we'll examine them carefully.

Part V is the book's conclusion. It is a look toward the future. It is a glimpse of the "very great and precious promises" that God has set before us (2 Peter 1:4). It is a fitting capstone of hope and confidence for the work of the Gospel in the world.

Change. That's the goal of Biblical charity. Its design is to pull people out of the poverty trap, out of the welfare muck and mire, and change their whole approach to life, family, and work.

Bringing in the Sheaves is offered in the humble hope that it may spur the faithful men, women, and Churches of this great nation and around the globe toward that change.

PART ONE

THE CRISIS

As long as there shall exist, by reason of law and custom, a social condemnation, which, in the face of civilization, artificially creates hells on earth, and complicates a destiny that is divine, with human fatality; so long as the three problems of the age — the degradation of man by poverty, the ruin of woman by starvation, and the dwarfing of childhood by physical and spiritual night — are not solved; so long as, in certain regions, social asphyxia shall be possible; in other words, and from a yet more extended point of view, so long as ignorance and misery remain on earth, books like this cannot be useless.

Victor Hugo (1862)

Sowing in the morning,
    sowing seeds of kindness;
Sowing in the noontide,
    and the dewy eve;
Waiting for the harvest
    and the time of reaping;
We shall come rejoicing,
    bringing in the sheaves!

Bringing in the sheaves,
    bringing in the sheaves;
We shall come rejoicing,
    bringing in the sheaves!

Sowing in the sunshine,
    sowing in the shadows;
Fearing neither clouds
    nor winter's chilling breeze;
By and by the harvest,
    and the labor ended;
We shall come rejoicing,
    bringing in the sheaves!

Bringing in the sheaves,
    bringing in the sheaves;
We shall come rejoicing,
    bringing in the sheaves!

Going forth with weeping,
    sowing for the Master;
Tho' the loss sustained
    our flesh often grieves;
But when our working's over,
    He will bid us welcome;
We shall come rejoicing,
    bringing in the sheaves!

Bringing in the sheaves,
    bringing in the sheaves;
We shall come rejoicing,
    bringing in the sheaves!

Knowles Shaw

ONE

A CRY FOR HELP:
THE BRIDGE

By the time I arrived on the scene, a crowd had already gathered. Some stood about uncomfortably talking in hushed and guarded tones. Others shouted up at the solitary figure perched between trusses of the bridge. Others had sauntered out into the knee-deep waters of the San Jacinto River, hoping for an unhindered view of the action.

Making my way through the oglers and the curiosity seekers, I got to within ten yards of the bridge when a voice split the air.

"Preacher, don't you come no closer. I'm gonna jump. I'm gonna jump, you hear?"

Squinting in the half-light, I recognized the huddled and desperate form clinging to the rusty girder. It was Johnny Porston. Instantly my mind began racing as I offered words of comfort, assurance, and Scripture. Shivering in the damp coolness of twilight, I talked, I pleaded, I exhorted, and I prayed.

Just as the police arrived, I decided I had best make a move before this whole affair raged out of control. I certainly didn't want Johnny to spend the night in jail. Slowly I extended my hand toward him and inched across the catwalk.

"Stop, Preacher! I swear to you, I'll jump! One more inch and I'm nothin' but mangled meat. Just save your time and save your breath; ain't nothin' gonna change my mind now. Things have gone too far. It's all over."

I turned to scan the scene behind me. The crowd was steadily growing, spilling over into the campsite that Johnny and his family had called home for the past three and a half months. The other two dozen or so residents were all standing by the river's edge, watching—heads hung in grief.

It seemed that just yesterday Johnny had come to my office for help. Two of his four children had dysentery and he had no money with which to secure medical attention. He had been in the Houston area for months, but had had only one good job prospect—and that one never panned out. When he had left Philadelphia, he had been full of optimism. After all, everyone knew that Houston was the job Mecca of the nation. It didn't take long for him to discover that that was nothing more than a cruel pipe dream. Ineligible for food stamps, welfare, or unemployment, Johnny and his family ended up living out of their battered old Torino wagon with no food, no job, no money, and, now, no hope.

Teetering sixty feet above the shallow waters, Johnny sputtered his tear-choked good-bye.

"Listen, Preacher, you take care of the kids, you hear? They'll be a lot better off in your hands. You know I tried. I just can't go on any more. I've been gagging on my old Philly pride for too long. There ain't no place in this world for me no more. Ain't no jobs and ain't gonna be either. Hey, put in a word for me, will ya? With the Man upstairs?"

The dull, sickening thud of Johnny's body on the surface of the sand bar still sounded in my ears weeks later. The shrieks and the gasps and the wail of the sirens invaded my every waking moment. And I knew that on that day and the one after and the one after that, I would be witness to the suffering of dozens more just like Johnny—homeless, jobless, penniless, and, worst of all, hopeless. I knew, too, that I had to do something, that I had to respond to the crisis of poverty.

But how?

Despite an ever-thickening veneer of growth and recovery, the shift from assembly lines to bread lines has become one of the most prominent features of the American economic landscape. According to the Census Bureau, 1980 saw a twelve percent jump in the number of persons living below the official poverty threshold.[1] In 1981, the rise was nearly nine percent,[2] and in recession-scarred 1982, the figures increased another eight percent.[3] In 1983, long-term unemployment—more than six months without work—hit a post-World War II record of nearly three million persons, one-fifth of all the unemployed workers currently on the dole.[4] And the much ballyhooed recovery did little to slow the slide of the bottom third of the economy into dire privation. In 1984, another half million workers became dependent on welfare and unemployment.[5] In 1985, nearly thirty-three million Americans were living below the poverty line — just over fourteen percent of the entire population. Another half-million were added in 1984.[6] And in 1987, the numbers continued to increase even though the percentage had at last begun to fall ever so slightly.[7] The additional tragedy of an estimated two million homeless poor scattered about in our alleyways, warehouses, and public parks only compounded an already obstinately complex crisis.[8]

How could I possibly make a difference?

I honestly didn't know. But I did know that I must try. I did know that it was my Christian duty to search the Scriptures and to find solutions. I knew that if the goal of building a Christian civilization out of the rubble of contemporary American culture was to be achieved in any measure, believers would have to tend to this all too obviously untended issue. We would have to hammer out a theology that was both Scriptural and compassionate. We would have to develop committed Churches. We would have to tailor our various outreaches and programs to specific local needs. And we would have to effect alternatives to the government's failing, flailing efforts. In short, we would have to develop a functioning model of Biblical charity — not just in theory, but in the tough realm of practice.

Much of what follows is the fruit of work toward just such an end at a small Church in Houston, Texas. We never had the luxury of sitting back and formulating our policies and programs at ease. We were in the midst of a crisis. When the oil economy crashed in the early eighties, our city went from boom to bust almost overnight. At one point in 1982 we had between thirty thousand and sixty thousand homeless, dispossessed poor camped about town in tent cities, living out of their cars.[9] At the same time, nearly fifteen percent of our metropolitan region was facing the trauma of unemployment.[10] Social service agencies, public and private, were buried beneath an avalanche of need. We had to do something. So we did.

We made mistakes. Lots of them. Sometimes we learned from them. Sometimes, for quite some time, we didn't. Eventually, however, a pragmatic model was constructed that fit both the Biblical precepts we'd discovered through diligent study and the obvious need we'd confronted through diligent labor.

What we achieved in Houston is not the panacea for all social ills from now 'til evermore. Not by any stretch of the imagination. But it is a start. What we learned in Houston is that functioning models of Biblical charity are not only necessary, they are *possible*. What we learned in Houston is that any Church — even if it must begin with little or no money, little or no resources, little or no staff, and little or no experience — can put together a formidable challenge to the modern notion that poverty is a problem too big for anyone but the government to handle. What we learned in Houston is that we can really make a difference in our world, if we would only take seriously our high calling as believers in the Lord Jesus Christ.

Johnny Porston's jump was a cry for help. It was a cry that none of us can afford the luxury to ignore.

At stake is nothing less than the integrity of the Church in our day — and perhaps even the viability of western civilization itself.

If even one American child is forced to go to bed hungry at night, or if one senior citizen is denied the dignity of proper nutrition, that is a national tragedy.

Ronald Reagan

It was the best of times, it was the worst of times, it was the age of wisdom, it was the age of foolishness, it was the epoch of incredulity, it was the season of Light, it was the season of Darkness, it was the spring of hope, it was the winter of despair, we had everything before us, we had nothing before us.

Charles Dickens

Do you hear the children weeping,
    O my brothers?
The young, young children,
    O my brothers?
They are weeping bitterly!
They are weeping in the playtime of others.

Elizabeth Barrett Browning

The line between hunger and anger is a thin line.

John Steinbeck

Nothing more overwhelms the human spirit, or mocks our values and our dreams, than the desperate struggle for sustenance.

Henry Kissinger

POVERTY: IN THE SHADOW OF PLENTY

The dark specter of poverty stalks the land.

Still.

Virtually unaffected by the erratic cycles of recession and recovery, its shade continues to haunt big cities and small towns, suburbs and farms, ghettos and rural communities, in both good times and bad.

Pitiful ragmen *still* haunt the garbage-strewn alleyways just off Michigan Avenue in Chicago.[1]

Ruthless teenage gangs, riven with hunger and hopelessness, *still* pillage the barrios of east L.A.[2]

Young mothers from Indiana's industrial "burned-over district," made over in skin-tight gold lamé and Spandex, *still* frequent the infamous "Lakeside Strip," supplementing welfare with a few "tricks" on the sly.[3]

With their every earthly possession crammed into filthy shopping bags, the homeless women of Manhattan's midtown *still* wander aimlessly through the rush-hour crowds in Grand Central Station.[4]

Tenement dwellers in East St. Louis *still* line up in swollen fury outside dilapidated government buildings after their food stamp allotments fail to suffice to the end of the month.[5]

Dispossessed farm families from the drought- and debt-ravaged Midwest *still* crowd into grange offices and emergency shelters, brokenhearted and disillusioned.[6]

In a tent city hugging the bank of the San Jacinto River just north of Houston's vast petrochemical complex, elementary school children *still* disembark from their buses and trudge slowly through the muck and mire toward the cardboard and plywood shanties they call "home."[7]

From the steel country of western Pennsylvania to Michigan's automobile towns, from the machine tool factories of Illinois to the red iron ore pits of Minnesota's Mesabi Range, all too many Americans *still* face the brute realities of silent machinery and boarded-up storefronts, with once proud men waiting in welfare lines and leaden-eyed women staring from their windows.[8]

The misery of privation is *still* the daily lot of millions of men, women, and children all across our land.

Still.

That fact offers vivid and irrefutable testimony to the fact that those on the bottom rungs of the economic ladder are immune to recessions and recoveries. It doesn't matter what the price of gold is on the international market, or how the dollar is faring against the pound, the yen, the mark. It doesn't matter what the trade deficits or budget deficits are.[9] For the hungry children in west San Antonio, for the single mothers in the Monogahela Valley, and for the migrant farm workers in Southern California, poverty is not merely a temporary setback. It is a way of life. For them, poverty is trading their dignity for a five-pound block of cheese. It is standing in line at an emergency food center for hours on end, ashamed and silent, but unable to let their children go hungry.

Poverty is *still* with us. It seems that it will be with us always (John 12:8).

Hard Luck in Good Times

According to statistics from the Bureau of the Census, almost thirty-five million Americans are perennially poverty-stricken.[10] More than ten percent of the White population, thirty percent of the Black population, and twenty-five percent of all Hispanics have become part of our society's permanent underclass.[11] More than one-fourth of all American children and almost eighty percent of elderly women living alone live in poverty,[12] all too often in abject poverty.

Despite the fact that one out of every five citizens receives some kind of means-tested public welfare, the stranglehold that poverty wields in their lives intensifies with every passing day.[13]

According to the U.S. Conference of Mayors, of all the problems facing American cities today, "hunger is probably the most prevalent and the most insidious. From all accounts, the numbers of people, including families with children, who have little or nothing to eat, have grown tremendously."[14] And *this* during an economic resurgence.

A recent study released by the Department of Health and Human Services suggested that as many as half a million children under the age of six in the United States suffer from malnutrition.[15] And *this* during a period of steady recovery.

Scattered anecdotes have given way to the cold hard evidence that during the last decade the incidence of infant mortality has begun to rise significantly. The number of low birth weight deliveries has begun to skyrocket, cases of children with stunted growth and "failure to thrive" symptoms have dramatically increased, and the incidence of neonatal water intoxication — infants who are ill from cheap or overdiluted milk — has increased exponentially.[16] And *this* during a time of unparalleled prosperity.

Clearly, a large sector of our society has fallen on "hard luck" in these "good times." In Detroit there has been an almost five-fold increase in households served by emergency food programs since 1980. In San Antonio, requests for food assistance are five times as high as at the beginning of the decade. Requests for assistance in Cleveland have increased by one hundred twelve percent. In New Orleans, calls for emergency assistance are up two hundred twenty-two percent. Almost twice as much food is distributed to the needy in Denver today as in 1980. Soup kitchens in Rochester have seen a seventy-five percent numerical increase. In Oakland, food programs served thirty-three percent more needy families. In Nashville, food bank deliveries have increased by sixty-six percent to meet demands. The National Conference of Catholic Charities, which includes seven hundred human service agencies and two hundred thirty specialized institutions, has doubled its caseload and reported increased requests for emergency aid by four hundred percent. And the Salvation Army has been forced to meet an estimated forty percent growth in requests for emergency relief.[17]

And if all that weren't bad enough, several new trends have emerged in recent years indicating that the stubborn problem of entrenched poverty has reached epidemic and crisis proportions: the feminization of the underclass, the collapse of the family farm, AIDS displacement, and the growth of homelessness.

Feminization

She was used to much better. Tanya Morrison had grown up in an upper-middle-class neighborhood, gone to excellent schools, and spent five years at a pricey women's college on the East Coast. She married a bright young professional with a promising career. They lived in an upscale condominium over-looking the ocean.

But all that is long gone now. "It all seems like a fantasy to me now," she said. "After Mike divorced me, I lost everything." Working sometimes as a waitress, sometimes as a typist in a sec-retarial pool, Tanya can barely make ends meet from month to month. Mike, on the other hand, is living the high life again. "I've only had to go on welfare a couple of times," she told me. "But toward the end of each month, things really get slim. Thank goodness, the kids have never missed a meal. Even if we have Cheerios or macaroni and cheese four or five days in a row, we eat. But it's hard. It's really hard. I don't think I'll ever be able to understand how this could have happened to a woman and her children — in *this* country. How could this happen to me — to us?"

But, of course, it happens all the time to people just like Tanya Morrison and her children. And to people even less fortu-nate. Sociologists call it the *feminization of poverty.*

Evidence everywhere abounds. More than seventy percent of women in the labor force today work out of economic neces-sity.[18] More often than not, they are single, widowed, or divorced. And more often than not, they are poor. An astonishing seventy-five percent of this nation's poverty is now borne by women and their children.[19]

The number of poor families headed by men has actually declined over the past fifteen years by a little more than twenty-five percent.[20] Meanwhile though, the number of women who headed poor families has increased nearly forty percent.[21] Thus, today, a full one third of all the families headed by women is poor, compared to only one tenth of the families headed by men, and a mere one twentieth of the intact, two-parent families.[22]

According to the *Thirteenth Annual Report* of the President's National Advisory Council on Economic Opportunity, "all other things being equal, if the proportion of the poor in female-householder families were to continue to increase at the same rate as it did from 1967 to 1987, the poverty population would be composed solely of women and their children before the year 2000."[23]

The fact is, the liberalization of divorce laws,[24] the elimination of preferential treatment in the workplace,[25] and the crisis in women's health care due to the brutal effects of abortion on demand[26] — all favored planks in the platform of modern feminization — have left women more vulnerable than ever before to the ravages of poverty.[27]

Tanya Morrison can certainly attest to that.

The Farm Crisis

John Tucker has always been a man of the land. "I've never wanted to do anything but farm," he told me. "Ever since I was a little tot, I've wanted to continue what my father had done before me, and his father before that, and on back as far as anyone could remember."

But that dream has been shattered for John, his wife, Lisa, and their four young children. Today they live in an emergency shelter established for families by the Salvation Army. Three years ago he lost his farm to foreclosure. "My family lived on that land, worked that land, and loved that land for seventy-two years," he said. "Now it's gone. And here we sit."

The plight of John Tucker is by no means an isolated incident. According to the Census Bureau, only about fourteen percent of this nation's poor live in the decaying inner cities.[28] Another forty-seven percent live in large metropolitan areas.[29] But all the rest — a frightening thirty-nine percent of the total poor population — live in rural regions.[30] Those nearly fourteen million poor Americans are our farmers, ranchers, loggers, hired hands, and migrant harvesters.[31] They are men, women, and children like the Tuckers.

All across the vast and fertile Farm Belt is mounting alarm that the grim harvest of failures and foreclosures that has threatened the family farm with extinction over the last decade will continue indefinitely.[32] The American farmer is facing the fiercest crisis in fifty years — since the Great Depression.[33] Almost half a million farms are currently threatened with bankruptcy.[34] Nearly seventy-two percent of all persons occupied with full-time agriculture have had to resort to some sort of federal welfare assistance.[35] And the numbers grow with every passing day.

Precipitated by a number of ill-advised political moves — artificial price support programs for farm commodities,[36] easy-to-get federal land bank loans,[37] billions in farm subsidies,[38] and protectionist trade policies[39] — the farm crisis had reached a fever pitch by 1988, leaving thousands, perhaps even millions, of rural families utterly destitute.

And then came drought. "I don't know what we're gonna do," John Tucker told me. "What I do know is that this isn't just my own personal tragedy. It's America's tragedy. And it's downright scary."

AIDS Displacement

Lance Crittendon was once a computer systems analyst for a large Silicon Valley technology consortium. He had a luxuriously comfortable six-figure income, with bonuses, programming royalties, and profit-sharing supplementing his ample salary. He lived alone in a magnificent home in an exclusive adult only planned community. He was living the great American dream.

That was just four years ago. Today Lance is jobless, penniless, and homeless. And if that weren't bad enough, he is dying. Lance has AIDS. "Who could have, or would have, ever imagined this?" he asked me. "I was once on top of the world. And now look at me. If it weren't for this free hospice I'm living in now, I'd be out on the streets. Out with the bag ladies, for heaven's sake. In fact, there are a lot of people that I once socialized with who *are* out there."

Indeed, there are a lot of AIDS patients "out there." According to the Centers for Disease Control in Atlanta, the number of reported AIDS cases is now doubling every twenty months.[40] And the number of people actually infected with the deadly virus may be "one hundred times higher than that of reported cases of AIDS."[41] That means that as many as four million people in the United States have AIDS. By the end of the century, C. Everett Koop, the U.S. surgeon general, estimates that one hundred million people will die of the disease.[42] According to British surgeon Dr. Wilson Carswell, "It is difficult to comprehend a disaster of such a magnitude. It is beyond the scope of one's experience, one's imagination."[43]

Medical care for each one of those patients ranges anywhere from seventy-five to two hundred thousand dollars, only a tiny fraction of which can be feasibly covered by Medicaid or other social welfare programs.[44] Couple that stark economic reality with the fact that AIDS patients are considered pariahs in the workplace and thus spend their final months, or even years, unemployed, and the destitution of a vast proportion of our population becomes a foregone conclusion.

Although research in this area remains somewhat scanty, it appears that more than half of all AIDS patients fall below the poverty line within six months of their diagnosis.[45] Nearly a third wind up homeless, living in welfare hotels, public shelters, charity hospices, or even "out there" on the streets.[46]

"Poverty in this country has taken a nasty turn," Lance said. "Whether this is God's judgment of our sin or not, may be important to determine on an individual level. But on the social level we'd best figure out what to *do*."

Homelessness

They have always been with us. From the glory days of ancient Rome to the high-tech decadence of modern New York, from the Protestant Reformation to the Industrial Revolution, from the Golden Age to the Space Age, they have always haunted our cities and our consciences.

The same beggar who stretched a suppliant palm toward the passing pilgrim outside ancient Jericho can be found today on Colfax Avenue in Denver, still thirsty for wine. The bruised and broken woman who slept in the gutters of medieval London now beds down in a cardboard box on Peachtree Street in Atlanta. The feeble-minded ragman who pillaged the alleys of seventeenth-century Rotterdam now collects tattered bits of rubbish in Macy's shopping bags on the corner of 34th and 7th in Manhattan's midtown. They exist on the fringes, taking meals and shelter when and where they can.[47]

Most of us view their very existence as a shame, a distasteful fact of life, faced, when it must be faced at all, with averted eyes. But the motley ranks of America's homeless are swelling and the recovery has yet to brighten their plight.

No region has been spared. Atlanta's first overnight shelter opened in 1979. Now the city has twenty-seven.[48] Salt Lake City's mayor insists his city has become a "blinking light" for wandering homeless,[49] while Phoenix and Tucson complain that hordes of transients have descended on Arizona and must be repulsed.[50] "Our shelters are full in September, long before it turns cold," says Audrey Rowe, commissioner of social services in Washington, D.C. With one hundred city beds for about twenty thousand homeless, Chicago, like most localities, relies on Church and community groups.[51] Unfortunately, the Churches and community groups have been either ill-equipped, or unwilling, to take on the ever-escalating crisis.

George Getschow of the *Wall Street Journal* has reported that: "Across the United States, tens of thousands of families and individuals . . . have joined the ranks of the new poor . . . homeless, jobless, and dispossessed. Not since the mass economic distress of the Great Depression, which drove the nation's destitute into tin-and-tent towns called Hoovervilles, have so many working-class people suddenly found themselves in such dire straits."[52] Getschow goes on to say, "A recent report by the U.S. Conference of Mayors says thousands of families have been evicted from their homes and are living in cars, campgrounds, tents, and rescue missions."[53]

It is estimated that there are now as many as two million homeless "new poor" in America today.[54] They crowd into tent cities, living out of their cars, under bridges, or, at best, in abandoned substandard shelters. In Pittsburgh, homeless men sleep in caves along the Allegheny River. In Los Angeles, homeless men and women go door-to-door in suburban neighborhoods peddling fruit. In our nation's capital, homeless women sleep on Pennsylvania Avenue in front of the White House. In Houston, the state director of the AFL-CIO tells the jobless to stay out of Texas: "There are no jobs here," he says, "and there are no beds."[55]

Though far from being a *Grapes of Wrath* situation, the crisis is still a formidable one. On the East Coast, Baltimore has nearly ten thousand homeless,[56] Philadelphia has eight thousand,[57] New York City has thirty-six thousand,[58] and the nation's capital has nearly eight thousand.[59] In the Midwest, where unemployment has been especially devastating, there are reportedly eight thousand homeless in Detroit,[60] and another ten thousand in the Hammond metropolitan area.[61] The West Coast has suffered with more than twenty-five hundred homeless new poor in Seattle[62] and over twenty thousand in the Los Angeles/Orange County region.[63] Because of the mass exodus of workers from the post-industrial Midwest and Northeast, the Sun Belt has been especially hard hit. Small cities like Abilene and Nashville struggle under the burden of two thousand homeless new poor,[64] while the Dallas-Fort Worth metroplex and San Antonio face catastrophic conditions with nearly fifteen thousand each.[65] Even cities like Phoenix and San Jose have not escaped. There, homelessness has claimed as much as five percent of the entire population.[66]

Remarkably, most of the homeless poor are not the typical hard-core unemployed. Most were, until the economic roller coaster ride of the seventies and eighties, solid middle-class working families in pursuit of the "American Dream." Most are former steel workers or auto workers, or coal miners, or oilfield workers, or other types of skilled industrial workers. Most have never known unemployment. In fact, most have been adamantly opposed to the welfare system in the United States. They were hard-working people.

These new poor are now crowding into public shelters and soup kitchens to the point where they often outnumber the bums and shopping-bag ladies, who, for years, have had the charities mostly to themselves.

"In Tulsa," says Roland Chambless, the Salvation Army commander there, "most of the people we fed a year ago were derelicts and alcoholics, but today it's mothers and small children."

Sergeant E. D. Aldridge of the Houston Police Department's Special Operations Division, has said, "It used to be that most of the homeless on the streets were alcoholics and things like that. Now, if you talk to them, most seem quite intelligent, middle-class types. They're just flat out and down on their luck."

A recent New York City survey of those staying in shelters there found an extremely high percentage of families and first-time applicants. Half of the men were high school graduates and twenty percent had attended college. They were primarily middle-aged secretaries unable to find work, young construction workers who hadn't worked in months, and laid-off department store clerks who had never been unemployed before.[67]

Gary Cuvillier, who operates a family shelter in New Orleans, says, "Most of the folks we deal with day in and day out are from the fringe of the middle class. Many owned homes before the big lay-offs. None had ever known real want before. What we're seeing is a change in the structure of American society, so fundamental that no one will remain unaffected."

"Lots of long-time indigents are landing in the streets," says Michael Elias, who is the administrator of a shelter near Los Angeles. "But so is a whole new class of people . . . families from Michigan and Ohio . . . middle-class people . . . it's a tragedy."

The Invisibility of the Poor

So, where are they? If there really is such drastic poverty in the shadow of plenty, why aren't we more aware of it? Why are the statistics so difficult to believe?

The fact is, the poorest of the poor are invisible,[68] or, at least, very, very hard to see.

The "invisibility" of the poor is due in part to the suburbanization of our culture. "We don't go to their neighborhoods. They don't come to ours," explains University of Houston political scientist Donald Lutz. "The suburbanization process has geographically stratified America. Thus, the poor are out of sight, out of mind." Except for the hard luck human interest stories that have become standard holiday fare, the poor almost never cross our path. The poor are "invisible" because of where they are.

But many of the poor are "invisible" because of who they are as well.

Of all those living below the official poverty line in America, thirty-five percent are elderly.[69] Despite Social Security benefits,

Medicaid, and Medicare, many of these elderly poor suffer severe privation in one form or another. Some have dropped out of the social care system, too immobilized by illness to travel the distance to the post office, or the grocery store, or the benefits centers. Alone, afraid, and afflicted, is it any wonder that the elderly poor all too often are shuffled off, by time and circumstance, beyond our line of sight? "Invisible."

Another forty-five percent of the poor in America are children.[70] They don't form lobbying groups. They don't march on Washington. They don't picket the unemployment offices. They don't crowd into the public shelters on cold winter nights. They don't line the sidewalks of Times Square wrapped in tattered rags that have known too many seasons. Like most children, they trot out each morning to meet the school bus. Like most children, they spend their days walking the corridors of America's public schools, except that they are poorly clothed, often ill, and unkempt. They are also hungry. And, more likely than not, they are unnoticed. "Invisible."

Another seven percent of the poor in America are mentally ill.[71] Due to overcrowding, understaffing, and budgetary restrictions, state mental hospitals release thousands of the psychiatrically impaired into the general population each year. Many of them have nowhere to go, so they end up in tenement houses, or abandoned warehouses, or out on the streets, but, always, out of sight. "Invisible."

Social activist Michael Harrington calls these "invisible" thousands "the other America." Bread for the World's Arthur Simon calls them "the new poor." George Getschow of the *Wall Street Journal* calls them "the dispossessed." But whoever and whatever they are, one thing remains clear: they are there. Whether or not we can see them, they are there.

Summary

Today there is stark poverty in the shadow of plenty. In spite of widespread economic recovery, the poorest of the poor continue to live in grave deprivation. The same cry of despair that rose above the clamor of Babylon's slums and Warsaw's ghettos rises today from America's urban sprawl. The poor are with us. Still.

Malnutrition is on the rise. Social service agencies are buried beneath an avalanche of need. Human suffering has reached unprecedented proportions.

But, the poor are out of sight and, thus, out of mind. So, despite the fact that their numbers are enormous, the poor remain remarkably inconspicuous. "Invisible." But just because the elderly, the disabled, the young, the sick, and the feeble have melted into the background of the urban milieu, that does not mean that they are any less needy. If anything, it demonstrates their helplessness all the more.

Jesus said, "The poor will be with you always." If we didn't believe Him before, we are compelled by the weight of evidence to believe Him now.

It is indeed possible that steps to relieve misery can create misery. The most troubling aspect of social policy toward the poor in late twentieth-century America is not how much it costs, but what it has bought.

Charles Murray

The federal government must and shall quit this business of relief. To dole out relief is to administer a narcotic, a subtle destroyer of the human spirit.

Franklin D. Roosevelt

We have apparently reached the point where government social spending may actually be generating poverty instead of reducing it.

Warren T. Brookes

Humpty-Dumpty sat on a wall;
Humpty-Dumpty had a great fall.
All the king's horses and all the king's men
Couldn't put Humpty back together again.

Mother Goose

Lo, this only have I found, that God hath made man upright; but they have sought out many inventions.

King Solomon

THREE

WELFARE: THE WAR
ON THE POOR

In his State of the Union message of 1964, President Lyndon Johnson declared an "unconditional war on poverty."[1]

Almost immediately, the full energies of the most powerful nation on earth were marshaled against the dark denizens of privation and want. Studies were authorized. Commissions were established. Images of Appalachian shanty towns and ghetto hovels filled the television screen. A helter-skelter of ambitious renewal and rehabilitative programs was launched. Governors and mayors set out on hopeful pilgrimages to Washington to lobby for their "fair share." The alms race had begun. And the federal coffers were loosed.

The Department of Health, Education and Welfare was given the monumental task of consolidating and administering all these scattered "wartime" initiatives. It began with a budget of two billion dollars,[2] actually a modest amount, less than five percent of the expenditures on national defense.[3] Fifteen years later, however, its budget had soared to one hundred eighty billion dollars,[4] one-and-a-half times more than the total spent by the Army, the Navy, and the Air Force.[5] In fact, its budget had grown to be the third largest in the world, exceeded only by the entire budget of the United States government and that of the Soviet Union.[6] The HEW came to supervise a gargantuan empire reaching every community in the nation, touching every life.

The "war" strategy developed by the HEW involved the creation or expansion of well over one hundred social welfare agencies.[7] Their grab-bag efforts included major programs like Social Security, Unemployment Insurance, Medicare, Medicaid, Aid to Families with Dependent Children (AFDC), Supplemental

Security Income (SSI), and Food Stamps, as well as a myriad of minor programs, including special supplemental feeding for Women, Infants, and Children (WIC), the Intensive Infant Care Project (ICP), Rent Supplements, Urban Rat Control, and Travelers' Aid.

By the time President Johnson relinquished the reins of power to Richard Nixon in 1969, the "war on poverty" had assumed an immutable, untouchable position in the federal agenda, consuming a full twenty-five percent of the gross national product[8] and employing one out of every one hundred Americans in one way or another.[9] Even when the new president appointed conservative strategists like Howard Phillips and William Simon to positions of authority, liberal crusaders had little to fear. The poverty programs had acquired such political clout that they not only survived, they thrived. In fact, the post-Johnson "war on poverty" saw the greatest increase in social welfare services since the Great Depression.[10]

The Food Stamp program, for instance, began in 1965 with less than a half million beneficiaries.[11] By 1967, the number in the program had quadrupled.[12] Under Nixon, that number was again quadrupled.[13] And, by 1980, the number of beneficiaries had grown to nearly twenty-two million,[14] fifty times the coverage of Johnson's original war on poverty legislative package.

Though the socioeconomic dogma of the HEW's legions gained consensus in Washington's corridors of power, it was not without its critics. Valiant voices of protest articulated the concern that the "war on poverty" was mismanaged, misdirected, and entirely mistaken, all to no avail. Dismissing such voices out of hand, the "war's" engineers continued to expand the bounds of their giveaway juggernaut.

Even Ronald Reagan — with a convincing conservative mandate to trim Washington's excess fat and eight years in the White House to do it — was unable to reform the welfare system, much less to end the "war on poverty." During his administration social welfare spending increased astronomically. In 1981 he spent nearly seventy billion dollars more than Jimmy Carter had the year before.[15] In 1982 he spent about fifty-four billion dollars more than that.[16] In 1983 he increased the spending another forty-six billion dollars.[17] And between 1984 and 1988 he upped the "war on poverty's" budget more than one hundred fifty billion dollars.[18] So, despite all the liberal moaning and groaning and the media hype over so-called budget cuts, it is obvious that the only thing Reagan cut was the rate of increase in spending. The "war on poverty" remained essentially untouched.[19]

In less than twenty years, the war on poverty had ceased to be an innovation and had become an institution. It had, indeed, become "unconditional."

The Consensus

Of course, civil concern for the poor did not begin with Lyndon Johnson and his economic strategists in the sixties. In fact, the "war on poverty" put asunder a long-standing consensus about the role and purpose of government sponsored social welfare programs.[20] It was a consensus that had remained virtually unchanged throughout the history of our nation, and, in fact, reached as far back as Parliament's enactment in sixteenth-century England of the Elizabethan Poor Laws. It was a consensus that operated on the basic premise that civilized magistrates do not let their constituents starve in the streets. Instead, they attempt to make some sort of decent provision for those who would otherwise languish helplessly in utter destitution.[21]

That decent provision was by no means promiscuously unqualified. It was, in fact, hedged round about with limitations, prerequisites, and stipulations. Our forebearers were unashamedly wary. Though perhaps necessary to the maintenance of civilized societies, government-sponsored emergency welfare was still looked upon as a hazard of compassion at best, a sentimental vice at worst.[22]

Why a hazard and a vice?

Because, despite the fact that some people are deserving poor — the "helpless" as the Poor Laws called them — many, many others are undeserving poor — the "vagrant" and the "sloth."[23] By extending government welfare, a society attracts and encourages both. A few desperate souls may be aided, but then the less savory are simultaneously spurred to corruption. So, our forebearers wisely gave heed to the Scriptural warning, "And on some have compassion, but making a distinction; save others with fear, snatching them out of the fire, hating even the garment defiled by corrupted flesh" (Jude 22-23).

Thus, welfare was, as a barely tolerable social and civil necessity, stripped down to the bare elementals. Nothing fancy. Nothing grandiose. Just adequate. No need to tempt fate or engender fraud. And no need to rush head over heels into policies that create and reward laziness, indolence, and dependency. Welfare was for emergency relief when every other support apparatus failed, and that's all.

This has always been the consensus view of government welfare in our country, even among the so-called "ultra-liberals."

Franklin Roosevelt and his New Deal legislative railroad may have radically altered the distribution of welfare with the introduction of Social Security, AFDC, Workman's Compensation, and Unemployment Insurance, but the purposes for social welfare remained unchanged. The consensus remained unchallenged. The concerns of character continued to hold sway over the uneasy conscience of compassion. In 1935, he told Congress, "The federal government must, and shall, quit this business of relief. To dole out relief is to administer a narcotic, a subtle destroyer of the human spirit."[24]

Harry Truman, heir to the throne of Roosevelt's welfare boondoggle often quipped, "No more soup lines, no more dole, and no more battlefields. That's what I want to see."[25] The consensus remained.

Even John Kennedy held to this view of welfare. In 1962, he launched a poverty assistance offensive with the slogan, "Give a hand, not a handout."[26] The program was based solidly on that old time-tested consensus that no lasting solution to the problem of poverty can be bought with a welfare check. He understood that the best welfare policy is the one that allows the poor to overcome poverty by the only means that have ever proven effectual: by conscientious *faith*, by a cohesive *family*, and by disciplined *work*.

The original Poor Laws, enacted in 1589, sought to "reinforce righteousness," to strengthen "the family bond," and to "set the poor to work" and turn the country into "a hive of industry."[27] Although far from ideal, the laws accomplished just that, and became the model for three centuries of unprecedented liberty and prosperity. If welfare was to be a compromise, it was to be a carefully conditioned compromise. Workhouses and labor yards were established so that those willing to work could "pull themselves up by their own bootstraps" while maintaining family integrity. Cottage apprenticeships were initiated so that the youth would "be accustomed and brought up in labor, work, thrift, and purposefulness."[28] Disincentives were deliberately incorporated so that unfaithfulness, irresponsibility, sloth, and graft could be kept to a minimum. From all but the disabled, industry was required.

This legacy of conditioning government welfare on faith, family, and work was carried across the sea by the early American settlers. Knowing that the Poor Laws were based on the fundamental Scriptural balance between discipline and responsibility, the colonists maintained the old consensus. As a result, the poor could expect justice and compassion even along the rough-hewn edges of the new frontier. But it was a justice and compassion that demanded responsibility, effort, and diligence of its beneficiaries. It was a justice and compassion rooted in the Biblical family and work-ethic. It was a justice and compassion that was administered, not by an army of benevolent bureaucrats, but by a gracious citizenry. It was a justice and compassion that created opportunities, not entitlements.

Alexander Hamilton wrote, "Americans hold their greatest liberty in this, our poor arise from their plight of their own accord, in cooperation with, but not dependent upon, Christian generosities."[29] Thomas MacKay wrote, "American welfare consists in a recreation and development of the arts of independence and industry."[30] And Benjamin Franklin was fond of paraphrasing the old Talmudic proverb, asserting that American charity "is the noblest charity, preventing a man from accepting charity, and the best alms, enabling men to dispense with alms."[31] So America came to be known the world over as the home of the free and the brave, the land of opportunity. The old consensus remained an unchallenged bastion in the determination of domestic social policy.

That old consensus died in 1964. It was the first casualty in the "war on poverty."

The members of President Lyndon Johnson's task force on poverty — including Michael Harrington, author of the influential book, *The Other America*, Bill Moyers, the high-profile tele-journalist, Sargent Shriver, pioneer of the Peace Corps, and Joseph Califano, later a chief aide to President Jimmy Carter — forged a new and invincible consensus.

This new consensus decried the old consensus as "harsh," "unrealistic," "insensitive," and "discriminatory." Rejecting the notion that poverty was in any way connected with individual or familial irresponsibility, the new consensus adamantly asserted that poverty was the fault of the system. Environment was the problem. Oppression, discrimination, materialism, and injustice were the cause. And society was to blame.

Thus, society would have to be made to do penance.

One day, Califano called reporters into his office at the White House to explain the president's legislative initiative increasing social welfare spending. He told them that, contrary to conservative rhetoric by the likes of then-Governor Ronald Reagan, a government analysis had shown that only fifty thousand people, or about one percent of the eight million people on permanent welfare, were capable of being given skills and training to make them self-sufficient. Of the other twelve million people on temporary welfare programs, only about half were trainable, he said.[32] Quite a dismal situation for this, the land of opportunity.

He went on to suggest that since *society* is to blame for creating such a mess, programs must be developed that go *beyond equality* of opportunity. Programs must be developed that will ensure equality of outcome.

This was the new vogue, the new consensus. Any and all other persuasions were quickly labeled "greedy," "racist," "unchristian," and "unjust."[33] Any public officials or political candidates daring to pass judgment on the effectiveness of the massive federal giveaways forged by the new consensus were then, and even are now, accused of "violating the rights" of the poor and then bludgeoned with the so-called "fairness issue."[34] If they persisted in their obstinate nonconformity, they were made to bear the wrath of near-universal rejection.[35] They were made out to be the enemies of civil rights, minorities, women, children, the elderly, the dispossessed, and the sacrosanct dolations of Social Security and Medicare.[36]

Something Went Wrong

But a funny thing happened on the way to Utopia. Before the "war on poverty," under the sponsorship of the old social welfare consensus, approximately thirteen percent of Americans were poor, using the official definition.[37] And the unemployment rate was running at less than four percent. Over the next twenty years, social welfare spending increased more than twenty times.[38] The result? Under the sponsorship of the new social welfare consensus, approximately fifteen percent of Americans were poor, using the official definition.[39] And the unemployment rate fluctuated between five percent and eleven percent.[40] Somehow, we were losing ground!

Something went wrong, terribly wrong. The "war on poverty" spawned a number of unintended side effects, second- and third-order consequences. Unintended. Unanticipated. But inevitable.

First, the "war on poverty" actually halted in its tracks the ongoing improvement in the lot of America's poor. Writers as diverse as Charles Murray,[41] George Gilder,[42] Thomas Sowell,[43] and Murray Rothbard[44] have shown conclusively that instead of enabling the infirm and the elderly to lead full and productive lives, and instead of empowering the poor to control their lives and rise from poverty, the social welfare programs rendered them impotent, dependent, and helpless. The sheer numbers ought to be enough to convince anyone. After billions upon billions of dollars spent, after a monumental effort that mobilized the ablest minds and the finest machinery, there are more poor than ever before.[45] There are more homeless than ever before.[46] There are more hungry than ever before.[47] Something went wrong.

Second, the "war on poverty" actually contributed to the disintegration of poor families.[48] The welfare system subsidizes idleness, provides institutional disincentives to family life, and reduces faith to a blind trust in the paternalism of the state.[49] Fatherless homes are rewarded with extra benefits and welfare perks, while intact homes are penalized and impoverished.[50] Illegitimate pregnancies are generously gratiated while moral purity is snubbed.[51] Something went wrong.

Third, the "war on poverty" actually provided incentives to avoid work. Each increase in welfare benefits over the past twenty years has resulted in a huge shift from the payrolls to the welfare rolls.[52] When entitlement programs become competitive with the salaries of lower—or even middle—income families, it is only sensible to expect that many, especially the poorly trained and poorly educated, will choose the path of least resistance.[53] In New York State, for example, an hourly wage of $4.87 would have to be earned in order to equal the welfare benefits available: hourly earnings one-and-a-half times the minimum wage.[54] Who's going to work in McDonald's at $3.35 an hour when they can "earn" $4.87 an hour on welfare? Something went wrong.

Fourth, the "war on poverty" actually contributed to the already enormous problem of governmental waste. Instead of helping to reduce waste by returning more and more citizens to productivity, the welfare programs have proven to be the most inefficient slice of the budgetary pie.[55] Only thirty cents of each anti-poverty dollar actually goes to help the poor alleviate their plight.[56] Shocking, but true. The other seventy cents is gobbled up by overhead and administration. So, in 1982, for example, one hundred twenty-four billion dollars was spent to reduce poverty, yet those expenditures reduced poverty by only thirty-seven billion dollars: not a terribly impressive return.[57] In theory, the one hundred twenty-four billion dollars should have been enough, not only to bring poor households up to the sustenance level, but also to bring these and all other households up to twenty-five percent above the sustenance level and still have forty-eight billion dollars left over for other purposes, such as reducing the deficit.[58] Something went wrong.

Fifth, the "war on poverty" actually reduced the opportunities of the poor in the open marketplace. Walter Williams, in his brilliant book *The State Against Blacks*,[59] and Thomas Sowell, in his equally insightful book *Civil Rights: Rhetoric or Reality?*,[60] have shown beyond any reason of doubt that many anti-poverty measures decrease work benefits through higher taxes, decrease job creation especially at the lower levels, and decrease entrepreneurial activity due to increased risk. Such measures as the minimum wage, occupational licensing, union supports, and the regulation of the taxi and trucking trades, instead of protecting the unskilled poor, only eliminate them from the marketplace. Upward mobility becomes impossible because the unskilled poor never get to square one. Something went wrong.

Sixth, the "war on poverty" actually contributed to the demise of American industry. Massive governmental interference in the marketplace has artificially sustained a whole host of antiquated businesses.[61] Instead of launching workers into new fields, new technologies, and new opportunities, the "war's" union guarantees, federal bailouts, and job placement programs have encouraged them to remain with stagnating industries, to be content with outdated skills, and to be fearful of innovation. Something went wrong.

The "war on poverty" had become, in fact, a "war on the poor." Welfare had become a trap, victimizing its supposed beneficiaries.

Crossover Victimization

Lachelle Washington was just twelve days away from her fifteenth birthday when the test confirmed her suspicions. She was pregnant. And she couldn't have been happier. The way she figured it, her timing was perfect.

Far from being an inconvenience, Lachelle's pregnancy was her ticket to "bigger and better things" — things her teenaged ghetto boyfriends could never hope to provide.

As a welfare mother, Lachelle would have a piece of the "good life." She'd be out on her own, with her own apartment, food and medical care for the asking, and even job training and day care if she wanted them. It was an offer she couldn't afford to refuse. Like her mother and three older sisters before her, she planned her whole life around her children and the federal benefits they'd accrue.

She knew that, under the current system, welfare mothers and their children can receive benefits simultaneously from as many as seventeen different programs:

- The Child Nutrition Program
- The Food Stamps Program
- The Special Supplemental Food Program
- The Special Milk Program

- The Lower-income Housing Assistance Program
- The Rent Supplements Program
- The Public Health Services Program
- The Medicaid Program
- The Public Assistance Grants Program
- The Work Incentive Program
- The Employment Services Program
- The Financial Assistance Program for Elementary and Secondary Education
- The Public Assistance Services Program
- The Human Development Services Program
- The Action Domestic Care Program
- The Legal Services Program
- The Community Services Program

Overlap is practically universal among all the hundred-odd welfare assistance programs, since only five of them limit eligibility on the basis of participation in other programs.[62] But even then, when overlap is considered, recipients are usually not turned away. In fact, many of the programs, including the basic cash subsidy programs like Aid for Families with Dependent Children (AFDC), Supplemental Security Income (SSI), Social Security, and Unemployment Insurance Compensation, actually will encourage applicants to multiply their benefits by applying for any and all overlapping programs.[63]

Lachelle's mother always used to say, "If the government's gonna be givin' it away, we might as well be in on the gettin'."

But, by the time she was twenty-six, Lachelle had made the startling discovery that life on the dole was not all it was cracked up to be. Her eleven-year-old son, Melvin, had already acquired a rap sheet longer than his thin, street-toughened arm, and her other three, James, Leslie, and William, were well on the road to trouble as well. There seemed to be no end to her medical problems: hypoglycemia, astigmatism, impacted wisdom teeth, allergies, bursitis, etc.

At one point, years ago, she'd tried to work. But her earnings jeopardized her welfare income and, since the minimum wage was no match for her federal benefits, she quit. Later, when she'd had a bellyful of welfare, not caring if she kept her benefits or not, she found that she couldn't keep a job. Even a minimum-wage job. She just couldn't adjust to the working life. Welfare had become a trap for her. A dismal, debilitating, disastrous trap.

For Lachelle Washington, the "war on poverty" had taken on a very personal dimension. She was one of its victims.

Welfare Reform

The "war on poverty" was supposed to reform the entire social fabric of our nation. The hungry were to be fed. The naked were to be clothed. The homeless were to be sheltered. The jobless were to be employed. The helpless were to be protected. Blacks, Hispanics, Indians, women, and the elderly all were to be brought to full equality. Through legislation and litigation, through education and communication, through taxation and distribution, the disadvantaged were to be unshackled from structural poverty.

But the "war on poverty" failed.

Twenty years and untold billions of dollars later, the hungry are hungrier than ever. The poor, the deprived, the weak, and the dispossessed are more vulnerable than ever. Instead of decreasing the incidence of infant mortality, the "war on poverty" only increased it.[64] Instead of decreasing the incidence of illiteracy, the "war on poverty" only increased it.[65] Instead of decreasing the incidence of unemployment, the "war on poverty" only increased it.[66]

Instead of training the chronically unemployed, instead of facilitating and rehabilitating the poor, the "war on poverty" built a massive bureaucratic machine. It increased Social Security spending so that its unfunded liability would soar to over two trillion dollars by 1980. It increased AFDC and other cash beneficient programs from fifty-two billion dollars to over three hundred fifty billion dollars. And still the poor suffer.

The "war on poverty" thus has indeed become a "war on the poor." It has actually added to the structures of structural poverty.

Even attempts to reform the welfare system have failed miserably. Reforming a "reformation" is not an easy thing to do. Every administration since Lyndon Johnson left Washington has attempted it.[67]

They have proposed various forms of means testing, voucher programs, work incentives, technical assistance, community development, workfare, decentralization, and privatization.[68] They have conducted studies, launched pilot programs, held conferences, sponsored research, hired consultants, and published surveys.[69] And still the problems persist, perhaps more obstinately than ever before.

And so the soup lines grow. The flophouses fill to over-flowing. The park benches are crowded at night as well as during the day. The newest token of welfare's failure is an indigent's cardboard box.

The Government's Role

What then, can the government do to reverse its dismal record in the "war on poverty?" What can the government do to *really* help the poor? According to economist Murray Rothbard, the only correct answer is, "Get out of the way! Let the government get out of the way of the productive energies of all groups in the population — rich, middle-class, and poor alike — and the result will be an enormous increase in the welfare and the standard of living of everyone, and most particularly of the poor who are the ones supposedly helped by the miscalled welfare state."[70]

In his book, *Welfare Without the Welfare State*, Yale Brozen points out, "With less attempt to use state power to compress the inequality in the distribution of income, inequality would diminish more rapidly. Low wage rates would rise more rapidly with a higher rate of saving and capital formation, and inequality would diminish with the rise in income of wage-earners."[71]

If the government were to reduce the level of taxation, remove industrial restraints, eliminate wage controls, and abolish subsidies, tariffs, and other constraints on free enterprise, the poor would be helped in a way that AFDC, Social Security, and Unemployment Insurance could never match. Jobs would be created, investment would be stimulated, productivity would soar, and technology would advance. If that were to happen, says Rothbard, "the lower income groups would benefit *more* than anyone else."[72]

The "war on the poor" can be turned around. It can be as it was intended to be from the start: a "war on poverty." But only if the government leaves the "war" machinery substantially alone. But only if the government leaves the "war" machinery substantially to us.[73]

Summary

In the face of the dire conditions of deprivation across America, an all-out "war on poverty" was declared by the Great Society Johnson administration. Marshaling a mind-boggling arsenal of social welfare programs, policies, and agendas, the Washington bureaucracy attacked poverty with all the zeal of crusaders outside Zion's Gate. The best minds, the greatest resources, and the grandest schemes were, thus, conscripted to fight helplessness, hopelessness, and lack.

The "war on poverty" not only marked a bold new initiative to improve the lives of the poor, it marked a dramatic new consensus about the nature and causes of poverty. The new humanitarian consensus held that earlier economic analyses, whether grounded in the individualism of classical civic liberalism or in the covenantalism of Christian orthodoxy, were altogether outmoded and reactionary. The brave new world would have to be forged from a brave new philosophy.

But, somehow, something went wrong. Instead of improving the lot of the poor, the "war on poverty" actually halted improvement. Worse, its programs contributed significantly to the disintegration of families, government waste, indolence, sloth, and the demise of industry. Apparently, the "war on poverty" was and is, more realistically, a "war on the poor."

A survey of American social policy, from the sixties to the present, reveals one outstanding fact: We're losing ground. The poor are worse off today than they were before the government grabbed the reigns of the economy.

PART TWO

THE SOLUTION

Are we not Christ's ambassadors? Are we not commissioned with the joyous duty: preach the Gospel to the poor, proclaim release to the captives and recovery of sight to the blind, to free the shackled? Is it not our sacred duty to comfort those afflicted with the very comfort with which we ourselves have been comforted by the God of all comfort: Are we not . . . the divinely ordained solution?

Nathaniel Samuelson (1671)

Having sole possession of the medicine of immortality, the Holy Church is the potion of hope, the elixir of life, and the nostrum of wholeness for all the world's woes and ills.

John Chrysostom

Rise up, O men of God!
    Have done with lesser things;
Give heart and soul and mind
    and strength to serve the King of kings.
Rise up, O men of God!
    The church for you doth wait,
Her strength unequal to her task;
    Rise up and make her great!

William P. Merrill

Alas, the Church has too often ignored the suffering and oppression of the poor and neglected her calling to help the needy and sick.

Hans Rookmaaker

We aren't the daily beggars
who beg from door to door
We are your neighbor's children
and we've been here before.

Wassail

It was the failure of the Church to practice community — first in its own circle but also to the neighbor — that really opened the door to much of the state's taking over what, in reality, the Church should have done.

Francis A. Schaeffer

AUTHENTIC CHRISTIANITY: WORD AND DEED

America's "war on poverty" is a dismal failure. The federally funded welfare program has become an incessant reminder that gross mismanagement, fiscal irresponsibility, misappropriated authority, and escalating calamity are the inevitable results of a society that attempts to solve complex human problems apart from the clear instruction of Scripture.

The welfare program cannot be reformed. Even a radical restructuring of the entire system from top to bottom would be inadequate.

The reason?

Welfare is not essentially or primarily the government's job. It never has been. And it never will be.

Welfare is our job. It is the job of Christians.

According to the clear instruction of Scripture, there is only one way to win the "war on poverty" — get the government out of primary welfare provision. And get the Church back in it.

Good Samaritan Faith

Notice I said "get the Church *back* in it." For centuries, Christians have been the primary agents of charity and compassion in Western culture.[1] From the first century forward to the founding of the American colonies, Christians took the lead in caring for the hungry, the dispossessed, and the afflicted.[2] This was, in fact, the hallmark of authentic Christianity.[3]

Even the enemies of the Church begrudgingly admitted that there was something about the Gospel of Jesus Christ that compelled Christians to perform extraordinary feats of selfless compassion. For instance, during his short reign as emperor in the fourth century, Julian the Apostate tried to restore the paganism of Rome's earlier days and undermine Christianity. But he just could not get around the Christians' works of love. Indeed, in urging his government officials to charitable works, he said, "We ought to be ashamed. Not a beggar is to be found among the Jews, and those godless Galileans feed not only their own people, but ours as well, whereas our people receive no assistance whatever from us."[4]

Christ modeled a life and ministry of compassion to the poor. He was forever mingling with them (Luke 5:1-11), eating with them (Luke 5:27-32), comforting them (Luke 12:22-34), feeding them (Luke 9:10-17), restoring them to health (Luke 5:12-16), and ministering to them (Luke 7:18-23). He even went so far as to use the dramatic words of Isaiah to summarize and epitomize His life's purpose: "The Spirit of the Lord is on me because He has anointed me to preach good news to the poor. He has sent me to proclaim freedom for the prisoners, and recovery of sight for the blind, to release the oppressed, to proclaim the year of the Lord's favor" (Luke 4:18-19).

It is not surprising, then, that His disciples, those called to "conform themselves to His image" (Romans 8:29), would similarly place a high priority on the care of the poor. Even a cursory glance through the New Testament "hall of fame" reveals a startling level of commitment to ministries of compassion.

Tabitha, for example, was a godly woman whose chief occupation was "helping the poor" (Acts 9:36-41).

Barnabas was a man of some means who made an indelible mark on the early Christian communities, first by supplying the needs of the poor out of his own coffers (Acts 4:36-37), and later by spearheading relief efforts and taking up collections for famine-stricken Judeans (Acts 11:27-30).

Titus was the young emissary of the Apostle Paul (2 Corinthians 8:23) who organized a collection for the poor Christians in Jerusalem (2 Corinthians 8:3-6). Later, he superintended further relief efforts in Corinth, and delivered Paul's second letter to the Church there, all on his own initiative (2 Corinthians 8:16-17). When last we see Titus, he has taken over the monumental task of mobilizing the Cretan Church for similar "good works" (Titus 2:3,7,12; 3:8).

The Apostle Paul himself was a man deeply committed to "remembering the poor" (Galatians 2:7-10). His widespread ministry began with a poverty outreach (Acts 11:27-30) and ultimately centered around coordinating the resources of Churches in Greece and Macedonia for relief purposes (2 Corinthians 8-9). In the end, he willingly risked his life for this mission of compassion (Acts 20:17-35).

The Good Samaritan is the unnamed lead character in one of Christ's best-loved parables (Luke 10:25-37). When all others, including supposed men of righteousness, had skirted the responsibility of charity, the Samaritan took up its mantle. Christ concluded the narrative, saying, "Go and do likewise" (Luke 10:37).

These early Christian heroes fully comprehended that "the religion our God and Father accepts as pure and faultless is this: to look after orphans and widows in their distress, and to keep oneself from being polluted by the world" (James 1:27). They knew that true repentance evidenced itself in sharing food and sustenance with the poor (Luke 3:7-11). And they understood that selfless giving would be honored and blessed (Luke 6:38; 2 Corinthians 9:6-8) as a sign of genuine faith (James 2:14-17).

The Diaconal Function

Biblical teaching concerning the believer's obligation to the poor permeated the thinking of the early Christians. They knew that if they were kind and generous to the poor, they would themselves be happy (Proverbs 14:21). God would preserve them (Psalm 41:1-2). They would never suffer need (Proverbs 28:27). They would prosper (Proverbs 11:25). They would even be raised and restored from beds of sickness (Psalm 41:3).

On the other hand, to refuse to exercise charity to the poor would have meant hurling contempt upon the name of the Lord (Proverbs 14:31). And for such an offense, they knew that their worship would have been rendered useless (Isaiah 1:10-17) and their prayers would have gone unanswered (Proverbs 21:13). They knew that they would in no wise escape punishment (Proverbs 17:5).

The result was that *every* aspect of their lives was shaped to some degree by this high call to compassion. From the ordering of their homes (Romans 12:13) to the conducting of their businesses (Ephesians 4:28), from the training of their disciples (Titus 3:14) to the character of their worship (James 2:2-7), they were compelled by the Author and Finisher of their faith to live lives of charity.

This is nowhere more evident than in the way their Churches were structured. Besides the elders, who were charged with the weighty task of caring for the flock (Acts 20:28) and ruling the affairs of the congregation (Hebrews 13:17), those early fellowships were also served by deacons — or, more literally, *servants*. According to Acts 6:1-6, the deacons were charged with the responsibility of coordinating, administering, and conducting the charitable function of the Church.

It seems that because of the spectacular growth of the Jerusalem Church, the distribution of food to the needy had gradually become uneven and inefficient. A number of the Grecian widows had been overlooked.

Since this situation was entirely unacceptable, the Twelve gathered all the Disciples together and said, "It would not be right for us to neglect the ministry of the Word of God in order to wait on tables. Brothers, choose seven men from you who are known to be full of the Spirit and wisdom. We will turn this responsibility over to them and will give our attention to prayer and the ministry of the Word" (Acts 6:2-3). Thus, these seven men, or *deacons* as they would later be called (1 Timothy 3:8-10), had as their primary duty the oversight of the poverty ministry of the Church. This was the essence of the diaconal function.

All throughout Church history, the diaconal function has been more or less faithfully carried out by men of passion, conviction, and concern — men like William Olney and Joseph Passmore.

Olney and Passmore were deacons for many years at London's Metropolitan Tabernacle during the pastorate of Charles Haddon Spurgeon. Their busy ministry in service to the needy involved the administration of almshouses, orphanages, relief missions, training schools, retirement homes, tract societies, and colporterages. In a lecture to young Bible college students in 1862, Olney stated, "Deacons are called of God to a magnificent field of service, white unto harvest. . . . Ours is the holy duty of stopping by the way, when all others have passed by, to ministrate Christ's healing. Thus, we take the Good Samaritan as our model, lest the pilgrim perish."[5] To that same audience, Passmore said, "It is ironic indeed that our type of diaconal faithfulness comes not from the life of a disciple of our blessed Lord. Nay, not even is our type from the ancient fathers of faith, the Jews. Instead, our type is from the life of a Samaritan. Mongrel, as touching doctrine, this Good Samaritan is all of pedigree as touching righteousness. Oh, that the Church of our day had such men. Oh, that the Church of our day bred such men, men of unswerving devotion to the care of the poor and brokenhearted. Oh, that the Church of our day was filled with such men, men driven by the Good Samaritan faith . . . offering both word and deed, the fullness of the Gospel."[6]

Sadly, in our Churches today we have virtually lost all sight of the diaconal function. Instead of meting out the succor of compassion to the needy, our deacons spend most of their time sitting on committees and launching building drives. Instead of spending and being spent on behalf of the needy, instead of modeling the Word and deed Good Samaritan faith, our deacons are waxing the floors of the fellowship hall or dusting the dampers, pew by pew, "and goodness knows what other trifles."[7] Consequently, the hungry, the naked, the dispossessed, the unloved, and the unlovable are left, at best, to their own wits, or at worst, to the benign benevolence of the "war on poverty's" welfare bureaucracy.

The condemnation written by John Calvin in 1559 is just as applicable in our own day as it was in his: "Today the poor get nothing more of alms than if they were cast into the sea. Therefore, the Church is mocked with a false diaconate . . . there is nothing of the care of the poor, nothing of that whole function which the deacons once performed."[8]

Love Is Something You Do

The Good Samaritan faith and the mandate to care for the poor and afflicted is by no means the sole domain of the diaconate. God desires us all to display the Good Samaritan faith by offering the needy a Gospel of Word and deed. The testimony of

Scripture is clear: All of us who are called by His name must walk in love (Ephesians 5:2). We must exercise compassion (2 Corinthians 1:3-4). We must live lives of service (Luke 22:24-30). We must struggle for justice and secure mercy, comfort, and liberty for men, women, and children everywhere (Zechariah 7:8-10).

In Matthew 22, when Jesus was asked to summarize briefly the Law of God, the standard against which all spirituality is to be measured, He responded, "You shall love the Lord your God with all your heart, and with all your soul, and with all your mind. This is the great and foremost commandment. And the second is like it; you shall love your neighbor as yourself. On these two commandments depend the Law and the Prophets."

Jesus has reduced the whole of the Law, and thus, the whole of faith, to love. Love toward God, and then, love toward man. But, at the same time, Jesus has defined love in terms of Law. In one bold, deft stroke, He freed the Christian faith from subjectivity. By so linking love and Law, Christ has unclouded our purblind vision of both. Love suddenly takes on responsible objectivity while Law takes on passionate applicability.

This sheds a whole new light on what it means for us to "walk in love." If our love is real, then it must be expressed; it *will* be expressed. If our love is real, then action will result because love is something you do, not merely something you feel. Love is the "Royal Law" (James 2:8). It is a Law that weds Word and deed (James 2:14-26).

Authentic Christian faith, according to Jesus, is verifiable, testable, and objective because it is manifested in a verifiable, testable, and objective love. Thus, Jesus could confidently assert that love is "the final apologetic" (John 13:34-35). And Paul could argue that all effort for the Kingdom is in vain if not marked by love (1 Corinthians 13:1-3). And James could disavow as genuine any and all loveless, lawless, workless faith (James 2:14-26).

True faith gets its hands dirty in the work of compassion because that is the way of love. Faith cannot be personalized, privatized, and esoteric because love cannot be personalized, privatized, and esoteric. True faith moves out into the push-and-shove of daily living and shows forth its authenticity via love.

It is not surprising then to find that Scripture repeatedly mentions love evidenced in faith in contexts that focus on service to the poor, the hungry, the dispossessed, and the lonely. "He who oppresses the poor reproaches his Maker, but he who is gracious to the needy honors Him" (Proverbs 14:31). "He who is generous will be blessed, for he gives of his food to the poor" (Proverbs 22:9). "The righteous is concerned for the rights of the poor, the wicked does not understand such concern" (Proverbs 29:7). "We know love by this, that He laid down His life for us; and we ought to lay down our lives for the brethren. But whoever has the world's goods and beholds his brother in need and closes his heart against him, how does the love of God abide in him? Little children, let us not love with work or with tongue, but in deed and truth" (1 John 3:16-18).

This is the faith, the love-evidenced faith, the Good Samaritan faith, the Word and deed faith, the authentic Christian faith to which God has called us.

Doing Things God's Way

To facilitate such a faith of compassion, God not only gives us commands to love objectively, but He gives us *structures* within which to love objectively. We find those structures in the Law (Exodus 22:21-24; Leviticus 19:9-10), in the Prophets (Isaiah 32:6-8; Jeremiah 21:11-12), in the Gospels (Luke 14:12-14; Matthew 25:31-46), and in the Epistles (2 Corinthians 8:1-9; Galatians 6:2-5). Living illustrations of those structures in action are woven into the narrative sections of Scripture (Ruth 2:2-18, 1 Kings 17:7-16), into the historical sections (Acts 4:32-35), into the poetic sections (Psalms 15:1-5; 72:12-14), into the liturgical sections (Isaiah 1:11-18), and into the didactical sections (Matthew 6:1-14; 2 Corinthians 9:1-15).

The reason Scripture is so specific about the implementation of charity is precisely because of the unique interrelationship of Law and love. Biblical love is not a naive, guilt-provoked sentiment. Biblical love is not a feeling. Biblical love is the compulsion to do things God's way, living in obedience to His unchanging, unerring purposes. It is Law's *motivation*. Thus, Biblical love does not strike out *blindly* in search of "truth, justice, and the

American way." At the same time, Biblical Law is not a passionless system of dos, don'ts, hows, and whys. Biblical Law is not a prison of rules and regulations. Biblical Law is the encoded mercy, grace, and peace of God. It is love's standard. Thus, Biblical Law does not lock us into heartless, soulless exercises in social control.

Law and love are inseparable, working in tandem to the glory of Christ and His Kingdom.

And when they are evidenced as such the needs of the poor will be met by faithful adherents of authentic Christianity — in Word and deed.

Summary

Welfare is not essentially or primarily the government's job. Welfare is our job. It is the job of Christians.

The hallmark of authentic Christianity, from the first century forward, has been its compassionate care of the poor and afflicted. Even a cursory examination of the ministry of Christ, and that of His disciples, reveals this as a dominant theme: Primary service to the needy is to be assumed, not by the state, but by the believer.

In fact, so central was welfare to the task of the Disciples that even the structure of the Church was custom-designed to facilitate its efficient execution. Thus, the office of deacon was established.

Of course, the work of caring for the needy is not simply and neatly relegated to the agency of the diaconate. Under its leadership, *all* believers are to live out the full implications of the Gospel. All believers are to walk in love.

Love is not just a sweet and soppy sentiment. Love is something you do. Christ's life was a crystal-clear translation of this fact into flesh and blood. As His disciples, we, too, must love, not "with words or tongue, but with actions and in truth" (1 John).

Not surprisingly, then, Scripture provides specific patterns for implementing love in the hard reality of daily life. Law and love are, thus, coordinated, ensuring the care of the poor, and the authenticity of the Gospel. The Law-love patterns of Word and deed *are* the Good Samaritan faith, the authentic Christian faith.

The only thing necessary for the triumph of evil is for good men to do nothing.

Edmund Burke

On the day the Church abandons its care of the poor, its fervent ministry of supplication, and its intently chosen fast, we will undoubtedly see its clergy dragged off in wickedness and promiscuity, its parishes awhoring after greed and avarice, and its congregates awash in every vain imagination and unspeakable perversions. On that day the Church will no longer be the Church. May it never be. May it never be. Stay the day with the hand of faithful diligence, I pray.

Otto Bhumhardt

No lasting solution to the problem of poverty can be bought with a welfare check.

John F. Kennedy

Our goal must be to help the helpless and the elderly so that they can lead full lives and empower the poor to control their lives and rise from poverty.

Congressman Newt Gingrich

But we can never prove
    the delights of His love
Until all on the altar we lay;
For the favor He shows and the joy He bestows
Are for those who will trust and obey.

John Sammis

The only dependable route from poverty is always faith, family, and work.

George Gilder

BIBLICAL CHARITY: FAITH, FAMILY, AND WORK

The practice of authentic Word-and-deed Christianity did not die with the last of the first-century disciples of Christ. Bible-believing Christians have long been committed to the care of the poor and afflicted. Throughout history, they have taken the lead in the establishment of orphanages and hospitals, almshouses and rescue missions, youth hostels and emergency shelters, soup kitchens, and community schools. From Polycarp to Penn, from Athanasius to Abelard, from Cranmer to Clarke, from Francis of Assisi to Francis Schaeffer, the Church has been led by godly men and women who lived out the full implications of the Gospel.

George Whitefield is best known for his role in sparking the great Methodist revival in England and the Great Awakening in the American colonies. But the chief concern of his life, and the labor to which all else was subverted, was the erection and maintenance of an orphanage in Georgia. As early as 1737, Whitefield's unflagging energies focused on the relief "of the deplorably destitute children, both fatherless and homeless, scattered in and about Savannah."[1] His lifelong fund-raising and zealous perseverance produced schools, hospitals, and homes for boys and girls that endure to this day.

Charles Haddon Spurgeon is commonly heralded as the greatest preacher to grace the Christian pulpit since the Apostle Paul. His Metropolitan Tabernacle was undoubtedly a dynamic force for righteousness in Victorian England. But his many years of ministry were marked not only by his masterful pulpiteering, but by his labors on behalf of the poor as well. In 1861, he erected an almshouse for the elderly. In 1864, he established a school for the needy children of London. In 1866, he founded the Stockwell Orphanages. And, in 1867, to these many enterprises was added still another, a private hospital. Explaining this furious activity on behalf of the poor, Spurgeon said, "God's intent in endowing any person with more substance than he needs is that he may have the pleasurable office, or rather the delightful privilege, of relieving want and woe. Alas, how many there are who consider that store which God has put into their hands on purpose for the poor and needy, to be only so much provision for their excessive luxury, a luxury which pampers them but yields them neither benefit nor pleasure. Others dream that wealth is given them that they may keep it under lock and key, cankering and corroding, breeding covetousness and care. Who dares roll a stone over the well's mouth when thirst is raging all around? Who dares keep the bread from the women and children who are ready to gnaw their own arms for hunger? Above all, who dares allow the sufferer to writhe in agony uncared for, and the sick to pine into their graves unnursed? This is not small sin: it is a crime to be answered for, to the Judge, when He shall come to judge the quick and the dead."[2]

Nathaniel Samuelson, a Puritan divine of some renown, was another great spokesman for Christ who devoted his life and ministry to the poor. He established a network of clinics, hospitals, and rescue missions that in later years served as the primary inspiration for William Booth in founding the Salvation Army. In a sermon that he reportedly preached more than three hundred times throughout England, he said, "Sodom was crushed in divine judgment. And why, asks me? Was it due to abomination heaped upon abomination such as those perpetuated against the guests of Lot? Nay, saith Scripture. Was it due to wickedness in commerce, graft in governance, and sloth in manufacture? Nay, saith Scripture. In Ezekiel 16:49, thus saith Scripture: 'Behold this, the sin-guilt of thine sister Sodom: she and her daughters wrought arrogance, fatness, and ill-concern, but neglected the help of the poor and need-stricken. Thus, they were caught, committing blasphemy before me. Therefore, I removed them in judgment as all see.' Be ye warned by Sodom's example. She was crushed in divine judgment simply and solely due to her selfish neglect of the deprived and depressed."[3]

Wherever committed Christians have gone, throughout Europe, into the darkest depths of Africa, to the outer reaches of China, along the edges of the American frontier, and beyond to the Australian outback, the Good Samaritan faith of authentic Christianity has been in evidence. In fact, most of the Church's greatest heroes are those who willingly gave the best of their lives to the less fortunate:

- Basil of Caesarea (330-379) established schools, orphanages, almshouses, and hostels for poor travelers, making his city a haven of hope for thousands of needy and neglected souls. But Basil is best known for his innovation in nonambulatory medical care that resulted in the first system of fully staffed hospitals.

- John Chrysostom (347-407) was renowned throughout the civilized world as an anointed and eloquent preacher of the Gospel. But his chief concern was not his pulpiteering but his service to the poor. He established innumerable Christian charities, hospices, and hospitals for the destitute.

- Augustine (354-430) changed the face of the Church with his brilliant theological treatises. But he also transformed the economic ecology of Northern Africa by establishing works of charity in thirteen cities — modeling authentic Christianity for the whole of the Roman Empire.

- Gregory the Great (540-604) spearheaded efforts to provide relief for those suffering from war, pestilence, and famine throughout his ministry. Both through his own personal generosity and through his administrative reform of Church revenues, he highlighted the priority of preaching the Gospel in both Word and deed.

- John the Almsgiver (560-619) became the pastor of the Alexandrian Church at a time when believers in that great city were demoralized by dissension, strife, and disarray. John restored their vision of orthodoxy by modeling for them a life of service: founding and endowing hospitals, maternity clinics, homes for the elderly, and hospices for refugees.

- Bernard of Clairvaux (1090-1153) not only launched one of the greatest monastic movements of all time, sparking evangelical fervor throughout France and beyond, but also established a charitable network throughout Europe to care for the poor. That remarkable network of hostels, hospices, and hospitals has survived to the present day, tending the needs of the unloved and the unlovely.

- John Wyclif (1329-1384) revived interest in the Scriptures during a particularly dismal and degenerate era with his translation of the New Testament into English. But he also unleashed a grass-roots movement of lay preachers and relief workers that brought hope to the poor for the first time in over a century.

- Jan Hus (1374-1415) shook the foundations of the medieval Church hierarchy with his vibrant evangelistic sermons and dynamic rapport with the citizenry. But what really struck fear into the hearts of his superiors was the fact that he had mobilized a veritable army of workers for emergency relief at a time when central Europe was stricken with one disaster after another. They feared him because he had gained the moral high-ground — through service to the poor.

- John Calvin (1509-1564) brought renown to the city of Geneva as the center of the Great Reformation. In so doing, he also transformed it into a safe haven for all of Europe's poor and persecuted, dispossessed and distressed.

- Dwight L. Moody (1837-1899) was America's premier evangelist throughout the dark days following the Civil War and Reconstruction. And although he is best known for pioneering any number of modern evangelistic norms, he was also responsible for the establishment of more than one hundred fifty different street missions, soup kitchens, clinics, schools, and rescue outreaches.

Each of these Christian heroes made the message of their lips manifest by the message of their hands — Word and deed. "And so the Word of God spread rapidly" (Acts 6:7).

The Great Commission

The Great Commission of Matthew 28:18-20 is familiar turf for most Christians. Its primary teaching is quite straightforward and commonly understood.

Jesus said, "All authority in heaven and on earth has been given to me. Therefore, go and make disciples of all nations, baptizing them in the Name of the Father and of the Son and of the Holy Spirit, and teaching them to obey everything I have commanded you. And surely I will be with you always, to the very end of the age."

All authority in heaven is His, of course. The heights and the depths, the angels and the principalities are all under His sovereign rule. But all authority on earth is His as well. Man and creature, as well as every invention and institution, are under His sovereign rule. There are no neutral areas in all of the cosmos that escape the authority of the Lord Jesus Christ (Colossians 1:17).

Therefore, on this basis, the Commission states that believers are to extend Christ's Kingdom, making disciples in all nations by going, baptizing, and teaching. This mandate is the essence of the New Covenant, which is but an extension of the Old Covenant: Go and claim everything in heaven and on earth for the Kingdom, taking dominion for His Name's sake (Genesis 1:28). We are called to be a part of that which will, in the fullness of time, "bring all things in heaven and on earth together under one Head, even Christ" (Ephesians 1:10). Our call is to win *all* things for Jesus. The emphasis is inescapable: We are not to stop with simply telling the nations that Jesus is Lord; we are to demonstrate His Lordship by taking dominion in our culture. We are to make disciples who will obey *everything* that He has commanded, not just in a hazy zone of piety, but in the totality of life.

This is the primary thrust of the Great Commission. It is the spiritual, emotional, and cultural mandate to win the world for Jesus. Whitefield, Spurgeon, Samuelson, and the others understood this and shaped their lives accordingly.

The tendency of modern Christians to sidestep all the implications of the Great Commission except soul-saving has, in stark contrast, paved the way for inhuman humanism's program to crush our liberties and steal away our freedoms. When the Christian's task is limited to merely snatching brands from the flickering flames of perdition, then virtually all Christian influence is removed from the world. There is little or nothing to restrain the ambitions of evil men and movements. There are no checks, no balances, no standards, and no limitations. God's counsel goes unheard and unheeded.

Commenting on this tragic tendency, Spurgeon said, "There are certain pious moderns who will not allow the preacher to speak upon anything but those doctrinal statements concerning the way of salvation which are known as 'the Gospel.' We do not stand in awe of such criticism, for we clearly perceive that our Lord Jesus Christ himself would very frequently have come under it. Read the Sermon on the Mount and judge whether certain among the pious would be content to hear the like of it preached to them. Indeed, they would condemn it as containing very little Gospel and too much good works. They would condemn it as containing all too much of the legal. But we must never let be forgotten Christ's emphasis: the Law must be preached, for what the Law demands of us, the Gospel produces in us, else ours is no Gospel at all."[4]

Biblical Christianity, authentic cutting-edge Christianity, as Spurgeon asserts, embraces the *comprehensive* implications of the Great Commission. It applies Scripture to every area of life and godliness. The fact is, the salvation of souls is an immediate aim of the Great Commission. But the more ultimate aim is the promotion of the glory of the Triune God (Romans 16:25-27). We must have a passion for souls (2 Corinthians 5:11). We must take every opportunity (Colossians 4:5), expend every energy (2 Corinthians 6 :4-10), and risk every expense (Acts 5:20). But personal redemption is not the do-all and end-all of the Great Commission. Thus, our evangelism must include sociology as well as salvation. It must include reform and redemption, culture and conversion, a new social order as well as a new birth, a revolution as well as a regeneration. Any other kind of evangelism is shortsighted and woefully impotent. Any other kind of evangelism fails to live up to the high call of the Great Commission.

Our monolithic humanistic culture, including the merciless "war on the poor," attests all too well that all our bumper-sticker, revival-meeting, door-to-door, and televangelism strategies are simply not sufficient in and of themselves for the task of satisfying the demands of authentic Christianity of fulfilling the Great Commission.

It is high time to release our evangelism from the restraints of passive Christianity in order to mount a full-scale assault on evil and privation.[5] It is high time we set our evangelistic visions by the Scriptural pattern.[6] It is high time evangelism becomes the invasion of lifestyle and society it was intended from the start to be.[7]

Blueprints for Living

Their tireless efforts on behalf of the poor and disadvantaged stand as vivid testimony to the fact that Whitefield, Spurgeon, Samuelson, and the others throughout Church history understood the comprehensive implications of the Great Commission, and hungered to see it fulfilled. Even a quick look at their organizational log books, charters, minutes, and other documents reveals that the primary motive behind their work was not to gratify the sympathies of human altruism. Nor was the motive a reluctant attempt to satisfy the fierce demands of Law. Their motive was to establish "a city upon a hill," "a light unto the nations," "a blessing unto all generations." Their aim was to build up the Kingdom by doing God's will on earth as it is in heaven (Matthew 6:10). They wanted nothing less than Christ's dominion, to effect change in all of life and culture in the only way that could make lasting differences — by giving it a Christianity that was authentically and comprehensively Biblical. In short, theirs was a desire to see to the fulfillment of the Great Commission.

For these latter-day Good Samaritans, there was not a single aspect of life or godliness that escaped the careful scrutiny of Scripture. The *whole* counsel of God was their rule. They took the battle cry of the Reformation — *Sola Fide, Sola Scriptura* — faith alone, Scripture alone — and made it their own. They knew that the Bible has much to say about bringing order to creation through law, art, economics, family life, commerce, the Church, music, literature, science, and, of course, poverty relief. Thus, they adamantly refused to segment or stratify the Gospel in order to favor a single darling doctrine. For them it was the whole Gospel for the whole man and the whole world.

These men and women throughout the ages believed the Bible. They didn't simply honor it. They didn't simply respect it. They didn't simply stand in awe of it. They truly believed it.

They believed that it was "God-breathed and useful for teaching, rebuking, correcting, and training in righteousness so that the man of God would be thoroughly equipped for every good work" (2 Timothy 3:16-17). They believed that "not one jot or tittle had in any wise passed from it" (Matthew 5:18). They believed that it was "settled in heaven" (Psalm 119:89) and "established on the earth" (Psalm 119:90). They believed the Bible, and so they ordered their lives and their message according to it.

If the Bible said that a particular sin was a crime, then they sought to have it codified as such in their legal system. If the Bible outlined a particular fashion of commerce, then they conducted their business accordingly. If the Bible demanded personal devotional disciplines, then they included them in their regular daily routine. If the Bible advocated a particular approach to relief of the poor, then they faithfully followed suit. Being mere men, they lacked perfect understanding, of course, so they made mistakes and they exercised poor judgment at times. But on the whole, they stuck to their conviction that in Scripture, and in Scripture alone, could the blueprint and safeguards for a wholesome society be found. Thus, undergirding all their efforts was the willingness to obey carefully the dictates of Scripture (Joshua 1:8), and the restraint never to go beyond its bounds (1 Corinthians 4:6). Such was the faith of our Christian forebearers. And such must ours be if the Great Commission is to be fulfilled in any measure.

To many Christian liberals, all talk of applying Scripture in blueprint fashion to the problem of the poor is scorned as woefully antiquated.[8] They much prefer the present insanity of government welfare.[9] Similarly, tenured humanists dismiss the Biblical plan of relief as dangerously demented.[10] So, well might we at this point adopt as our own the words of R. L. Dabney, first uttered over a century ago, "A discussion of a social order now totally overthrown . . . will appear as completely out of date . . . as the ribs of Noah's ark, bleaching amidst the eternal snows of Ararat, to his posterity, when engaged in building the Tower of Babel. Let me distinctly premise that I do not dream of affecting the perverted judgments of the great . . . party which now rules the hour. Of course, a set of people who make success the test of truth, as they avowedly do in this matter, and who have been busily and triumphantly engaged for so many years in perfecting a plain injustice, to which they had deliberately made up their minds, are not within the reach of reasoning. Nothing but the hand of retributive Providence can avail to reach them. The few among them who do not pass me by with silent neglect, I am well aware will content themselves with scolding: they will not venture a rational reply . . . The only office that remains . . . is to leave testimony for . . . righteous fame, feeble it may be now, amidst the din of passion and material, yet inextinguishable as Truth's own torch. History will some day bring present events before her impartial bar."[11]

For the record, the federal government's "war on poverty" is a dismal failure. It has become a "war on the poor." By ignoring Scriptural wisdom, by asserting its universal responsibility to care for the poor, by centralizing the criteria of poverty, by bureaucratically administering relief, by reducing the importance of local conditions and accountability, and by institutionalizing the apparatus for care, the state has, created "a permanent welfare class which owes its survival — it thinks — to the continued generosity of the state."[12] The "war on poverty" will never be met with anything except devastation and defeat simply because it does not, and cannot, help people get on their feet. It is but a salve to momentarily succor mortal wounds. It is but a drop in the bucket.

But it is the program that "now rules the hour." And the liberal Church, in its zeal to procure mercy for the broken and justice for the downtrodden, goes awhoring after more statist intervention and, thus, is busily and triumphantly engaging in "perfecting a plain injustice."

Clearly, the only hope for the poor lies in the Church's returning to the Great Commission compulsion that drove Whitefield, Spurgeon, Samuelson, and others throughout Church history. The only hope for the poor lies in the establishment of functioning models of Biblical charity.

So, what alternatives to the federal welfare system and its Social Gospel cousin does the Good Samaritan faith mine from the inimitable and inestimable riches of love and Law? What is the Scriptural blueprint for poverty relief?

Very simply it is the promotion and implementation of three elements in the lives of the poor: faith, family, and work. According to economist George Gilder, "upward mobility depends on all three."[13] Indeed, "these are the pillars of a free economy and a prosperous society."[14]

Faith

What a person thinks, what he believes, what shapes his ultimate concerns, and what he holds to be true in his heart—in other words, his faith or lack of it—has a direct effect on his material well-being. And it has a direct effect on whether or not he can alter that well-being. "For as a man thinketh in his heart, so is he." (Proverbs 23:7 KJV).

In 1905, Max Weber, the renowned political economist and "founding father" of sociology, affirmed this fundamental truth for modern social scientists in his classic work, *The Protestant Ethic and the Spirit of Capitalism*.[15] He argued that the remarkable prosperity of the West was directly attributable to the cultural, personal, and ethical prevalence of the Christian faith. In contrast to pagan cultures, where freedoms and opportunities were severely limited and where poverty and suffering abounded, Weber found that commitment to the Gospel brought men and nations both liberty and prosperity.

According to the Bible, the reasons for this are multitudinous:

First, the Christian faith reorients fallen men to reality. Because of sin we are naturally blind (2 Peter 1:9), foolish (Titus 3:3), ignorant (Isaiah 56:10), and self-destructive (Proverbs 24:2). We are ruled by our passions (James 5:17), our lusts (James 1:14), and our delusions (Isaiah 53:6).

Commitment to Christ, however, removes the scales from our eyes (Acts 9:18) and the shackles from our lives (Romans 5:12-21). In Him we are at last acquainted to what is right (2 Thessalonians 1:6), what is real (1 John 2:29), and what is true (John 8:32).

"Men without faith in the Savior," said the great Puritan divine Richard Baxter, "are damned to rootless lives of fantasy, frustration, and failure. For indeed, apart from the Light of His Life, all men must needs be ever in darkness."[16]

The poor need Jesus Christ. They need the "Bread of Life" (John 6:48-51). The ultimate poverty engendering perpetual deprivation is a lack of faith.

Second, the Christian faith counteracts the destructive effects of sin. *Sin* is not a concept that has much currency with the modern social scientists, economists, politicians, community organizers, civil rights activists, and social service providers that administer our government's programs for the poor. Which may account for their utter and dismal failure.

Sin is, in fact, one of the chief causes of poverty. Surely injustice (Isaiah 58:6), calamity (Genesis 47:13-19), famine (Leviticus 25:25, 39, 47), and exploitation (James 5:1-2) cause poverty, and Christians must meet those causes and that poverty with unmitigated mercy (2 Corinthians 8:1-15). But we must realize as well that a vast amount of poverty is self-inflicted. Men who do not know Christ and do not walk in faith are more often than not immoral, impure, and improvident (Galatians 5:19-21). They are prone to extreme and destructive behavior, indulging in perverse vices and dissipating sensuality (1 Corinthians 6:9-10). And they are thus driven over the brink of poverty (Proverbs 23:21).

On the other hand, "if any man be in Christ, he is a new creation; the old things are passed away; behold new things are come" (2 Corinthians 5:17). The Christian faith reforms sinners with new and constructive values. We are provoked to moral and upright lives of diligence, purity, sober-mindedness, thrift, trustworthiness, and responsibility (Colossians 3:5-15).

Where poverty germinates in the rotting soil of sin, productivity flourishes in the fertile field of faith.

Third, the Christian faith establishes a future orientation in men. All too often the poor either flounder in a dismal fatalism or they squander their few resources in an irresponsible impulsiveness. They are short-sighted (Proverbs 6:6-11), unmotivated (Proverbs 28:19), and naive (Proverbs 7:6-23). And "where there is no vision the people perish" (Proverbs 29:18).

The Christian faith teaches men to live thoughtfully (Matthew 25:13-30), to plan (Matthew 7:24-27), to exercise restraint (Ephesians 4:25-32), and to defer gratification in order to achieve higher ends (James 5:7). We are provoked to self-control (Galatians 5:22-23), wisdom (James 3:13-17), and careful stewardship in order to build for the future (Genesis 1:28). According to Thrasymachos of Trace, a fifth-century Church historian,

"Christless lives are goalless lives. And goalless lives are wealthless lives."[17]

In order to break the yoke of poverty we must invade the culture of the moment with the dynamic escalation of Christ.

Fourth, the Christian faith provokes men to exercise responsibility. Outside the grace of salvation and sanctification men are naturally prone to selfishness, wastefulness, and sloth (2 Peter 2:2-3).

In Christ though, men grow into selfless maturity (Philippians 2:3-4). We are responsible to redeem our time (Ephesians 5:16). We are responsible to make the most of every opportunity (Colossians 4:5). We are responsible to fulfill our calling in life (1 Peter 4:10). We are responsible to use our money wisely (Deuteronomy 8:18), to care for our families (1 Timothy 5:8), to serve the needs of others (Luke 22:25-30), and to be an example of redemption before all men (1 Peter 3:1-17).

It is this very kind of diligent responsibility—this very fruit of faith—that the poor most need if they are ever to climb out of the broken cistern of dispossession.

Fifth, the Christian faith empowers men with confidence in the "very great and precious promises of God" (2 Peter 1:3-4). God blesses obedience (Deuteronomy 28:1-14). He curses wickedness (Deuteronomy 28:15-68). So even though every believer suffers through life's normal setbacks, struggles, sicknesses, and strife, we have the assurance that in the end God's sovereign hand will set it all aright (Romans 8:28). We can confidently claim the magnificent benefits of the covenant (Hebrews 4:16). We can appropriate the glorious riches of the heavenly realm (Ephesians 1:3).

The poor need God's blessing. They need the rewards of His favor. But "without faith it is impossible to please Him, for he who comes to God must believe that He is, and that He is a rewarder of those who diligently seek Him" (Hebrews 11:6).

If Biblical charity is a genuine attempt to transform poverty into productivity, its agenda will necessarily include discipleship in the essentials of the Christian faith—beginning with soteriology and carrying on through to complete maturity. Neither a transfer of wealth, nor a massive reeducation agenda, nor an impenetrable economic safety net, nor a comprehensive social welfare program, nor all of these things together can substitute for this. "It is faith," says George Gilder, "in all its multifarious forms and luminosities, that can by itself move the mountains of sloth and depression that afflict the world's stagnant economies; it brought immigrants thousands of miles with pennies in their pockets to launch the American empire of commerce; and it performs miracles daily in our present impasse."[18]

Authentic Christianity goes to work equipping the poor to walk in faith. That's Biblical charity.

Family

The family is the basic building block of society. When the family begins to break down, the rest of society begins to disintegrate. This is particularly evident in the lives of the poor. A full seventy-five percent of those living below the poverty line in this country live in broken homes.[19] In times of economic calamity intact families are ten times more likely to recover and ultimately prosper than broken families.[20]

There is no replacement for the family. The government can't substitute services for it. Social workers can't substitute kindness and understanding for it. Educators can't substitute knowledge, skills, or understanding for it. The poor need the family. They need fathers, and mothers, and brothers, and sisters. They need grandparents, and aunts, and uncles, and cousins. "There is no other place," wrote John Chrysostom in the fourth century, "where the human spirit can be so nurtured as to prosper spiritually, intellectually, and temporally, than in the bosom of the family's rightful relation."

There are several reasons for this:

First, family life provides men with a proper sense of identity. In the midst of our families we can know and be known. We can taste the joys and sorrows of genuine intimacy. We can gain a vision of life that is sober and sure. We are bolstered by the love of family (Luke 11:11-13). We are strengthened by the confidence of family (John 1:39-42). We are emboldened by the legacy of family (Genesis 49:3-27). And we are stabilized by the objectivity of family (Hebrews 12:7-11).

The poor desperately need this kind of perspective. They desperately need to be stabilized in the gentle environs of hearth and home.

Second, family life provides men with a genuine social security. There's no place like home. In times of trouble our greatest resource will always be those who know us best and love us most. Because family members share a common sense of destiny with one another and a bond of intimacy to one another they can—and will—rush to one another's sides when needed. And well they should. That is just as God intended it (1 Timothy 5:8).

"Caesars and Satraps attempt to succor our wounds and wants with opulent circuses and eloquent promises," said Methodius, the famed seventh-century missionary to the Slavs. "All such dolations are mere pretense, however, in comparison to the genuine Christian care afforded at even the coarsest family hearth."[21]

Third, family life provides men with the accountability and discipline they need. Families are an incubator for sound values (Deuteronomy 6:4-9). They reinforce the principles of authority (1 Peter 3:1-7), structure (Ephesians 5:22-33), liability (Hebrews 12:7-11), obedience (Ephesians 6:1-9), and selflessness (Ephesians 5:21).

According to economist Michael Novak, family accountability and discipline bring out the very best in us. He says, "A typical mother or father without thinking twice about it would willingly die—in a fire or accident, say—in order to save one of his or her children. While in most circumstances this human act would be regarded as heroic, for parents it is only ordinary. Thus . . . the Creator has shaped family life to teach as a matter of course the role of virtue."[22]

If the poor are to be equipped in any measure to rise up from their beds of affliction and prisons of addiction and ghettos of restriction, then Biblical charity must retrain them in the fine art of family living. It must be the aim of Biblical charity to strengthen marriages, equip parents, encourage intimacy, and heal brokenness.

Authentic Christianity goes to work establishing the poor in stable families. That's Biblical charity.

Work

Work is the heart and soul, the cornerstone, of Biblical charity. In fact, much of the outworking of Biblical charity is little more than a subfunction of the doctrine of work. Its operating resources are the fruit of work: the tithe, hospitality, private initiative, and voluntary relief. Its basic methodologies are rooted in the work-ethic: gleaning, training, lending, and facilitating. Its primary objectives revolve around a comprehension of the goodness of work: productivity, rehabilitation, and entrepreneurial effect.

This is because work is the heart and soul, the cornerstone, of man's created purpose. God's first Word to man was definitive: "Be fruitful and increase in number; fill the earth and subdue it. Rule over the fish of the sea and the birds of the air. Have dominion over every living creature that moves on the ground" (Genesis 1:28). In other words, work.

Throughout Scripture this emphasis is not only maintained, it is amplified: "Ill-gotten gains do not profit, but righteousness delivers from death. The Lord will not allow the righteous to hunger, but He will thrust aside the craving of the wicked. Poor is he who works with a negligent hand, but the hand of the diligent makes rich" (Proverbs 10:2-4). "The soul of the sluggard craves and gets nothing, but the soul of the diligent is made fat. Wealth obtained by fraud dwindles, but the one who gathers by labor increases it" (Proverbs 13:4,11).

The Bible is replete with teaching on work. But its basic thrust may be fairly reduced to four points:

First, the Bible teaches that all honorable work is holy. "A man can do nothing better than find satisfaction in his work" (Ecclesiastes 2:24; 3:22). Far from being a bitter consequence of the Fall, work is a vital aspect of God's overall purpose for man in space and time. For that reason, He has typically used workmen, ordinary laborers, in the enactment of that purpose. He has used shepherds like Jacob and David. He has used farmers like Amos and Gideon. He has used merchants like Abraham and Lydia. He has used artists like Solomon and Bezalel. And the men He chose to revolutionize the Roman Empire in the first century were a motley band of fishermen and tax collectors. The great Puritan, Hugh Latimer, best captured the Biblical emphasis on the holiness of man's work when he wrote, "Our Saviour, Christ Jesus, was a carpenter and got His living with great labor. Therefore, let no man disdain . . . to follow Him in a . . . common calling and occupation."[23]

The Fourth Commandment, though commonly and correctly understood as prohibition against working on the Sabbath, has another all-too-often neglected injunction: "Six days you shall labor and do all your work" (Exodus 20:9). And so Richard Steele, another of the great Puritans, could confidently write that it is in the shop "where you may most confidently expect the presence and blessing of God. Work is holy unto the Lord, ordained by His immutable Way."[24]

Everyone, even the partially disabled, reaps honor from industrious, productive work.

Second, the Bible teaches that God calls each person to his or her work. "There are different kinds of gifts, but the same Spirit. There are different kinds of service, but the same Lord. There are different kinds of working, but the same God works all of them in all men" (1 Corinthians 12:4-6). The doctrine of calling was once the cornerstone of the Reformation. And rightly so. As Martin Luther wrote long ago, "The world does not consider labor a blessing, therefore, it flees and hates it . . . but the pious who fear the Lord, labor with a ready and cheerful heart; for they know God's command and will, they acknowledge His calling."[25]

Similarly, Cotton Mather, the great American colonial preacher, wrote, "A Christian should follow his occupation with contentment. . . . Is your business here clogged with any difficulties and inconveniences? Contentment under those difficulties is no little part of your homage to that King who hath placed you where you are by His call."[26]

And William Tyndale wrote, "If we look externally there is a difference betwixt the washing of dishes and preaching of the Word of God; but as touching to please God, in relation to His call, none at all."[27]

Third, the Bible teaches that work is intended for the benefit of the community. It is not just to benefit ourselves. By work, we are to uphold our responsibility to provide for our family (1 Timothy 5:8), and build the work of Christ's Kingdom (Deuteronomy 8:18), and share with those in need (Ephesians 4:28). As John Calvin so aptly asserted, "We know that all men were created to busy themselves with labor . . . for the common good."[28] And Martin Luther wrote, "All stations are so oriented that they serve others."[29]

Fourth, the Bible teaches that, because of sin's devastation, the high ideals of the work-ethic can be attained only through Christ's restoration, imparted to us in the Gospel, and through the ministry of the Church.

The Fall has disrupted and obstructed the blessings of work. Man cannot, and will not, work as he should (Genesis 3:17-19). Sin blinds and binds us, so that our divine commission is left unfulfilled. "Adam refused to work as priest of God's creation," says theologian James B. Jordan. "He rejected the true meaning and direction of his life. As a result, he became dead and impotent, his work was cursed to futility, and he was cast out of the pleasant land of Eden into a howling wilderness."[30]

In a very real sense, everything that the Bible teaches about the benefits of work can stand only as a condemnation to fallen man (Romans 7:10-11). And the poor are but standing reminders of this fact.

Thanks be to God, in Jesus Christ we are restored (Romans 7:24-25). In Him, our lives and our work are redeemed from futility and made meaningful once again (Ephesians 2:10). As Langdon Lowe, a nineteenth-century Southern Presbyterian, wrote, "Man was made for work. The Fall unmade him. Now, in Christ made anew, man can once again work. But he must be ever mindful of the salvific connection: The call to work must not, cannot, go out unaccompanied by the call to salvation."[31]

Now, the practical implications of those four basic points are quite astounding. As David Chilton points out, "The earthly victory of God's people will come about through diligent work. Ungodly powers must and shall fall through the daily work and prayer of the godly. Like the spider in Proverbs 30:28, if we take hold with our hands, we will someday find ourselves in the palaces of kings. But Scripture never countenances the idea that we are to attain dominion by demanding our 'fair share' of resources owned by others, or by using governmental coercion to redistribute wealth. We must encourage ourselves and each other to labor diligently in obedience to God's commands, in the confident expectation that God will honor His promises—that we and our seed will inherit God's good blessings in this life and the next. The reason for Western prosperity is not accidental. It is the direct outgrowth of the 'Puritan ethic' which involved diligent labor, saving, investment, and the philosophy of free enterprise and initiative. God's Law clearly promises external blessings in response to external obedience."[32]

Work is a primary aspect of that external obedience.

In his seminal work entitled *Idols for Destruction*, Herbert Schlossberg states, "Christians ought not to support any policy toward the poor that does not seek to have them occupy the same high plane of useful existence that all of us are to exemplify, 'Serving the poor' is a euphemism for destroying the poor unless it includes with it the intention of seeing the poor begin to serve others."[33]

Whereas humanitarian social policy keeps people helplessly dependent, Biblical charity seeks to remove them from that status and return them to productive capacity. Biblical charity seeks to put them back to work because Biblical charity should never be anything other than a prod to full restoration of the poor to their God-ordained calling. Paul makes it plain: "If a man will not work, he shall not eat" (2 Thessalonians 3:10).

A handout does not charity make!

Every effort must be made to ensure that our helping really does help. A handout may meet an immediate need, but how does it contribute to the ultimate goal of setting the recipient aright? How does it prepare him for the job market? How does it equip him for the future? How does it strengthen the family? How well does it communicate the Law of God and the precepts of Biblical morality? The kind of evangelical myopia that envisions the Scriptural duty to the poor as a simple transfer of funds simply misses the boat. When the Church mimics the government by promiscuously dispensing groceries and other goods and services, it hurts the poor more than it helps. Adherents of such short-sighted thinking only perpetuate the "war against the poor."

Authentic Christianity goes to work putting the able poor to work. That's Biblical charity.

Sheaves for the Provident

In practice, how are these three elements—faith, family, and work—coordinated into a coherent program of care for the poor? Can these Biblical ideals be satisfactorily implemented in a coherent and compassionate fashion?

Although contemporary examples abound, perhaps the best illustration of Biblical charity in action is the Scriptural narrative in the Book of Ruth. It is a story of compelling beauty and romance, of faithfulness and intrigue, of tragedy and hope. Set during the time of the judges, it provides for us an intimate glimpse of covenant life in ancient Israel.

The main characters in the story, Ruth and Naomi, are widows living on the edge of destitution (Ruth 1:6-13). Determined to take responsibility for her elderly mother-in-law (Ruth 1:14) and to accept the terms of God's covenant for herself (Ruth 1:16-17), Ruth does the only thing she can do. She professes her faith, she preserves her family, and then she goes out to find work (Ruth 2:2). In many ways, though, this was a good news-bad news situation for her. The bad news was that Ruth was a stranger to the ways and customs of Israel, being a Moabitess (Ruth 1:4) and, furthermore, she did not appear to have any readily marketable skills. The good news was that God's Law made abundant and gracious provision for strangers (Exodus 23:9; Leviticus 19:33-34; Deuteronomy 24:17-18), as well as for unskilled, destitute workers (Leviticus 19:9-10; 23:22; Deuteronomy 23:24-25; 24:19-22). Gleaner laws stipulated that farmers and landowners leave the edges of their fields unharvested and that overlooked sheaves remain uncollected. Any among the poor or the alien who were willing to follow behind the harvesters and gather that grain were welcome to it, thereby "earning" their own keep. Ruth took advantage of just provision and was thus able to uphold her responsibility to Naomi.

Several basic principles concerning Biblical charity emerge from Ruth's story.

First, it is clear that the benefits of covenantal charity come into Ruth's purview only after she professed faith in the Lord. Whereas her sister-in-law, Orpah, turned away to the pagan gods of Moab, Ruth clung to Naomi, saying, "Do not urge me to leave you, or to turn back from following you; for wherever you go, there I will go, and wherever you lodge, there I will lodge. And your people shall be my people, and your God will be my God" (Ruth 1:16).

Ruth's whole way of thinking was transformed. Her vision of the future was corrected. Her hope was set on nothing less than the Lord of the covenant and His righteousness.

This element of faith was essential in Ruth's rehabilitation from poverty to productivity. Biblical charity cannot successfully operate on any other basis.

Second, the apparatus for care that Ruth took advantage of was uniquely rooted in family life. Ruth didn't go out gleaning just anywhere. She went to the field of Boaz—having bonded herself to Naomi's family—she then invoked the Levirate Law of redemption (Deuteronomy 25:5-10).

Biblical charity always relies on the principle of the kinsman redeemer as the first course of compassionate action. It attempts to rebuild and restore the natural bonds of the home and thus to provide a genuinely effectual safety net.

Third, Ruth worked. And she worked hard (Ruth 2:2-7). Gleaning the fields involved backbreaking labor.

Biblical charity does not attempt to smooth over economic crisis by making privation somewhat more acceptable. It attempts to solve economic crisis. Biblical charity does not attempt to help families adjust to their situation. It attempts to change their situation. Biblical charity does not strive to make poverty and dependence more comfortable. It strives to make productivity and independence more attainable.

The framers of the Elizabethan Poor Laws understood this when they sought to "set the poor to work." Similarly, Whitefield, Spurgeon, Samuelson, and the others throughout Church history understood this and implemented it in their poverty relief programs.

If we are to have any success in our own day in fighting the scourge of poverty, then we must follow this Scriptural mandate.

Fourth, Ruth did not turn to the government for help in her time of distress. She looked to the private sector. Biblical charity is portrayed as a privately dispensed mercy ministry by the landowners, not by an overarching state institution (Ruth 2:4-16). Welfare in the Bible is invariably private in nature. As a result, the apparatus of charity is kept simple. Accountability is enhanced. Flexibility is made possible. Local conditions are maximized. And personal attention is more likely. By keeping charity decentralized, deinstitutionalized, and private, everyone concerned is saved from the anguish of graft, corruption, and red tape.

In our cosmopolitan culture of vast concentrations of urban poor, many have suggested that the private initiative gleaning model is simply out of date. But as John Naisbitt has pointed out in his highly regarded vision of the future, *Megatrends*, gleaning is as up to date as the latest high-tech Silicon Valley breakthrough: "Americans, especially senior citizens, are helping themselves by salvaging the vast food resources usually wasted in production and harvesting — about twenty percent of all food produced, according to the United States Agriculture Department. Gleaners' groups in Arizona, California, Michigan, Oregon, and Washington State go into the fields and find food passed over by the harvest, then distribute it in community groups. St. Mary's Food Bank in Phoenix, Arizona, which collects cast-aside and gleaned food, sent two million pounds of food to schools and social service groups and fed forty-eight thousand emergency victims for three days during 1979. Now St. Mary's helps other groups all across the country to learn the self-help approach to cutting waste and feeding the poor."[34]

Other gleaners' groups, like Goodwill Industries, the Salvation Army, and Light and Life Resale Shops, collect discarded commodities and then repair them for sale by using unemployed and handicapped workers. And groups like HELP Services in Texas and the St. Vincent de Paul Society in New Hampshire have put unemployed workers out on the city streets cleaning up litter, rubbish, and overgrowth in exchange for groceries. All without federal subsidies. All without bureaucratic interference. As R. J. Rushdoony has pointed out, "The rise of welfarism has limited the growth of urban gleaning, but its potentialities are very real and deserving greater development."[35]

Fifth, Ruth obtained mercy. But that mercy was not a "right" that she claimed. It was not an entitlement. In fact, Biblical charity is discriminatory (Ruth 2:7). Biblical charity knows nothing of promiscuous handouts to sluggards. "The lazy and improvident," David Chilton has said, "could expect no saving intervention by a benevolent bureaucrat."[36] If he worked, he ate. If he chose to laze about, then he and his family went hungry. Biblical charity discriminates. Ruth received genuine mercy, but it was a mercy freely given and rooted in merit.

Discrimination. Just mention the word and suddenly visions of bigotry, pogroms, and stiff-necked lovelessness dance in our heads. But Scripture teaches that discrimination, far from being a villainous vice, is very often a venerable virtue. Our confusion comes when we automatically associate discrimination with racism, unfairness, and oppression. But whereas the Bible explicitly condemns racism, unfairness, and oppression, it condones discrimination.[37]

The dictionary defines discrimination as "making a clear distinction, to differentiate." Thus, to discriminate Biblically is to make distinctions and to differentiate utilizing God's unchanging Law as the standard. As such, discrimination is nothing more than the fruit of discernment. While the racist may abuse discrimination by judging the world around him in accord with his vile prejudices, the Christian is called to exercise spiritual discernment, godly discrimination, judging the world around him in accord with God's unerring Truth.

This pattern of holy discrimination is illustrated and implemented throughout Scripture.

God Himself differentiated between Abram's seed and the rest of mankind (Genesis 12:1-3). God discriminated. His love was not promiscuous. That, of course, does not mean that He acted unfairly or partially in judging men. It simply means that He judged them. Impartially. According to His standards. He distinguished between those within the covenant and those without. He differentiated between believers, those destined for the throne, and unbelievers, those doomed to damnation. God discriminated.

Again, God differentiated between Jacob and Esau (Genesis 25:23; Romans 9:10-13). God discriminated. His love was not promiscuous. God made a distinction between the arrogant, selfish, and gluttonous Esau and the provident, industrious, and enwisened Jacob. His judgments were not indiscriminate or standardless philanthropic exercises in sentimentality. God discriminated.

On Mount Carmel, Elijah was commanded by God to differentiate between the followers of Baal and the disciples of the Lord (1 Kings 18:20-40). Elijah exercised spiritual discernment, godly discrimination. Shunning human prejudice and fleshly sympathies, he judged the world around him according to God's standards. Thus, justice was preserved. God's Truth was upheld and vindicated because Elijah discriminated.

The Apostle Paul admonished the elders of the Ephesian Church to exercise discriminatory oversight in their congregation (Acts 20:18-35). And that admonition is echoed by Peter and Jude and John in their various letters (2 Peter 2:1-22; 1 John 4:1-6; Jude 5-23). The wolves must be distinguished from the sheep. The false professors must be differentiated from the true professors. And because discrimination is the fruit of discernment, discrimination must, of necessity, play a central role in the life of the obedient Church.

Jesus Himself discriminates. On the last day Christ will distinguish the sheep from the goats (Matthew 25:31-48). Utilizing God's impartial standard of justice, He will send the goats off to their eternal perdition. On that day, He will not collapse into indiscriminate sentimentality. He will not throw off God's holy requisites in favor of a pity-provocated promiscuity. He will discriminate: The sheep will go to the right; the goats, to the left.

In this time of institutionalized guilt and federalized pity, we must make certain that we measure our conceptions of justice, mercy, and compassion against God's standards in Scripture. Justice that does not discriminate between the worthy and the unworthy is not true justice. Mercy that does not discriminate between the deserving and the undeserving is not true mercy. Compassion that does not discriminate between the provident and the improvident is not true compassion.

God desires for us to discriminate. Not by the sinful standards of racism or sentimentality or nationalism. God desires for us to exercise spiritual discernment, utilizing the unchanging standard of His Holy Word. Thus, Herbert Schlossberg can appropriately assert, "No theory of helping the poor may be said to be Christian if it does not discriminate among the poor. The old distinction, now despised among social workers, between the deserving and undeserving poor, is a reflection of a Biblical theme."[38]

This distinction becomes more than evident as we note the Law's provision for gleaners as opposed to sluggards (Leviticus 19:9-10; 23:22; Deuteronomy 24:19-21; Proverbs 6:6-11; 19:15; 21:25-26). Standing within the covenant, the gleaner—whether he was converted or not—had the privilege of provision and care. Standing outside the covenant, the sluggard did not. Willing to labor long and hard, the gleaner was the recipient of regular charity. Unwilling to lift a hand, the sluggard was not.

Boaz discriminated in the case of Ruth (Ruth 2:8-16), and rightly so. He was following the pattern of Biblical charity.

Other Biblical Patterns

The Scriptural principle of gleaning, illustrated in the story of Ruth, is one of the primary means of implementing Biblical charity, but it is certainly not the only means. Faith, family, and work are compassionately reinforced in a number of other ways in Scripture as well.

Every town in Israel was commanded to keep a benevolence fund in case of calamity or emergency. Every third year, special tithes were collected for this fund, which was then to be used to care for "the orphan and the widow" (Deuteronomy 14:29). In addition, any unspent Levitical tithes were also returned to the local communities for the fund (Numbers 18:24). In the New Testament, this concept of alms was continued by the local Churches in order to care for the needy in their midst (Acts 4:35; 1 Corinthians 16:2; 2 Corinthians 8-9).

Another method of dispensing Biblical charity is private giving. This was the approach the Good Samaritan took on the road to Jericho (Luke 10:30-37), and it was the impulse that motivated Barnabas and others in the early Church when emergency relief became necessary (Acts 4:32-37). Private giving has the advantage of being totally unencumbered by any and all regulatory agencies. It springs from a Spirit-provoked desire to match available resources with pressing need, above and beyond the requirements of Law or responsibility.

Still another approach to Biblical charity is the interest-free loan (Exodus 22:25; Leviticus 25:35-37). Charitable loans are not intended to be business transactions; they are instead simply to ensure that poor families are able to secure the barest necessities: food, shelter, and clothing. To further protect the poor from harassment or long-term liability, these charitable interest-free loans are to be canceled by the lender after seven years (Deuteronomy 15:1-2).

A modern model of Biblical charity may include aspects of the alms, private giving, and interest-free loan patterns in Scripture as well as gleaning. But whatever methods it utilizes, it will always focus on reinforcing in the lives of the poor the triumvirate values of faith, family, and work.

Long-term Efforts

Sifting through all the verses that constitute the Scriptural blueprint for relieving the poor, it is readily apparent that Biblical charity is not built upon the flimsy foundations of guilt-edged sentimentality. It is built upon God's Law. It is built upon a bootstrap ethic of covenantal faithfulness, family cohesiveness, hard work, determination, productivity, and personal responsibility.

Sustaining a life through a handout or two is quick and easy. But such short-term efforts create a permanent welfare underclass. Equipping a life through counsel, training, accountability, and referral is time-consuming, financially demanding, and difficult. But such long-term efforts create self-sufficient, productive workers. Thus, anything less than the time-consuming and the difficult is an unadulterated waste and deserves our boisterous repudiation. Anything less is something other than Biblical charity. "If history teaches us anything," says author Gary DeMar, "It is that governments increase the effects of poverty (Genesis 47:13-19; 1 Samuel 8). Civil governments continue to exact a greater portion of our incomes through taxation to fund social programs that do not work over the long run. God placed the responsibility to care for the really poor with each individual, family, Church, and those institutions voluntarily supported by our tithes and gifts. The conquest of poverty will come when people are obedient to the commandments of God."[39]

God has a plan. He has the blueprints. If and when we follow them, "not turning to the left or to the right" (Deuteronomy 24:14), then we will experience the fullness of His promise:

> There shall be no poor among you, for in the land the Lord your God is giving you to possess as your inheritance, He will richly bless you, if only you fully obey the Lord your God and are careful to follow all these commands I am giving you today. For the Lord your God will bless you as He has promised and you will

lend to many nations but will borrow from none. You will
rule over many nations but none will rule over you (Deuteronomy 15:4-6).

Summary

Authentic Word-and-deed Christianity has had its exemplars
since the first century, in the likes of George Whitefield, Charles
Haddon Spurgeon, Nathaniel Samuelson, and a whole host of
others. Their orphanages, hospitals, almshouses, rescue missions, schools, and soup kitchens all spoke eloquently to the
world of the exacting compassion of Christ, and bore stark testimony to the obedience of His servants. These holy men and
women clothed their faith with works of compassion that not
only changed their world, but continue to affect lives and cultures to this day.

They understood that Christ's Great Commission commands
the Church to much more than mere soul-saving: we are to *disciple* the nations by teaching them to obey *everything* that He has
taught us. Our call is to win *all* things for the Lord Jesus. Whitefield, Spurgeon, Samuelson, and the rest lived their lives to that
end. Unfortunately, the modern tendency to ignore all our
Scriptural responsibilities *except* soul-saving has resulted in the
gradual takeover of Western culture by an insipid humanism.

Since the Bible is a blueprint for living, providing models,
structures, and systems for the godly ordering of every aspect of
life, we can fully expect to find in it answers to even the most
monolithic of problems, like an encroaching humanism and an
endemic poverty. And we can fully expect that when we adhere
to those models, structures, and systems, our evangelism will
then become the invasion of lifestyle and society that it was intended from the beginning to be.

The Biblical alternatives to the massive giveaway programs
enacted by the federal government especially show the blueprint
character of Scripture. Grounded in a family and work-ethic
that encourages faith, responsibility, industry, productivity, and
self-sufficiency, those Biblical alternatives are systematically outlined in innumerable places throughout the Scriptures. Methodologies like gleaning, the tithe-alms, and lending are protected
from abuse by the tempering conditions of discernment, dis-

crimination, and discipline. From A to Z, the Bible lays out, in blueprint fashion, the models, structures, and systems necessary for the task of transforming poverty into productivity.

Like Whitefield, Spurgeon, Samuelson, and the others, we can turn back the tide of humanism by reclaiming the full implications of the Great Commission. Like them, we can meet the grave dilemmas of our day with the full confidence that Scripture has the answers.

PART THREE

THE STRATEGY

The battle plans were laid before Joshua, long before he took to the field of Jericho. The plans were inscribed upon time's scroll by the holy predetermination of the Sovereign Lord. Joshua had but to follow, to obey. Indeed, no less could be said of the plans laid before us. We have but to follow, to obey. Such is the strategy.

Langdon Lowe (1882)

We, in the Church, are going to have to take over charity and welfare, as well as preaching the Gospel. A new standard is set before us as the day of the easy Christian grinds to a halt.

Marshall Foster

When the Church of Jesus
        shuts its outer door,
Lest the roar of traffic
        drown the voice of prayer,
May our prayers, Lord,
        make us ten times more aware
That the world we banish
        is our Christian care.
If our hearts are lifted
        where devotion soars,
High above this hungry
        suffering world of ours;
Lest our hymns should drug us
        to forget its needs,
Forge our Christian worship
        into Christian deeds.

F. Pratt Green

The real issue that divides Liberals and Conservatives is not whether to help the poor, but how to help them.

John Eidsmoe

O Master, let me walk with Thee
In lowly paths of service free.
Stir me, Lord, that I might bear
The strain of toil, the fret of care.

Washington Gladden

The contemporary explosion of human need may present the Church in North America with its greatest opportunity to make a lasting impact on this continent. But this will only happen if individual Christians and local Churches act.

Bernard Thompson

SIX

FAITH: DEVELOPING
A MISSION

Jeff Wharton was struggling with his responsibility as a young adult Sunday School teacher. He felt as if he just wasn't getting anywhere.

"I'm so excited about the things I've been teaching. I just don't understand why no one else is. I mean, we'll talk about the horrors of abortion, or the public school mess, or the problems of the poor, and then, after class, everyone just trots off happy as you please. Doing nothing. I wish I could motivate them some-how. I wish I could get them into gear, making a difference in the world. You know, if we Christians don't really get on the ball soon, everything we hold precious and dear will vanish before our very eyes." After a long, frustrated silence, he concluded, "We must begin to develop a sense of mission. We've got no time to waste."

But how? How do we motivate Christians to tackle huge problems like homelessness, hunger, and welfare waste?

There are thousands of Christians like Jeff all over America. Frustrated by their own inaction and by the inaction of others. Fearful that we may have let things go a little too long. Wonder-ing if there is any way to turn things around, to unleash the peo-ple of God as a force of healing and righteousness.

After all, the poor *need* the Church. They don't just need food or clothing or job counseling. They need the Church.

That is because the Church is the only institution on earth that can actively nurture the values of faith, family, and work in the poor — or anyone else for that matter — through the Word re-vealed, the Word made manifest, and the Word incarnate.

The Word renews the minds of the poor. Through the teaching of Scripture, the way and will of God is revealed. Right doctrine shatters old habits, explodes bad thoughts, and establishes real hope. The Gospel changes people. Thus, the agenda of Biblical charity must not simply be an institutional alternative to the federal "war on poverty." It must be forthrightly centered in the Church. The poor need good news. They need *the* Good News.

The Word readjusts the poor to reality. True worship is not an arcane indulgence in abstract rites. It is a tangible offering *to* God, a consecration *before* God, a communion *with* God, and a transformation *in* God. It is thus a conscious drive at the heart of ultimate reality. It is the Word made manifest. In it, the meaning and value of all life is revealed and fulfilled. The poor — like all men — need a double dose of reality. And only the Church can serve up that reality as it gathers together each Lord's Day.

The Word also reforms the lifestyles of the poor. The discipling and the disciplining process of life in the local Church repatterns men's ways according to the ways of the Lord, confronting them with the Word *incarnate*. It retrains them in humility, joy, perseverence, diligence, and responsibility. Their expectations and desires are slowly brought into conformity with the expectations and desires of the righteous. They are reformed. And they are reformed in the midst of other people who likewise are in the process of being reformed. These other people then become a lifestyle context that not only reinforces the ongoing reformation, but also provides a community of concern and care.

The poor need the Church.

Sadly though, the Church in our day has not made itself available to the poor — as Jeff Wharton and thousands of Christians like him have discovered in frustration. Biblical charity has become — like the poor themselves — a forgotten and neglected ideal. Were it not for people like Jeff — a small but faithful remnant — it seems that the Church would be swallowed up in a catatonic apathy, and the ideals of faith, family, and work would be lost to us entirely.

Thankfully, the Bible assures us that it is never too late (Psalm 37:9-11). We *can* stir men's passions and loose the strength of the Christian community on the problems that plague our culture.

Jeff and the others like him need to be assured that our Churches *can* be motivated to take action. We *can* make a difference.

But how? How can we effectually break the bonds of listless complacency? How can we stir up passions for authentic Christianity?

Very simply, if we are going to help our Churches develop a sense of mission — if we are going to motivate them to take action on behalf of the distressed, the oppressed, the unborn, or the poor — then we must first help them think Biblically. Right thinking precedes right action. We must help them develop a Biblical worldview. Then, and only then, will they be ready, willing, and able to undertake action agendas.

Right Thinking

Our worldview is simply the way we look at things. It is our perspective of reality. It is the means by which we interpret the situations and circumstances around us. Whether we know it or not, we have a worldview. Everyone does. Alvin Toffler, in his landmark book *Future Shock*, said, "Every person carries in his head a mental model of the world, a subjective representation of external reality."[1] This mental model is, he says, like a giant filing cabinet. It contains a slot for every item of information coming to us. It organizes our knowledge and gives a grid from which to think. You see, our mind is not blank and impartial and our viewpoint is not open and objective. "When we think, we can only do so because our mind is already filled with all sorts of ideas with which to think," says economic philosopher, E. F. Schumacher.[2] These more or less fixed ideas make up our mental model of the world, our frame of reference, our presuppositions — or, in other words, our worldview.

"A worldview is a map of reality," James Sire tells us. "And, like any map, it may fit what is really there, or it may be grossly misleading. The map is not the world itself, of course, only an image of it, more or less accurate in some places, distorted in others. Still, all of us carry around such a map in our mental makeup and we act upon it. All of our thinking presupposes it. Most of our experience fits into it."[3]

One of the basic demands of Christian discipleship, of following Jesus Christ, is to *change* our way of thinking. We are to "take captive every thought to make it obedient to Christ" (2 Corinthians 10:5). We are "not to be conformed to this world but be transformed by the renewing of our minds" (Romans 12:2). In other words, we are commanded to have a Biblical worldview. All our thinking, our perspective on life, and our understanding of the world around us, is to be comprehensively informed by Scripture.

God's condemnation of Israel came because "their ways were not His ways and their thoughts were not His thoughts" (Isaiah 55:8). They did not have a Biblical worldview. When we begin to think about law or biomedical ethics or art or business or love or history or welfare or anything else apart from God's Revelation, we too have made ourselves vulnerable to condemnation. A Biblical worldview is not optional. It is mandatory.

So, how do we develop a Biblical worldview? How do we go about replacing our old ways of thinking with God's way of thinking? How do we go about helping others develop such a Scriptural outlook on all of life?

Obviously, the place to start is with the Bible itself. We need to read the Bible with new eyes of awareness, with a new hunger for comprehensive Truth. We need to familiarize ourselves with its full contents, with its whole counsel. Then we need to teach others the new insights we have discovered.

This is precisely how godly men and women throughout the ages provoked their congregations, friends, neighbors, and families to apply authentic Word-and-deed Christianity to the problems of poverty. Whitefield, Spurgeon, Samuelson, and the others had a Biblical worldview. In other words, everything they did, everything they thought about, all that they aspired to, and all that they passed on in legacy to their children was shaped by the clear teaching of Scripture and the mandates of the Great Commission. The Bible for them was a blueprint for every area of life and culture. The ministries that they built — the ministries that we inherited — were thus influential, powerful, and always poised for righteous action. They were not perfect, of course. Far from it. As mere fallen men and women, they made mistakes. Often. Even so, they were insistent on obeying Scripture to the best of their ability across the board. And with their belief in the totality of the Bible's message and unwavering trust in the promises of God, they were able to succeed dramatically.

Not only did those Biblical charity pioneers take the Bible to be their blueprint for living, but they passed it on to their children in blueprint form. They believed that the revelation of God to men in the Bible was the authoritative starting point and the final court of intellectual appeal on earth. They would have wholeheartedly concurred with Cornelius Van Til when he asserted, "The Bible is authoritative on everything of which It speaks. And It speaks of everything."[4] Thus, they taught every educational discipline to their children on the assumption that all forms of secular knowledge had been constructed on foundations of philosophical, moral, and spiritual sand. This meant that children learned to read straight from God's Precepts. They began to hammer out principles of economics in terms of God's Word. They began to develop political perspectives based upon God's Commands. They pioneered art, music, and ideas that were Scripturally grounded. Everything, in every field, on every front, was built on a fundamental rejection of the notion that there might be areas of moral, intellectual, or cultural neutrality. They understood that every realm of human endeavor must flow from Biblical principles: mathematics, biology, literature, sociology, law, music, physics, and welfare. Because God has ordained that the Bible govern them all.

It has been so terribly long since Christians have maintained that kind of stand, that kind of educational program. It is little wonder then that Western culture has lost, or is losing, all its Biblical distinctives. And all its Biblically wrought blessings to boot.

Are there compassionate Scriptural alternatives to the state welfare system? Are there judicious Scriptural alternatives to wage and price controls in the face of runaway inflation? Are there viable Scriptural alternatives to the monolithic abortion industry? Are there equitable Scriptural alternatives to government-regulated public schools? The Bible says *yes* on every count, but you'd never know it by looking at the Church. Christians, befuddled and bewildered, have not looked to Scripture for anything more than personal solace and salvation. We have not developed a Biblical worldview. We have not applied the Scriptures to all areas of life as the blueprint for living.

Now is the time to begin serious work toward building Biblical worldviews. Now is the time to reclaim our lost legacy. Now is the time to return to the blueprints. Right thinking precedes right action.

A Blessed Hope

Not only did the Biblical charity pioneers of centuries past believe the Bible, they trusted it. Not only did they faithfully conform every aspect of their lives to its pattern, they had every expectation that such faithfulness would be met with divine favor. They believed that God was personally and intimately involved in the affairs of men, and thus, His promises were dependable and sure. This was the cornerstone of their worldview.

They believed that His Law would actually be "a lamp unto their feet and a light unto their path" (Psalm 119:105) and enable them to "walk about in freedom" (Psalm 119:45). They even believed that if they were "careful to do everything written in it, then they would be prosperous and successful" (Joshua 1:8) and "productive and effective" (Psalm 1:3). Thus, they were able to approach life and culture with a very healthy Christian hope. They knew God would honor His Word. They knew they could trust His "very great and precious promises" (2 Peter 1:4). They knew that their efforts for righteousness would not be in vain. In short, they were an optimistic people. They looked forward to the days ahead with great anticipation. And, perhaps most importantly, they taught others to do the same thing.

If we are to have any hope of motivating others to take action, if we are to develop in them a sense of mission, then we must emulate our elders. We too must trust God and His Word enough to see the future in an optimistic light. For far too long we have wallowed in the mire of a paralyzing dread. For far too long we've seen "hope" as nothing more than a last-second rescue from the jaws of destruction.

The Bible says that we are "more than conquerors" (Romans 8:37), "overcomers" (1 John 5:4), and "victorious" (1 Corinthians 15:57). "For greater is He that is in us than he that is in the world" (1 John 4:4). So why do we carry on as if we were a defeated and dispersed band of vagabonds? The Bible says that our hope is not bound to the subjective. It is clearly objective as well. It is not bound to the individual. It is clearly corporate as well.

Humanism's hope of peace on earth has been shattered time and time again on the battlefields of Europe, Southeast Asia, Central America, and the Middle East. Humanism's hope of political Utopia has been shattered in the streets of Paris, Moscow, Gdansk, and Tehran. Humanism's hope of medical and genetic perfectibility has been shattered in the ovens of Auschwitz, the abortuaries of New York, and the nurseries of Bloomington. Humanism's hope of winning the "war on poverty" has been shattered in the ghettos of New York, Chicago, and Detroit. But the Biblical hope has never yet been found wanting. In fact, as history marches ever forward, that hope becomes ever more secure.

Like our Good Samaritan forefathers, we must develop an optimistic view of the future if we are to, in any form or fashion, be faithful to the call of God and thereby motivate others to action. We must expect great things and, thus, attempt great things, so that we may accomplish great things.

War-Zone Mentality

The Biblical charity pioneers were a peace-loving people. Above all else, they desired to see their families and congregations live long and harmonious lives. But, at the same time, they nurtured a war-zone mentality. It is not that they harbored latent paranoia. Far from it. It is simply that they viewed all of life through the lens of Scripture. And Scripture teaches that Christians are in a war. It is a war that crosses all boundaries and invades all ages. It is a life-and-death struggle of cosmic proportions. Those early, faithful Christians believed that and lived accordingly, and their worldview was shaped accordingly.

They took seriously the Apostle Paul's admonition to "put on the full armor of God" in order to prepare for conflict with the dastardly forces of darkness (Ephesians 6:10-18). They understood it to be their calling to "wage war," to "demolish strongholds," and to "tear down fortresses" (2 Corinthians 10:4-5). They were more than willing to "suffer hardship as good soldiers of Christ Jesus" (2 Timothy 2:3). Of course, they comprehended that their primary enemies were not "flesh and blood" (Ephesians

6:12) and, thus, they were "not to wage war as the world does" (2 Corinthians 10:3).

Those stalwart men and women who willingly gave their all for the poor and the broken made great spiritual and cultural advances because they understood the concept of warfare. If we are to make similar advances in our own day, then we must not shirk our war-zone duties.

Throughout the Scriptures, the issue of conflict is undeniably prevalent. Opponents are disarmed (Colossians 2:15). Victories are won (1 John 5:4). Captives are taken (2 Corinthians 10:5). Casualties are exacted (1 Peter 5:8). Strategies are formulated (Revelation 5:1-8). Commissions are extended (Mark 16:15). Ambassadors are engaged (2 Corinthians 5:20). Weapons are dispensed (2 Corinthians 10:4). Espionage is exposed (Acts 20:29-30). Battle cries are sounded (1 Corinthians 14:8).

And the war that is described in Scripture is not some metaphysical, esoteric, invisible war. On the contrary, the war involves cultures, civilizations, institutions, powers, and principalities. It involves men and nations, not simply and exclusively demons and hobgoblins (Genesis 1:28; Matthew 28:19-20). The army of God is to conquer the earth, to subdue it, to rule over it, to exercise Christ's dominion. Christians are called to war. And it is a war we are expected to win.

The blessings of liberty and prosperity in Western culture have softened us in this matter. The war-zone mentality is alien to us. Thus, even when humanism's monstrous assault upon the innocents reaches to our own backyards, we remain hesitant, uncertain, and recalcitrant. While Christian schools are attacked, unborn children are slaughtered, pastors are jailed, prayerful children are silenced, and the helpless poor are entrapped, the vast Christian army, meek and mild, goes virtually unnoticed. This must change.

That change will only come when we are faithful in motivating others to right action through right thinking. We must instill vision in those who see no future.

A Call to Excellence

There is one catch. Even if our congregations, families, and friends are riled and ready for action, there is a further element of the Biblical worldview that must be fully comprehended before action can be appropriately undertaken. Our program to help the poor, or any other activity for that matter, cannot be slopped together in a rush. Vision or not, the implementation of authentic Christianity must be marked by excellence. The answers, alternatives, and models we develop must bear the seal of Christ's handiwork.

A great obstacle to the Christian reclamation of Western culture is shoddy craftsmanship. It has almost become an evangelical legacy to churn out sloppy literature, sloppy music, sloppy social action, sloppy scholarship, and sloppy worship. As Franky Schaeffer has so accurately stated, we have become "addicted to mediocrity."[5]

Arresting this tragic triviality trend can only be accomplished as Christian leaders renew their heretofore unshakeable commitment to excellence. But how does a leader develop a spirit of excellence in a day of compromise and accommodation, when almost anything can be passed off as good enough? The answer is that he must start with God Himself. He must consider and emulate the excellence of God's character and attributes.

Not surprisingly, the Bible has much to say about the subject:

- God's Name is excellent: "O Lord, our Lord, how excellent is Your Name in all the earth" (Psalm 8:1). "His Name alone is excellent, His glory is above the earth and heaven" (Psalm 148:13).

- God's lovingkindness is excellent: "How excellent is Your lovingkindness, O God" (Psalm 36:7).

- God's power is excellent: "Praise the Lord. Praise God in His sanctuary; praise Him in the excellence of His power" (Psalm 150:1).

- God's salvation is excellent: "Call upon the Name of the Lord, declare His doings among the people, make mention of His exalted name. Sing unto the Lord, for He has done excellent things" (Isaiah 12:4-5).

- God's will is excellent: "Do not be conformed to this world but be transformed by the renewing of your mind that you may test and approve the good, and acceptable, and perfect will of God" (Romans 12:2).

- God's way is excellent: "As for the Lord, His way is perfect" and "The Word of the Lord is tried" (2 Samuel 22:31).

And so the story goes, on and on throughout the Scriptures, a never-ending hymn of praise to the excellence of the Living Lord.

Now, if we are to follow after Him — and we are (Matthew 4:19); if we are to be of the same mind as He — and we are (1 Peter 2:21); if we are to emulate His very attributes — and we are (1 Peter 1:16), then it only stands to reason that excellence must be a universal distinguishing characteristic of disciples of the Lord.

The fact is that the same God who demanded sacrificial excellence (Malachi 1:8-10); the same God who demanded artistic excellence (Exodus 28:2); the same God who demanded cultural excellence (Genesis 1:28); the same God who demanded evangelistic excellence (Matthew 28:18-20); the same God who demanded economic excellence (Matthew 25:14-30) demands that you and I manifest something significantly more than the current status quo of mediocrity.

Elton Trueblood, the esteemed Quaker scholar, has noted that "Holy shoddy is still shoddy."[6] And there is no room for any thing shoddy in the glorious Kingdom of our God and King. Isn't it about time we acknowledged as much by striving for excellence in our Churches? In our preaching? In our thinking? In our work on behalf of the poor? We must motivate our congregations, not just to action, but to effective action, excellent action.

Mission Strategy

Obviously, a full-scale frontal assault on complacency and reticence in our congregations will be required if Biblical charity is to be implemented with any real success — if a consistent Biblical worldview is to be ingrained to any degree. Authentic Christianity is not easily nurtured. Congregations are not easily catalyzed. Nothing less than a missions strategy that encompasses every aspect of Church life will do.

First, the preaching program of the Church must be mobilized to motivate, equip, and educate the saints so that they can then undertake the work of the ministry (Ephesians 4:12).

All too often though, our preaching — the primary means of reproducing Scriptural convictions in others — has been entirely inadequate. Our focus on homiletics has either been doctrinal and exegetical to the near exclusion of specific, practical application, or it is awash in an existential piffle, drivel, and swill. As a result, our sermons have lost their life. They are either dry or soppy. They are either intangible or incorrigible. But either way, they lack both heart and art. The chief end of preaching is to proclaim God's Truth and to thus give Him glory. And there is no glory in either dead didactae or flash-in-the-pan contentlessness.

In order for Biblical charity to see resurgence in our day, in order to mobilize our congregations for Good Samaritan effectiveness, our preaching must emphasize both content and passion. Our homiletical art must match the level of excellence in our homiletical exposition. Men's minds must be informed, and their hearts must be stirred. A sermon's intent is not simply to transfer information or to provoke metaphysical fireworks. It is to motivate. It is to change. It is to ignite zeal. It is to reproduce convictions. It is to set into action the army of God. It is to lay the foundations for a Biblical worldview among God's own.[7]

Why not encourage your pastor to undertake a series of sermons on the subject of Biblical charity? Perhaps an exposition of Ruth? Or, if he is hesitant, maybe you could begin to give him a few books on the subject. Keep him informed about the works of compassion that faithful followers of Christ the world over are undertaking. Encourage him. Support him.

When the pulpits of America begin to sound the strains of authentic Word-and-deed faithfulness, a vast army of motivated, dedicated warriors for Truth *will* emerge. When missions-oriented sermons ring forth once again, then we *will* have committed congregations.

Second, the worship of the saints must become missions-oriented if Biblical charity is to become a reality.

Much of the work of stirring a congregation's soul rests on the shoulders of worship. It is not the sole responsibility of the sermon. In fact, the whole service of worship, from the beadle to the benediction, should ideally work together toward that goal. Of course, the chief end of worship is not to be entertaining or enthralling or enthusing. It is to give God glory. It is to be structurally and Scripturally faithful. But there is no glory or faithfulness in dead orthodoxy. Sadly, our Churches have uncritically

mimicked either traditional or contemporary liturgical forms with
no eye toward Biblical, theological, cultural, or situational appro-
priateness. Thus, there is little motivation and even less glory.

In order for Biblical charity to see resurgence in our day,
worship must receive the same kind of careful scrutiny it received
in the eighth century, during Byzantium's ascendency, or in the
sixteenth century, during the Reformation. Creativity must
combine structurally with Biblical and historical faithfulness.
Vision and conviction must hammer out forms that will unite
the people of God in undetermined activity for the Kingdom.

A whole catalogue of hymns has been gathered over the
years that underscores the precepts of the Good Samaritan faith.
Why don't we begin to sing such classics as *Bringing in the Sheaves,*
Where Cross the Crowded Ways, Ne'er Empty Handed, Rise Up, O Men
of God, To the Work, Make Me a Channel of Blessing, and *Forward*
Through the Ages once again? What happened to the Psalms that
our Word-and-deed forefathers made such an integral aspect of
their song-worship? Why have the Psalms of victory, compassion, imprecation, and exhortation been all but retired from the
life of the Church? Whatever became of the dynamic liturgical
services of John Chrysostom, Basil the Great, John Knox, or
Martin Luther? Why don't we loose the motivating and equipping power of worship against the forces of privation?

The Book of Revelation makes clear that the activity of
God's people in worship actually and ultimately changes the
course of history.[8] To slough through worship means that we will
have to slough through history. To participate dynamically in
worship means that we will be able to participate dynamically in
history. Worship then must be marshaled to the task of defeating
the scourge of poverty.

Third, the missionary implications of the sacraments, especially the Lord's Supper, must be recovered.

James B. Jordan reminds us, "Historically, the Church has
particularly remembered the poor in connection with the Lord's
Supper. That's because this is God's gift to the starving. It is not
the gift of philosophy or of theology, or of ideas or of inward feelings. First and foremost, it is the gift of food. Thus, for instance:
the Christian Reformed Churches traditionally have a special
collection for the poor right after the quarterly communion

meal. And the historic orthodox Churches take up food and cloth-ing for special gifts at Christmas and Easter, that all may feast."[9]

Thus comprehended, the Lord's table, where we reap His bounteous grace provisions, becomes a continual provocation to missions. Thus comprehended, the Lord's table becomes an ever-present reminder of our earthly task.

God's people have always been cared for by God's own hand. And that has, in turn, been provocation for them to care for others. Whenever believers have been hungry, for instance, God has fed them. He fed them in the Garden (Genesis 2:16). He fed them manna in the desert (Exodus 16:4). He fed them bread in the morning and meat in the evening (Exodus 16:12). He fed them on the fat of a bounteous land flowing with grapes, figs, and pomegranates, dripping with milk and honey (Numbers 13:23-27). He fed them in times of famine (Ruth 1:1-16), in times of oppression (Ezekiel 34:13-14), in times of distress (1 Kings 19:1-8), in times of drought (1 Kings 17:1-16), and in times of war (1 Samuel 21:1-6). "The Lord will not allow the righteous soul to famish" (Proverbs 10:3).

When Jesus came, He came to feed. The people were starv-ing. So He fed them loaves and fishes (John 6:1-14). And He fed them the "bread of life." He invited them to His banqueting table (1 Corinthians 11:23-25). He came to sup with them, and they with Him (Revelation 3:20). He came to prepare a table before them in the presence of their enemies, to anoint their heads with oil, and to fill their cups to overflowing (Psalms 23:5). He came to feed them at the glorious marriage supper of the Lamb (Reve-lation 19:7-9).

Ever since, Christians have made the focus of their weekly worship the Lord's Supper. They have come together to eat. And God gathers them about Him and feeds them from His bounty.

Then, because they have been satisfied, they can turn to the world to feed the hungry there. Because they have before their eyes constant reminders of man's need and God's provision, they are able to go forth with grace, mercy, and compassion. "Blessed is he who shall eat bread in the Kingdom of God" (Luke 14:15).

It is terribly tragic then that the Church in our day has lost sight of these orthodox truths. Because we have minimized the Lord's Supper to make room for "more important matters," we have become like salt that has lost its savor (Matthew 5:13). Because we have trivialized the Lord's Supper to magnify "more pressing concerns," we have begun to starve, and with us, the rest of the world (Amos 8:11-12).

If Biblical charity is to see any kind of resurgence in our day we will have to return to canonical and sacramental integrity.

Fourth, the Sunday School also must be utilized as a dynamic prod for mission once again.

Instead of being a dilapidated vehicle for watered-down moralisms, the Sunday School could serve as an intensive training camp for dedicated Kingdom activists. Rescued from banality, Sunday School could be the platform from which strategies are plotted, tactics are launched, and reclamation is begun.

Why not start a weekly elective Sunday School class or training series to explore what Scripture has to say about poverty and the appropriate Christian response to it? If we start small and take our learners along in smooth, carefully plotted stages, it won't be too terribly long before we have a whole slew of Christians champing at the bit, raring to jump headlong into the battle against hunger, homelessness, and the welfare trap.

Fifth, special events and meetings must be held periodically to stir the passion for, and instill the vision of, Biblical charity. Since most Churches already schedule special revivals or Bible conferences or prophecy seminars or missions conferences each year, why not devote some of the time to the problem of poverty and its Scriptural solutions? Why not invite a speaker or two who have actually begun the work of Biblical charity to detail the ins and outs, the ups and downs of their ministries?[10]

During the heyday of modern foreign missions, just before the turn of the century, missionaries visited in our Churches on a very regular basis, sharing their experiences and inspiring many to follow in their footsteps. Why not renew that old and venerable tradition? But this time, why not mix in a few "home missionaries" who are working with the poor as well as those called by God to foreign fields? The distressing trend away from an emphasis on missions has impoverished the Church and has diminished the motivations of our congregations to fulfill the Great Commission. But special meetings, conferences, and seminars can help change all that.

Sixth, the deacons of the Church must be mobilized for the work of missions. Since their Scriptural task is almost exclusively defined by the work of Biblical charity, they are a natural starting place.

Capture the hearts of the deacons, and you capture many a Church. Encouraging deacons to read books on Biblical charity or having time set aside in each deacons' meeting to study the Scriptural injunctions concerning the care of the poor would go a long way to achieving that end.[11] Or, what about having a deacons' retreat where a pastor, an evangelist, or a Biblical charity pioneer can lead in an intensive training session? Or, perhaps a series of Saturday morning prayer-and-study breakfasts, where the issue of welfare and poverty and the Church's response can be discussed?

If the Church is to be motivated to undertake the monumental task of building alternative structures of Scriptural compassion, the deacons' support is critical. Don't push. Don't shove. But, by all means, don't bypass the deacons.

Seventh, the youth of the Church must be enlisted in the work of missions.

Many of the great revivals the Church has experienced throughout history and many of the great missions movements began with the young. But, aside from that very obvious lesson, Church history also teaches us that any effort that ignores the youth is a short-lived effort, lasting only one generation. That simply won't do in the case of Biblical charity. Its complexity and magnitude requires us to think in multigenerational terms.

The punch-and-cookies approach to youth ministry is a tragic waste of time, money, and lives. Why not involve the youth of the Church in Biblical charity projects instead? Why not orient the youth ministry to the service of others? Why not channel the standard youth ministry fare of fund-raising, missions trips, fellowships, etc., into the fulfillment of the Good Samaritan mandate? Why not unleash the creative and productive labors of Christian kids on problems that really matter?

After all, if we win the hearts and minds of the next generation, we've won the future.

Eighth, even counseling can be enhanced by giving it a missions orientation.

It is a common understanding among pastoral counselors that service to others is the best therapy in which a person can engage. Many difficulties that Christians bring into counseling sessions have, as their best solutions, discipline, activity, selfless giving, and dedication. In the work of Biblical charity, people can exercise their spiritual gifts. They know they are accomplishing something important. Body life begins to flower spontaneously. Involvement intensifies. What better way to infect a congregation with authentic Christianity? What better way to begin to motivate Christians to action?

Ninth, other media also must be marshaled to the cause if we are to have committed, convicted congregations forming the framework for Biblical charity.

Though preaching, teaching, worship, the diaconate, the youth, etc., are central, the performing and graphic arts must by no means be ignored. Nor must we slight newsletters, books, videotapes, audiocassettes, films, radio broadcasts, data basing, and cable television.

Obviously, these diverse suggestions only touch upon the many and various ways that congregations can be motivated to take action on behalf of the poor. In fact, no matter how many pages might be devoted to the subject, we could no more exhaust the possibilities than we could drain the deep. But the point is, and hopefully it is a point well taken, any and every means the Church has at its disposal must be dispatched to the end of stirring up families with a zeal to flesh out the fullness of the Gospel.

Biblical charity requires an army. A couple of people here and a couple there simply won't cut it. If our objective is to supplant entirely the federal welfare folly with genuine Scriptural forms, it will take the framework of entire congregations, entire families, a whole host of dedicated, committed believers to do it.

Nothing short of a comprehensive missions strategy, encompassing every aspect of Church life, can enlist that kind of response.

If, on the other hand, we are unwilling to make the sacrificial effort necessary to motivate our congregations and ultimately to roll back the debilitating effects of welfare by equipping the poor through Biblical charity, we'd better admit it. We'd better stop complaining about the federal dole, "if not out of a sense of decency," says journalist Tom Landess, "at least out of a healthy regard for the vicissitudes of modern industrial life and the fickleness of the electorate." That way, "if we run across a battered and penniless stranger while traveling from Jerusalem to Jericho, we won't have to stop and help him ourselves. We can just call the appropriate agency and tell the bureaucrats where along the road to look for the body."[12] We can then wash our Levitical hands clean of blood-guilt and scamper on our merry way.

Bits and Pieces

Jeff Wharton was preparing for his next Sunday School lesson. The opening words of Francis Schaeffer's classic, *A Christian Manifesto*, leapt off the page and gripped his attention: "The basic problem of the Christians in this country in the last eighty years or so . . . is that they have seen things in bits and pieces instead of totals."[13]

"That's it!" he thought to himself. "That's the problem. Christians aren't going to get motivated, they're not going to make a difference in our world, if all they ever get is a confused smattering of facts and issues. We need an overall perspective, a driving sense of mission that pervades all of life and spirituality."

Throughout the rest of the week, Jeff went to work mapping out a strategy to inform and motivate the people in his Church. He contacted the pastor and several of the deacons. He set up a few preliminary meetings. He made arrangements to rent a series of films from a local Christian distributor. And he began some serious work on bringing focus to his Sunday School teaching.

Before long, Jeff's Church had begun to implement a comprehensive missions strategy. An outreach to the poor had been initiated and a study group was investigating ways to address the problem of abortion. "Things are finally beginning to happen," Jeff said, "and I couldn't be happier. The families in this Church will never go back to the old piecemeal approach to issues. We're ready to take on the world!"

Summary

In order to facilitate Biblical charity, we must mobilize entire congregations, educating and motivating them to get involved. We must free them from the bondage of apathy and complacency. We must develop a sense of mission in our Churches.

The first step in this process, of course, is to nurture a Biblical worldview, because right thinking precedes right action. We must study the Bible with an absolute certainty that it provides a plan for every area of life, including a viable model for charity. Only then can we begin to structure an agenda for action. Only then can we maintain confidence in the possibility of victory for the Church on earth as an earnest of the ultimate and objective victory of the risen, returning Christ. Only then can we develop a war-zone mentality that will prepare us for confronting and defeating the forces of darkness. Only then will we be able to accomplish our work with any measure of godly excellence.

To be certain, to effect such a worldview, the Church will need a comprehensive missions strategy: the preaching program of the Church must emphasize both doctrinal content and holy passion; congregational worship must convey both the heart and the art of the Biblical faith; the sacraments must be restored to their full Scriptural function of defining and catalyzing the people of God; the Sunday Schools, Bible conferences, and youth groups must be reclaimed from banality and set to the work of developing discipline, compassion, and missionary zeal.

It is critical that we not put the cart before the horse. We must develop a sense of mission in our Churches, but in order to do that, we must first help them to think Biblically. We must help them develop a Biblical worldview by marshaling every aspect of Church life to the task.

In this world a person can only be complacent if he or she is young enough, has money enough, is well enough, and, at the same time, lacks compassion for those about him. As soon as we face reality, the obscenity of the present situation strikes us in the face.

Francis A. Schaeffer

The solstice is called by the seasonal Voice,
So comes Your summons to me
    and the clarity eats at my choice.
The brethren clouds hang
    and inhabit the chill,
So I subsist in Your love,
    impaled on Your will.
The winded years carve Your Name
    on the face of the land,
And I am graven upon the palms of Your hands.

Kemper Crabb

The word "ministry" has become a clerical-collar word that most believers never apply to themselves. It seems too grand for ordinary, unordained believers. But the exact opposite is true! "Ministry" is not a professional word. It is one of humility which Christ applied to Himself. It speaks of the joy that goes with us as we obey Christ to minister to a world in need. "Ministry" is a term of caring and loving. It is a word for others, a word that liberates us from ourselves, a sculpting word to fashion us into the image of Christ Who came "not to be ministered unto, but to minister."

Calvin Miller

You are meant to incarnate in your lives the theme of your adoration, you are to be taken, consecrated, broken, and distributed, that you may be the means of grace and vehicles of the eternal charity.

Augustine

FAMILY: CHARITY BEGINS AT HOME

A recent survey conducted by the National Conference of Mayors indicates that a full twenty percent to twenty-five percent of the homeless street people in our cities suffer significant psychiatric disorders.[1] Among the estimated two million homeless poor in the United States are thousands of mentally retarded, autistic, and clinically insane persons.

For many years, tax-supported institutionalization kept the psychiatrically impaired out of sight and out of mind. But dire overcrowding, gross mismanagement, misappropriation of funds, and bureaucratic irresponsibility have worked together to dismantle the effectiveness of state programs. As a result, thousands of patients are released into the general population by this social service system gone awry.

So where do these handicapped ex-patients go? Many are reabsorbed into society quite successfully. Others are sheltered by their families. But, unfortunately, the vast majority simply end up in the streets.[2] Some are young, some are old, but almost all are dressed in rags stained dingy yellow by life in the streets. The pockets of their tattered overcoats and their shopping bags bulge with all the little bits of rubbish they collect and live on. They are filthy and suffering . . . bent and twisted by the downward curve of hunger, desperation, feeblemindedness, and want. These are our nation's untouchables . . . America's pariahs: invisible, disposable, and surplus. They are the destitute waste of our failing, flailing welfare society.

What can be done to solve the problem of our handicapped exiles?

In Geel, Belgium, is an interesting model of care for the unwanted, discarded mentally handicapped. It is a system that has been in effect since the middle of the fifteenth century.[3]

Over the course of five hundred-plus years, thousands of pilgrims have visited the Shrine of St. Dimpna in Geel. Mentally impaired or handicapped supplicants often travel long distances to the site in hope of a cure. Although records of the Church attest to the many miracles performed by the Lord, many of the pilgrims are not cured. In such cases, all too often the natural family, in despair and frustration, returns home, leaving the supplicant behind. Invariably, local families will then open their rooms to those abandoned. Again and again, the same sad scenario is replayed.

As time passed, word spread throughout Europe that the people of Geel had hearts of compassion and mercy, and would open their rooms to the distressed, unwanted, and feebleminded.

To this very day, over a thousand families within this town of thirty thousand exercise hospitality and provide medical care for one or more impaired boarders.

There has never been a recruitment program, never a central bureaucracy, and never a central administration. There have been only Christian families, generation after generation, demonstrating Christ's love, compelled by the Word-and-deed mandate of the Gospel. There are no mentally retarded, no autistic, no handicapped outcasts on the streets of Geel, because there, the people of God take seriously the Biblical mandate to care for the helpless and equip the poor.

In the United States, there are thousands of psychologically broken victims cluttering our alleys and flophouses. The reason? Christian families have failed. We can't blame "deficit-conscious politics." We can't even blame welfare's "war on the poor." The Bible teaches us that the family — provoked and equipped by the Church — is the primary agent of charity in a society. It is not the state's job to take care of the poor, the unemployed, the dispossessed, the untouchables, and the aliens. Nor is it the job of the social service agencies. It is Christian families that are to provide environments of stability, healing, nurture, encouragement, and responsibility.

The Primacy of the Family

If families fail—because the Church has failed to mobilize, motivate, equip, and enlist them—not only do the hungry and helpless suffer, we all suffer.

Christians in our day had best pay heed to an interesting scenario played out in the life of Samuel. Scripture gives us an intriguing glimpse at his family life and the role it played in the national arena.

It seems that, as judge over Israel, Samuel was a very busy man. Each year, we are told, he made the long and arduous "circuit from Bethel to Gilgal to Mizpah" (1 Samuel 7:16). His duties left little time for the diligent oversight of his home life in Ramah, and thus, he attempted to rule his family from afar. The result of that course, so sincerely undertaken, was nothing short of disastrous.

The Bible informs us that Samuel's neglect of family affairs was readily apparent in his sons. They failed consistently to walk in a manner befitting righteousness. "They turned aside after dishonest gain and accepted bribes and perverted justice" (1 Samuel 8:3). From their judicial seat in Beersheba, they exasperated the people and defiled judgment.

This personal tragedy, as bad as it was, was just the beginning of Samuel's woes. You see, the Israelites, seeing the wickedness of Samuel's family and the senescence of Samuel, began to panic. They began to fear for the future. They began to fret over the stability of their political and cultural order.

In time, the elders came together in Ramah to confront Samuel with their fears and to present him with their demands (1 Samuel 8:4). Samuel's failure in his home had undermined the foundations of the national security. Thus, they wanted him to take immediate political action in order to preserve life and liberty in the land. They wanted a king. Like all the other nations around them, they wanted a king (1 Samuel 8:5).

Not surprisingly, Samuel was grieved. His entire life's work had been committed to preserving the standard of Biblical Law and justice in Israel. And now it seemed that his undersighted neglect at home was nullifying his every accomplishment.

In desperation, Samuel attempted to warn the people of the inherent dangers of a monarchy (1 Samuel 8:11-18). There would be taxation. There would be conscription. There would be coercion. There would be tyranny. It was inevitable. But still the people could not be moved (1 Samuel 8:19). Even the prospect of tyranny down the road looked better to them than an eroding social order under Samuel's debauched progeny. A king and his tyranny it would be.

The Bible teaches us that the family — guided and shaped by the Church — is the primary agent of stability in a society. It is the family that is charged with the responsibility of infusing children with the principles of God's Law (Deuteronomy 6:6-7). It is the family that is charged with the responsibility of upbraiding, restraining, and rebuking behavior (Proverbs 23:13-14). It is the family that is charged with the responsibility of being culture's basic building block (Genesis 9:1-7). It is the family that is charged with the responsibility of balancing liberty with justice, freedom with responsibility, and license with restriction (Deuteronomy 11:18-21). It is the family that is charged with the responsibility of relieving want and destitution within their own ranks (1 Timothy 5:8). Thus, when the family fails, the entire social order is jeopardized. When family worship, family discipleship, family solidarity, and family responsibility are surrendered to the expediency of the moment, freedom is surrendered as well. Tyranny is the direct result of the failure of families.

Throughout his life, Samuel wandered hither and yon, weaving a social and political fabric impervious to the rending attacks of lawlessness, godlessness, and truthlessness. He poured himself into this work to the exclusion of all else — only to discover late in life that his sorely neglected family was unraveling his every stitch. He was chagrined to discover that the "important" things in life were overtaken by the "trivial" and, subsequently, tragically subdued. Matters of "great" consequence were subverted by matters of "little" consequence.

Samuel learned too late that families are the primary agents of stability in society. Not judges, not constitutions, not manifestos, not prophets, not bureaucrats, not kings — but families.

Scripture teaches that the family is the moral and institutional foundation upon which all human relations are built. It is central to every social endeavor from education (Proverbs 22:6) to governance (Deuteronomy 6:20-25), from economics (Deuteronomy 21:17) to spirituality (Ephesians 6:1-4), from the care of the aged (1 Timothy 5:3-13) to the subduing of the earth (Genesis 1:26-28). To all these responsibilities is added another. Economist Gary North says: "The family is designated by God as the chief agency of human welfare. It is the agency that is most effective in solving the problems of poverty, sickness, and crisis. It is the only agency which knows its limitations and strengths, for the self-interest of every household head is to count the costs of every project undertaken by the family. No other human agency links mutual self-interest, mutual understanding, mutual obligations, and mutual support in the way that a family can. Members are close. They know each other's weaknesses and strengths. The family is also an extended institution, with brookline contacts that can spread out widely. It can call upon related families for help in a crisis."[4]

For centuries, the Christians in Geel have provided, for all the world to see, living proof that no other institution, agency, or program can care for the poor and afflicted as effectually and as securely as the family. They have demonstrated what Christians should have known all along: as society's safety net, the family cannot be supplemented or supplanted in the work of charity without distorting and ultimately destroying charity. In her blockbuster book, *The Way Home*, Mary Pride relates: "When I was young, even though TV had exploded into every house, parents still told their sons and daughters that charity began at home. Those were the days before the Great Society and the 'war on poverty,' before it was discovered that charity begins in Washington. Americans had not yet learned to be ashamed of taking care of their families first, and then branching out to help other people. We did not yet feel responsible for solving the entire world's problems before solving our own. But the family is now out of the running when it comes to charity. Private, personal charity has, in our generation, largely been replaced by institutions whose professional job is to do good."[5]

Yet those institutions, those usurpers of the family have utterly failed.

The reasons for this are legion:

First, family charity is personal. No matter how benevolent, no matter how philanthropic, and no matter how altruistic a social service agency may be, it can never hope to match the personal intimacy of a family. Except in the rare and extreme cases where strife and bitterness have completely disintegrated familial identity, there is no replacement for the close ties of brothers and sisters, fathers and mothers, husbands and wives, parents and children, aunts and uncles, kith and kin.

Charity is people helping people by the grace of God. Charity is personal. Charity is the merciful expression of love and hope and life from one person to another. So when, in our attempts to aid the poor, we depersonalize and institutionalize charity, it ceases to be charity. When we begin to delegate away all our familial responsibilities to bureaucracies and professional humanitarians, the "war on poverty" inevitably turns ugly and becomes the "war on the poor."

Second, family charity is flexible. Care can be carefully adapted to fit each unique need. The federal welfare system can't afford that luxury. Their procedures must remain nationally uniform. They are bound to an endless array of charts, graphs, budgets, time limits, rules, and regulations. The family, on the other hand, can custom-design charity. It can specify and pinpoint the precise kind of aid for the precise length of time so that the needy are genuinely helped. There is less waste, so the cost is significantly lower. There are fewer delays, so the agony of waiting is eliminated. And the aid can be stopped at any time if it appears that that may be the best course of action.

The federal system is a lumbering, uncoordinated monster, unable to react to new situations, unable to change directions when circumstances so warrant. The family, on the other hand, is agile and flexible. So, while the social workers are forced, out of sheer necessity, to treat a street person from downtown Detroit the same way as an unemployed auto worker from Flint, the family is not so encumbered. The family can meet needs and solve problems. The welfare system can only create dependencies—as if poverty weren't bad enough.

Third, family charity facilitates accountability. Because the benefactor knows the beneficiary on a personal, intimate, one-on-one basis, there is far less room for sly manipulation and fraud. Income is harder to conceal. Sloth is next to impossible to hide. Everything is out in the open. Again, this is a luxury the social service system cannot afford. Its nameless, faceless operation is entirely incapable of engendering anything more than a stiff, statistical accounting of its clients. The magnitude of its caseload makes an investigation for graft impractical, and even an enforcement of basic regulations becomes increasingly impossible, and perhaps illegal, depending on the whims and fancies of tomorrow's judicial finagling.

Accountability in charity is only possible one-on-one. And one-on-one charity is only possible in the family.

Fourth, family charity reinforces positive values and moral fidelity. As R. J. Rushdoony has pointed out, under the welfare system, "there is a disintegration of the individual and of the family, and extensive demoralization." Under the family system, however, "untold millions are supported able and well, with the best of social consequences."[6]

Welfare breeds guilt, bitterness, sloth, envy, and vice. Family charity breeds loyalty, gratefulness, initiative, and productivity.

A recent survey of unemployed workers in Utah showed that those who chose to go on the federal dole were ten times more likely to suffer divorce, three times more likely to turn to crime, and twice as likely to abuse alcohol or drugs than those who did not.[7] But then, we didn't need a survey to tell us that. One look around a government housing project should be enough to convince anyone that there is something wrong, something terribly wrong, with the values that welfare breeds.

Fifth, family charity is effective. "Welfare agencies maintained by state and federal agencies have provided some kind of economic existence for as many as fifteen or more millions at one time," says Rushdoony. "But, daily, far more than a hundred million are supported by the family system."[8] Families can do the job, and do it well.

A U.S. Senate subcommittee report estimated that if every Christian family would only take care of its own, the federal dole would decrease a full thirty percent. If every Church would then take care of *its* own, the dole would decrease another twelve percent. And then, if each of those Churches would provide a sponsoring family to exercise charity to a single outsider, the federal dole could be eliminated completely.[9] Just like that. Families simply fulfilling their Christian responsibility to their own (1 Timothy

5:8), to their brethren in Christ (Galatians 6:10), and to the stranger and alien (Exodus 23:9), can so effectively do the work of charity that no back-up system, no federal bureaucracy, no matching funds, and no professional humanitarians are necessary. Families can do the job.

When Churches mobilize and motivate, equip and enlist families to practice authentic Christianity, they have not only gotten God's people out where the needs are and seen those needs met in accord with the Great Commission mandate, they have also set into motion the power of body life. They have catalyzed the practice of the priesthood of believers.

The Priesthood of Believers

From the dawning of the Church on the day of Pentecost, virtually all Christians have held, at least in theory, to the practice of the priesthood of believers. When the orthodox Churches of the East broke with Rome in the eleventh century, it was primarily over this issue. And later when Martin Luther, John Calvin, Ulrich Zwingli, and other sixteenth-century Protestants challenged the authority of Rome, it was again the priesthood of believers that was at issue. The reformers in both cases asserted that the people of God were not merely recipients or spectators, but also vital participants in the affairs of the Church. Thus, the heretofore inactive and immobilized believers were unleashed to do the work of the ministry (Ephesians 4:12) and to exercise their gifts (Romans 12:6).

Wherever the orthodox message reached, the priesthood of believers was emphasized. New Christians were taught early on that they were "being built into a spiritual house to be a holy priesthood, offering spiritual sacrifices acceptable to God through Jesus Christ" (1 Peter 2:5). They learned that they were "a chosen people, a royal priesthood, a holy nation, a people belonging to God," called to "declare the praises of Him who called them out of darkness into His wonderful light" (1 Peter 2:9).

Church history affirms that whenever this truth has been actively taught and practiced, there has been great revival and renewal. However, when the Church has narrowed its view of ministry to the point where only certain people at certain times with certain training can perform God's work, there has been only atrophy and decline.

In recent years, despite the countering effects of the body life movement, the home Bible study movement, the charismatic movement, the parachurch movement, and the reconstruction movement, the Church has drifted away from its reformed and orthodox moorings and its practice of the priesthood of believers. Christianity has become, by and large, a spectator sport. It has become an institution, an organization, a vast complex of properties. Senate Chaplain Richard Halverson has estimated that even after taking into account Sunday School teachers, choir members, youth sponsors, ushers, and committee members, fewer than one out of every twenty Church members ever actually participates in the work of the ministry. All the rest come to Church just to watch.[10] Since the Church can only "grow and build itself up in love, as each part does its work" (Ephesians 4:15-16), this institutional drift has impoverished the work of the Gospel. It has resulted in a Church that is, according to pastor and author Frank Tillapaugh, "ministry-helpless."[11]

A new emphasis on the priesthood of believers in our day would bring about at least three major changes in our Churches:

First, Christians would begin to understand and accept their Scriptural responsibilities. They would spring into action. Liberated from institutional limits, innovative and powerful ministries would blossom from newly unfettered gifts. They would function as priests, accountable directly and individually to the Lord and Giver of Life. They would move out beyond institutions and traditions and become salt and light, sharing the Gospel, reaching the lost, and mobilizing their families to care for the hungry, the naked, and the infirm.

Second, Christians would begin to think and act in terms of the covenant. Knowing that they were not merely individual priests, but a priesthood, they would begin to work together. They would cooperate. They would coordinate. They would network. As a people bonded together by the covenant of God, they would see all their work, all their ministries, and all their responsibilities in terms of the whole, in terms of the many. As a priesthood, and not just a collection of isolated priests, each going separately to God, they would be a community of priests.

They would be priests to each other. Monolithic problems like hunger and homelessness would not be left to a catch-as-you-can haphazardness, but would be confronted by the unified resources and the coordinated faithfulness of all the families of the covenant.

Third, Christians would begin to look outward with optimism once again. They would comprehend that priesthood is not just for the internal life of the Church; it is for the world. They would see themselves as ambassadors. They would move out to claim the earth for their Master and King. They would become Kingdom-conscious instead of program-conscious. They would begin to measure success by the standard of Scripture instead of the standard of the world, and thus would willingly commit to difficult, multigenerational tasks like the total reconstruction of social welfare. Knowing that a priesthood has the responsibility of both representing God to men and men to God, they would begin to minimize petty differences and move with confidence toward victory.

The One and the Many

The practice of the priesthood of believers is a practical reflection of the Biblical balance between the one and the many.[12] It is the application of both individual responsibility and corporate life. What this means for Scriptural compassion should be obvious: Families are the primary agents of charity in society, but anarchy need not reign. Families are responsible and accountable to God to live out authentic Christianity, but they need not tackle poverty alone, isolated and uncoordinated. God's people are called together in the New Covenant (Hebrews 7:22). They are to act covenantally (2 Corinthians 3:6). They are to synchronize their efforts and maximize effect through cooperation (1 Corinthians 12:7).

The Christian school movement had its genesis when parents began to take seriously their responsibility to educate their children, thus raising them "in the nurture and admonition of the Lord" (Ephesians 6:4). Yet, usually those families did not just strike out alone—even when they taught their children at home. They worked in tandem with other families and with their Churches, pooling resources, sharing expenses, and delegating functions.

Very similarly, families can be coordinated by Churches to take up their responsibilities in caring for the poor. The Churches can maintain the records, initiate the programs, administer the resources, and make the referrals, freeing the families to concentrate on personal ministry, succor, and relief. The Churches can provide security, expertise, and supervision, while the families begin the arduous task of restoring the needy to self-reliance and productivity.

The Church is charged with the responsibility of equipping the saints (Ephesians 4:12) and motivating believers with a sense of mission (Titus 3:8). The individual believers and their families are then to do the work of the ministry (Ephesians 4:12) and to bear the burdens of others, "thus fulfilling the Law of Christ" (Galatians 6:2). Any modern model of Biblical charity will see this balance between the one and the many deliberately implemented from the start—individual, faithful families and networking, convenantal Churches serving in unison to provide hope for the hopeless.

Putting It All Together

Carl W.lch was convinced. For some time, he had watched, listened, and learned. Now he was ready to act. "At first, when the elders and deacons began to encourage the families of the Church to care for the poor, I was quite skeptical," he admitted. "But the more I saw and heard, the more convinced I became."

He and his wife, Betsy, began by volunteering two evenings a week handling calls at the Church office, posting jobs on the bulletin board, and distributing food to the prescreened applicants. "The way the program has been set up by the Church, famili:s can begin right away making a difference in the lives of the needy. I, for one, finally feel as if I'm doing some good. Never in all my days have I had so many opportunities to share the Lord and to exercise my gifts. Betsy and I are closer than ever. This whole program is just fantastic. It's as if I'm really putting it all together: evangelism, discipleship, compassion, spiritual gifts, cooperation, and family togetherness."

Summary

Scripture teaches that the family is the primary agent of stability in society, providing as it does the moral and institutional foundation upon which all human relations are built. Thus, when the family fails, society itself fails. Similarly, when the family is supplanted or suppressed in the work of charity, true charity is distorted and ultimately destroyed.

The family is the best agent for the dissemination of charity because it is personal, flexible, accountable, reinforcing, and effective. As a result, the family can perform the task of charity efficiently and discriminately without welfare bureaucracies, matching federal funds, or professional humanitarians.

But, in order for the family to accomplish this feat of daring, it will need some help. In order for the place of the family to be restored to its proper function in society, the Church must once again emphasize the orthodox and reformed doctrine of the priesthood of believers. Only when the Church enables the family to comprehend its centrality to the work of the ministry will any real progress be made toward solving the great problems of our day. Only then will a balance be forged between individual liberty and corporate responsibility. Only then will deprivation and lack meet their match.

Thus, individual, faithful families and networking, covenantal Churches, serving hand in hand, form the infrastructure around which a functioning model of Biblical charity is built.

The failure of the welfare state requires that we change our rational assumptions, our hopes, and dreams at the visionary level, then implement our new vision with new strategies and, finally, develop new operations and tactics for the implementation of those strategies.

Congressman Newt Gingrich

The Christian Social Union here
Was very much annoyed;
It seems there is some duty
Which we never must avoid,
And so they sang a lot of hymns
To help the unemployed
Then Canon Holland fired ahead
Like fifty cannons firing
The way he made the windows jump
We couldn't help admiring.
I understood him to remark
(It seemed a little odd)
That half of his friends
Had never been in quod.
He said he was a Socialist himself,
And so was God.
To which (I couldn't help myself) I said,
"Pshaw! Pshaw!"

G. K. Chesterton

Without charity, no work profiteth, but whatsoever is done in charity, however small and of no reputation it be, bringeth forth good fruit.

Thomas à Kempis

EIGHT

WORK: FACILITATING PRIVATE INITIATIVE

In Terre Haute, Indiana, executives of the Great Scot super-market chain and several area Churches have joined forces to help the needy. "The Samaritan Food Project enables families to harness the resources of the private business sector for the benefit of the less fortunate," says John Holdren, Great Scot president. "We've set up collection containers in each of our stores where customers can donate canned goods, staples, and other nonperishables. At the end of each week, the food is distributed, and we pay a matching cash donation to the various food pantries and Church charities involved."

The project was started when leaders of the Greater Terre Haute Church Federation began to look for more systematic and effective ways to care for the poor. "We were constantly running short of groceries," said project supervisor Frank Volkers. "We needed to find ways to standardize our intake and packaging, and we needed to smooth out a lot of kinks in our distribution system. Great Scot's involvement was a godsend. We had the willing families, the workers. They had the expertise, the space, and the resources." The Samaritan Food Project is a prime example of how Churches can motivate families, who can then mobilize community forces to help the poor Scripturally.

In Minneapolis, Minnesota, a once-elegant and bustling Francis Drake Hotel is alive again, this time as a shelter for recovering alcoholics and homeless people. Dick Danielowski and John Treiber, both former alcoholics, decided to pool the resources of their family businesses so that they could better implement the Scriptural mandate to help the down-and-out rebuild their lives. "If it hadn't been for the godly concern of others, I probably wouldn't be alive today," says Treiber. "Dick and I and our families just wanted to comfort others with the very comfort we'd received. So we kind of mixed and matched our business assets and our family holdings with the constant encouragement of our Churches and, well, this is what we came up with."

When it first opened in 1926, the old hotel was a glittering two-hundred-room showcase with a basement supper club. Now, it is a showcase of a different sort. It, too, is a prime example of how Churches, motivating families and mobilizing businesses, can offer a valuable alternative to the federal welfare system.

In Houston, Texas, executives of the Igloo Corporation teamed up with a local Church charity to provide homeless families with ice chests, vacuum jugs, and pure-water containers. According to Igloo executive Joe Decker, "Most manufacturers of consumer goods have large supplies of unsalable inventory. The items may be seconds, they may be outdated, or they may just be the wrong color. But, regardless, the stock must be disposed of somehow." Most manufacturers destroy such inventory. "If Churches and other charities could organize a reputable and efficient distribution system," he said, "then I'm sure most of the waste would cease immediately and the goods could be had by those who probably need them most."

Manufactured goods are not the only commodities that would be available in abundance for distribution to the poor if only families, private businesses, and Churches could work together. On a busy day, manager D. L. Stone estimates that his busboys throw away half a ton of food at a Wyatt's Cafeteria in suburban Dallas. At the Borden Dairy Plant in New Orleans, workers returning outdated milk from stores every week dump five tons of dairy products into tanks so they can be shipped to the Midwest to be used in animal food. At supermarkets throughout Des Moines, store managers say they throw out day-old bread and other food "by the dumpsterful." They say if it is of no value to the store, it's probably of no value to anyone. In the Rio Grande Valley, citrus farmers leave tons of unsalable oranges and grapefruits to rot on the trees every year. And, amidst all this plenty, the poor hunger still.

According to one hunger researcher and lobbyist in Washington, "If even one-fourth of the edible food disposed of each day in the United States could be saved, hunger would be, for all intents and purposes, conquered. Unfortunately, charities haven't yet learned how to utilize the resources around them. More often than not, they'll go looking for some kind of federal grant instead of just checking in with the guy down the street. It's ridiculous, really."

Our Historical Legacy

Long before there were federal grants, special endowments, and cash subsidies—long before government paternalism became normative—Christians knew how to coordinate community resources to effect Scriptural mercy. They saw to it that their Churches maintained a missions emphasis and that their families did the work of the ministry. Then, from that base, they orchestrated community forces, from industry to city services, in order to rebuild broken lives competently.

Charleston, South Carolina, was still reeling from the effects of the Civil War and Reconstruction when Langdon Lowe began his work with the poor in 1881. Hundreds of former sharecroppers and plantation slaves had made their way into the city, hoping to find jobs as dock hands, or perhaps even serving in the merchant marine. But jobs were few and far between. The city was deeply depressed. The corruption and decay of Reconstruction had left the city treasury thoroughly depleted, so that the streets, the docks, the harbor, the sewers, and the financial district had fallen into near ruin. That, of course, inhibited business growth and reinvestment. For a time, it looked as if Charleston, once "the emerald of the South," would go the way of Carthage and Troy and slowly die. But Lowe had other ideas.

The former Confederate colonel had been converted to faith in Christ during the great revival among the Southern armies in 1863.[1] Over the next eighteen years, the dashing Southern gentleman devoted his energies to Church, family, business, and politics, rising to a place of moderate prominence in the community. But a chance encounter one evening along the Charleston strand with a destitute family of nine forced him to reevaluate his life completely. Not only did that disturbing encounter revitalize his Christian devotion, but it lit a fire of compassion in his heart that would ultimately spark Charleston's revival.

Lowe began by organizing work crews to repair the streets and docks. In exchange for a day's food and shelter, plus a few coppers, unemployed and homeless workers would gather rubbish, clear away debris, cut down overgrowth, and do light repairs. Lowe solicited financial and material assistance from the various benefiting businesses. Before long, not only were many of the city's poor working again, but a full-scale revitalization had begun. Several other groups similar in scope to Lowe's sprang up, and suddenly Charleston was on the road to becoming a hive of industry, activity, and prosperity again.

Just three years after beginning his ambitious private initiative program of Biblical charity, Langdon Lowe died. But the legacy he left Charleston and all Christendom lives on; "he, being dead, still speaks" (Hebrews 11:4). His diary, first published in 1896, is not only a classic glimpse into the spiritual vitality of this Southern Presbyterian layman, but it is a detailed description of how Churches, businesses, families, and community coalitions can coordinate their efforts and pool their resources for the benefit of the needy. "The Lord God on High has ordained and prescribed obedience in all matters," Lowe wrote just a month before his death. He continued, "Huddled against the cold of the ocean, shivering urchins and penniless Confederate widows are but prods to the fullest expression of that obedience, drawing from the unified strengths of mercantilists, Churchmen, craftsmen, and seamen. Akin to the primordial Gospel society in Jerusalem following Pentecost, our work corps allows the attention of each concern to be focused on provisions of mercy, grace, and peace. For the welfare of our own, we turn, not to Rome or Babylon, or Washington, we turn to hearths of our own making."[2]

Langdon Lowe did not travel a solitary way. His approach to Biblical charity was common among believers during the first one hundred fifty years of American history. Edwin Caedman in St. Louis, Lucas Shepler in Chicago, Nan Rastolic in Oakland, and Oscar Oberholtzer in Columbus similarly devoted their lives to coordinating private enterprise and the strength of American industry so that the hungry could be fed, the naked could be clothed, and the idle could be put to work.[3] According to Lowe, this basic strategy of Biblical charity shared by believers throughout every age was "part and parcel with the Nehemiah mandate and its fulfillment."[4]

The Nehemiah Mandate

The task before Nehemiah, son of Hacaliah, was a formidable one. The walls of Jerusalem had lain in ruins for more than seventy years (Nehemiah 1:3). The gates of the city had been consumed by fire (Nehemiah 2:13), the remnant of her citizens were in great distress (Nehemiah 1:3), and her magnificent architecture had been reduced to little more than dusty rubble (Nehemiah 4:2). But Nehemiah had a mandate (Nehemiah 2:12). It was a mandate to rebuild the walls, restore the gates, and remove the reproach (Nehemiah 2:17).

In a miraculous display of cooperation, industry, diligence, and faithfulness, the people of Jerusalem under Nehemiah's leadership were able to succeed (Nehemiah 6:15). Overcoming discouragement (Nehemiah 3:5), outside opposition (Nehemiah 4:1-8), apathy (Nehemiah 3:5), and shortages of manpower (Nehemiah 4:16-21), time (Nehemiah 4:22-23), and resources (Nehemiah 5:1-5), they demonstrated that obedience to God's Precepts is invariably undefeatable (Joshua 1:8).

The enterprise of rebuilding the wall was organized around a private initiative coordination of families, guilds, tradesmen, clergy, aristocracy, and merchants (Nehemiah 3:1-32). Each group provided its own unique gifts, skills, resources, and expertise. Individually, they would have had very little effect on the prevailing climate of despondency and defeat. But, together, they were able to reclaim from the rubble their city and their mission. They fulfilled their mandate.

Several aspects of "the Nehemiah Mandate" and its fulfillment are especially significant in light of America's current crisis of privation and need.

First, Nehemiah's effort was marked by a constant dependence on God. Friend and foe alike acknowledged that Nehemiah was a man of unwavering devotion and that his successes could only be attributed to the blessing of the Lord (Nehemiah 6:16). He yielded at every turn to the will of God (Nehemiah 2:12; 5:15; 7:5). He was constant in prayer (Nehemiah 1:4; 2:4, 8; 4:4, 9; 5:19; 6:14). He was forever publicly acknowledging God's sovereignty and providence (Nehemiah 2:8, 18; 4:14-15, 20; 7:5). And he served selflessly, with no eye toward personal gain (Nehemiah 5:14-19; 13:15-22). He was a man of God. In our own day, if we are to meet the formidable challenge of the poverty crisis with any measure of Nehemiah's success, we must emulate Nehemiah's devotion. We, too, must nurture a holy boldness before men and an attentive meekness before God.

Second, Nehemiah's effort relied primarily on family structures. Instead of stratifying work assignments geographically, occupationally, socially, or politically, each *family* was given total responsibility for a section of the wall (Nehemiah 3:1-32). Besides reinforcing basic Biblical discipleship and authority, Nehemiah's reliance on families provided greater commitment, initiative, solidarity, and productivity from the people. Taking his cue in this matter is critical to the effort of Biblical charity. As we have seen, any system, be it governmental, ecclesiastical, or commercial, that tries to sidestep the primacy of the family is doomed to frustrated failure. On the other hand, any system that follows Nehemiah in exalting the primacy of the family will enjoy success.

Third, Nehemiah's effort relied primarily on resources at hand. The raw materials for the rebuilding of the walls were whatever the people could salvage from the smoldering rubble. They did not have a vast treasury from which to draw on. They did not even have a resource-rich land they could mine. They were forced to be innovative, scavenging creatively for every need. Though Asaph, the keeper of the king's forest, provided timber to make beams for some of the gates (Nehemiah 2:8), no other help was forthcoming. Even so, necessity, that sly old mother of invention, proved sufficient for the task. In our own day, the instant-everything mentality has robbed us of the creative provocation to make do. A hodgepodge of thrown together programs will not be adequate if poverty is to be Scripturally addressed. But, at the same time, we needn't be crippled by an apparent lack of resources. We need only to follow Nehemiah's lead in coming up with innovative solutions to monolithic problems.

Fourth, Nehemiah's effort was marked by selflessness and sacrifice. He eschewed all the privilege and station that was his due as governor (Nehemiah 5:14). He broke with tradition by refusing to accumulate for himself land (Nehemiah 5:16) or ill-gotten gain (Nehemiah 5:15). He did not even request reimbursement for his living expenses (Nehemiah 5:18). Instead, he and his household devoted themselves to the labor at hand. Side by side with the others, they rebuilt the walls.

Nehemiah was a servant. He sacrificed for the sake of the Kingdom, and this example of selflessness encouraged and motivated all the rest of the people to sacrifice as well. The greatness of Nehemiah's achievement lies in this: He was able to lead the people in a staggeringly difficult endeavor without guilt-manipulation, without despotism, and without bureaucratic finagling. He did it with righteous sacrifice. In order to motivate families and mobilize private initiative to hammer out practical models of Biblical charity, we need servant leaders like Nehemiah. We need men and women who can inspire sacrifice.

Vishal Mangalwadi and Sabutu Mariam are such men.

Nearly two decades ago, Vishal Mangalwadi and his wife, Ruth, founded the Association for Comprehensive Rural Assistance near Delhi in their native India. Besides operating farms, schools, textile mills, and evangelistic camps, the association assists lower-caste Hindus to rise above the bitter lot of destitution through industry, cooperation, and creativity.

After graduation from Wheaton College, the Mangalwadis were led by God to begin erecting models of Biblical charity sufficient to supplant the structures of injustice, corruption, sloth, and despair that were so much a part of India's economic ecology. The Gospel imperative to care for the afflicted compelled them to look for solutions deeper and more abiding than mere relief. They sought out long-term answers.

Since Scripture teaches that right thinking precedes right action, they began a comprehensive program of Christian education. Since Scripture teaches that gleaning is one of the primary means of effecting Biblical charity, they began to organize work crews, separating the deserving from the undeserving. Since Scripture teaches that charity is to be family-centered, Church-provoked, and community-supported, they did the hard work of equipping, motivating, and facilitating. But perhaps their greatest achievement has been the coordination of local business concerns for the benefit of the needy. In that regard, they have indeed fulfilled the "Nehemiah Mandate."

Unlike the Mangalwadis, Sabutu Mariam has lived all his life in his homeland, the tiny East-African land of Eritrea. Federated with Haile Selassie's Ethiopia by the United Nations after World War II, the former Italian colony has been troubled by poverty, restlessness, and insurrection ever since. But it wasn't until the Selassie government was overthrown in 1977 by a brutal Marxist dictatorship that Sabutu and his countrymen began to suffer extensively. Since then, a planned famine, designed by the Communist ideologues to crush Eritrean reformers, rebels, and separatists, has cost over a million lives and has devastated the nation.

Though emergency relief for his famine-wracked people was first and foremost in his mind when Sabutu established the Eritrean Relief Association in 1979, the organization quickly developed into a comprehensive Biblical charity outreach. Operating from small headquarters in the nearby French protectorate, Djibouti, the group not only smuggles in fruit, grain, and medicines to the famine victims, they also have marshaled Western commercial support for a network of Christian schools, clinics, and refugee reception centers. In several isolated regions where government forces rarely venture, Sabutu's workers have even been able to establish a number of successful cottage industries and redevelopment ventures through the cooperative efforts of Christian missionary groups, local Churches, the Separatist leadership, the Eritrean exile community, and business interests throughout free East Africa. Thus, they, too, have fulfilled, in an exemplary fashion, the "Nehemiah Mandate."

The strategy for implementing Biblical charity involves first, motivating our Churches to emphasize compassion through a comprehensive missions orientation and second, equipping our families to do the work of the ministry. Both tasks will require a complete reordering of our way of looking at the world, so that our thoughts, our hopes, and our deeds conform with Scripture.

But, because the poverty crisis is so gargantuan, it will be necessary to supplement our committed congregations and our active families with cooperating initiatives from business, commerce, banking, and industry.

If Vishal Mangalwadi and Sabutu Mariam can facilitate private initiative charity in India and Africa, surely we can do it here. If Langdon Lowe, Edwin Caedman, Lucas Sluper, Nan Rastolic, and Oscar Oberholtzer were able to do it around the turn of the century, surely we can do it today. By depending on God, relying on families, maximizing existing resources, and serving selflessly, we can. Without a doubt.

Summary

A vast plethora of resources existing in the private industrial and corporate sector of society can be directed to Biblical poverty relief — surplus food, factory seconds, remaindered product lines, medical and dental services, rent-for-work plans, etc. All it takes to release there resources for Scriptural charity is determined effort and creativity by individuals, families, and Churches.

History demonstrates that Western culture has a legacy of committed Christians who know how to coordinate the resources of the community for the benefit of the poor. Langdon Lowe was such a man, and it was largely due to his vision and initiative that the commercial interests of post-Civil War Charleston were able to rebuild their city for the glory of God and good of their neighbors.

Patterning his efforts on those of Nehemiah, and thus fulfilling what he called the "Nehemiah Mandate," his charity outreach remained distinctly Biblical. It was totally and self-consciously dependent upon the direction and blessing of Almighty God. It was family-oriented. It was creative and resourceful. And, it was marked by selflessness and sacrifice.

Modern examples of Nehemiah-like charity pioneers may be few and far between, but they do exist. And where they exist, whether in the United States, India, or Ethiopia, God has blessed their faithfulness with success and great favor.

PART FOUR

THE TACTICS

I humbly beg and implore . . . that you will not decline to read, and diligently ponder, what I have to lay before you. The magnitude and weightiness of the cause may well excite in you an eagerness to hear, and I will set the matter so plainly in your view that you can have no difficulty in determining what course to adopt. Whoever I am, I here profess to plead in defense both of sound doctrine and of the church. . . . There are two circumstances by which men are wont to recommend, or at least to justify, their conduct. If a thing is done honestly and from pious zeal, we deem it worthy of praise; if it is done under the pressure of public necessity, we at least deem it not unworthy of excuse. Since both of these apply here, I am confident, from your equity, that I shall easily obtain your approval of my design.

John Calvin (1544)

I have six faithful serving men
Who taught me all I know.
Their names are what and where and when
And how and why and who.

Rudyard Kipling

Unwilled observation is soon satiated and goes to sleep.
Willed observation, vision with executive force behind
it, is full of discernment and is continually making discoveries which keep the mind alert and interested. Get a
will behind the eye and the eye becomes a searchlight,
the familiar is made to disclose undreamed treasure.

Robert Traina

Peering into the mists of gray
that shroud the surface of the bay
Nothing I see except a veil
Of fog surrounding every sail.
Then suddenly against a cape
A vast and silent form takes shape.
A great ship lies against the shore
Where nothing has appeared before.

Who sees a truth must often gaze
Into a fog for many days;
It may seem very sure to him
Nothing is there but mist-clouds dim.
Then suddenly his eyes will see
A shape where nothing used to be.
Discoveries are missed each day
By men who turn too soon away.

Clarence Edward Flynn

NINE

WHO AND WHAT: IDENTIFYING NEEDS

Greg Davies could barely believe his own eyes. "Honey, have you seen the front page of the paper yet?"

"Are you kidding?" replied his wife, Evelyn. "With three kids to clothe, feed, and get off to school?"

"Look. It's Freddie Johnson."

"So who, pray tell, is Freddie Johnson?"

"Don't you remember? Freddie was one of the fellas who worked the line on the sonic project. Good worker. Real industrious. One of the best I ever had. Well, when the government canned the sonic . . ."

"Boeing canned him."

"Right. And now look at him. Here in the paper. On the front page, no less. Standing in line for free government cheese and butter."

Alternate waves of guilt and pity washed over Greg as he looked up from the paper. The breakfast room's bay window afforded him an almost unobscured view of Puget Sound. From this vantage point, he could see dozens of other homes, not at all unlike his, flanking the downgrade, "like the castles of the Danube." He imagined that within each of them a similar scene was being played out: kitchens all abustle with kids clad in the latest fashions, the rich aroma of coffee and doughnuts luring moms and dads into reluctant wakefulness, and last-minute planning for the coming afternoon's frenzied shuttle between piano lessons, orthodontist appointments, and slumber parties.

The contrast was a bit much for him. "Something has to be done."

"About what, dear?" Evelyn had succeeded in getting the kids out the door and on their way, and had joined Greg at the table.

"About Freddie. And the others here," he said, pointing to the ragtag group in the picture. "Scripture is plain enough about caring for the needy. But as far as I can see, we don't ever do anything about it. I'm sure our missions fund at the Church goes to help feed the starving in India or someplace. And that's great. But what about people like Freddie? Look at him, for goodness' sake!"

"He doesn't look too terribly good, does he?"

"I mean, is dropping a few dollars in a basket every so often all we can do for the poor? Considering how blessed we are," he said, as his hand swept across the comfortably furnished room, "there ought to be more."

Over the next several weeks, Greg succeeded in convincing the Church board to initiate an outreach to Seattle's poor. They set up a food pantry, stocking a storage room behind the Sunday School department with canned goods and staples. They made the gym available each evening for the homeless, investing in several dozen cots, blankets, pillows, towels, and assorted toiletries. They even established an informal job referral network.

But after several months of serving only "drifters, dead-beats, and drunks," everyone involved with the project was thoroughly discouraged, including Greg. "I practically guilt-and-pitied myself to death over the plight of the poor. And for what? Last night, for instance, we had three winos and a German shepherd show up at the gym for shelter. I ended up letting the dog stay, but the winos were so unruly, filthy, and ungrateful, I had to kick them out. It seems as if we haven't even touched the needs of the people who really need help, because we spend all our time dealing with the riffraff. I don't know if we've even *seen* the people who really need help. I mean, where are the Freddies? How can we help them? How can we reach them?"

Countless attempts to help the poor have ended in a similar flutter of resignation. The programs began with bright-eyed enthusiasm and altruistic idealism, with all the promise of a spring monarch's premiere flight, but, they failed, nonetheless.

Why? Why was Greg Davies unable to help Freddie and the others like him, the people he had so intently set out to help?

Part of the reason is that guilt and pity, the primary impulses behind Greg's outreach and many, many others like it, are insufficient for the task of Biblical charity. Guilt and pity are, in fact, crippling emotions because they are measured by and against man.[1] Ethical obedience to God's love and Law, on the other hand, liberates and empowers, because it is measured by and against God. The compulsion to exercise compassion is invariably exhausted if it has no deeper root than a metaphysical or existential burden.

But, beyond that strategic philosophical defect, Greg's outreach and others like it that floundered and died shortly after inception, were based on a serious tactical error as well. In order to be successful, a program of Biblical charity must be focused. It cannot simply be designed to "help the poor." It must be pinpointed toward a precise target group. Needs must be identified. Relationships must be developed, goals set, and priorities established. The circumstances of local privation must be carefully weighed against the resources of the caring community. The kinds of help that are most needed must be discovered.

Stop, Look, and Listen

So how do you go about discovering and identifying needs in the community? How do you go about properly focusing Word and deed for maximum effect?

The answer is so simple, so obvious, that it is invariably overlooked: Know your community. Look about. Examine the highways and byways of your area with new eyes of awareness and discernment. Do your homework.

What is the local unemployment rate? Is it rising or falling?

Do dilapidated Torinos and Bonnevilles, loaded to the hilt with the tattered remnants of precious possessions, dot the roadsides?

Are firelit camps scattered about the fringes of your town, under bridges, along the river, or beside the lake?

Do abandoned warehouses give sanctuary to the dispossessed against the night?

Are the public shelters, soup kitchens, and rescue missions filled to overflowing?

Have the newspaper help-wanted ads shrunk from a thick bundle to a few truncated notes tacked to the end of the business section?

How many retail failures have marred the glittering track record of your local Chamber of Commerce?

What is the vacancy rate at the various apartment mega-complexes in town? And how busy has the constable been in enforcing evictions?

Know all the whos, whats, whens, wheres, and whys of your community. Talk to people. Find out what's going on at the social service agencies that maintain nearby offices. Swap stories with other Churches. Read the local news. In short, stop, look, and listen.

Every community is different. In order to be effective, therefore, your charity outreach must be precisely tailored to your unique situation. Obviously, a Church in a posh suburb of San Jose is not going to be able — or willing — to duplicate the charity programs of an inner-city Church in Chicago. A small rural Church in Southern Ohio will want a substantially different approach in implementing Biblical charity than a large urban Church on the edge of Houston's petrochemical complex. Although the Scriptural prescriptions for the exercise of charity are immutable, their applications are extremely flexible.

Demographics

Demographics is the science of vital statistics. It is the gathering, sorting, and evaluating of data so that informed projections can be made about the future and wise decisions can be made in the present. Demographics have in recent years become an essential tool of any and all who wish to have a successful impact on the American cultural apparatus.

But, except for an occasional evangelistic survey,[2] our Churches have left demographics to the domain of the pollsters, the sociologists, the advertisers, and last, but not least, the liberal bottom-rung bureaucrats. Why? Demographic acumen can provide the raw materials for an informed, precise, effective, focused, efficient, and productive charity outreach. No need to administer by guess and by golly. No need to flail about in uncertainty. No need to mimic mindlessly the "proven successes" of others. No need to duplicate services and ministries ably provided elsewhere. Demographics can take the foundation of good theology and the framework of committed believers and channel them to appropriate effect. Demographics can mean the difference between a powerful social and spiritual impact and a "Gospel Blimp."

Anytime the Church ventures into unknown and unexplored realms, there will be elements of risk. We will, of necessity, have to learn from our multitudinous mistakes. But, by informing ourselves about the community about us, those risks are reduced and those mistakes are minimized. Demographics are, thus, of prime importance.

It is clear that Christians in our day need to pioneer Biblical charity outreaches. We are to jump into the struggle for genuine justice and mercy with both feet. But we are to look before we leap.

Before you commit to a plan of action, why not do a bit of preliminary footwork? Why not gather some information?

First, contact the Churches in your community. Virtually all Churches in America have some kinds of benevolence programs. But even if they don't, they'll at least be able to tell you what kind of people come around looking for help and what kind of help they're looking for. So, ask lots of questions and take notes. Do they have poverty outreach programs? Have they ever thought about starting them? Why or why not? How much money do they spend annually on benevolence? What kind of records do they keep, if any? Do they participate in seasonal charity, dispensing Christmas presents or holiday baskets? What kinds of successes can they share? What about failures? Do they refer persons to other agencies? Which ones?

A treasure trove of information can be mined from just a few calls. Not only are you better able to gauge the climate of poverty in your area and to assess what services are already available, but you've made a good contact for future cooperative efforts as well.

Second, contact all the social service agencies, both private and public. You may find yourself being transferred from phone to phone, but the information you can glean is invaluable and, thus, worth the hassle. See if they can send you literature detailing their activities and services. Even general information brochures can tell you a great deal. Ask them to send you every-thing they've got, from year-end reports to promotional pieces, from financial schematics to appeal letters. Then, sort through all the material to find out what you need to know. Again, ask lots of questions. Take notes. And be sure to obtain their referral lists. That way you've not only acquired information about the individual agencies, you've discovered how each agency net-works with other groups and you have even learned a bit about its philosophical bent.

Third, contact the police department. No one knows more about the nature and needs of a community than the police. Thus, no demographic survey worth its salt will neglect this im-portant source of information. The police can point out tiny pockets of poverty that you may have overlooked. They can direct you to the truly needy like nobody else can. They can also probably tell you about the various programs and services that are available to the poor, and which ones have proven to be effective and which ones haven't. They can warn you of pitfalls and perennial problems, and they can steer you clear of danger.

Fourth, contact the schools, especially the elementary schools. It is possible to hide the face of poverty from Churches, social agencies, and police. But is it impossible to hide from second-grade teachers. It's not that the long-held suspicion about "eyes in the backs of their heads" is true, it's just that the closeness of the elementary school environment causes them to be more at-tentive and aware. Teachers know which of their pupils are mal-nourished. They know which ones come from broken homes. They know which ones are unbathed and need medical atten-tion. They know. And, very often, they are willing to talk about it. So, don't neglect their expertise and range of vision.

Finally, contact the various merchants, shop owners, and businessmen in the community. They can probably give you a fairly good idea about the kinds and numbers of applicants they've had for jobs. Be especially inquisitive at fast-food restau-rants, convenience stores, service stations, and other places where the unskilled poor might be inclined to seek employment. Also, grocery stores that accept food stamps may be able to help you evaluate the nature and magnitude of poverty in your area.

Use every inductive and deductive device you can think of to determine just where and what the needs are.

Straight from the Horse's Mouth

But even after you've conducted a thorough demographic survey of your community, you still haven't successfully discovered and identified the needs of the poor until you actually talk to the poor. Find out what *they* think. Find out how *they* feel.

Robert Thompson is the pastor of First Baptist Church, Evanston, Illinois. Several years ago, he began an outreach to the unemployed. But instead of structuring a program based on what *he* thought the poor needed, he gathered them together, on a weekly basis, to let *them* explore, share, plan, and formulate strategies of compassion. "In spite of the fact that each person's experience of unemployment is unique," he said, "all unemployed people do share some common feelings . . . a sense of alienation, a loss of self-esteem, and a feeling of powerlessness . . . These need to be identified and understood if one hopes to make the most of a troublesome situation."[3]

Thompson's group meetings not only enabled him to put together informed and effective tactics of Biblical charity, they also provided support, encouragement, and evangelistic opportunity for the poor themselves. In fact, the group meetings continued long after Thompson's fact-finding mission had been completed, just for that reason.

Max Harfield is the director of the Calvary Mission Center in New York City. For eight and a half months in 1982, he lived on the streets with the homeless. Sleeping in phone booths, subway stations, and public shelters; eating in soup kitchens, abandoned warehouses, and city parks; and wandering almost aimlessly throughout lower Manhattan, he came to know the poor in a way most of us never will. He probed their deepest fears, their greatest ambitions, and their clearest needs. Then he established the center. Starting with the Scriptural strategies for charity, and taking into account all that he had learned from the poor themselves, from his life on the street, he began to build a dynamic model of Biblical charity that changes lives for the Kingdom.[4]

Of course, it's not necessary to go to the extreme of living on the street for eight and a half months simply to discover what the

poor need in your community. But, it is necessary to build relationships with the poor. It is necessary to hear what they have to
say so that your charity outreach avoids the pitfalls and the per-
plexities of uninformed humanitarianism.

Precautions

Everyone is an expert. As you go about your task of discovering and identifying needs, you'll find that people cannot resist
sharing their opinions with you. That's all right, except that
you're bound to wind up with a whole lot of divergent and contrary opinions.

Opinions and demographics should not shape the work of
Biblical charity. Only Scripture can do that. Opinions and
demographics should only inform and focus the attentions of
Biblical charity. They should simply help Christians to discover
and identify needs in the community. The temptation to baptize
circumstances and situations over Biblical imperatives must be
resisted at all costs.

The guilt-and-pity approach to compassion shows its weakness at just this point. Instead of allowing Scripture to be the
starting point, the frame of reference from which all of life is
judged, it starts with a particular situation and then goes only to
Scripture for "support," "encouragement," or "inspiration." This
sort of Scripture-twisting may not be a deliberate attempt to sub-
vert the Bible's authority, but it is subversive, nonetheless.

Thus, we must take great pains to ensure that our demographics do not deter us from the primary task at hand: stridently
obeying the high call of God to submit our lives, our work, and
our ministries to His revealed will. Demographics are just tools.

It was essential that Peter know that he was walking amidst
the waves (Matthew 14:28-29). It was important that he take
into account the nature of his situation (Matthew 14:25-28). But
all the while, it was necessary for him to keep his eyes fixed on
the Standard, and not to be swayed (Matthew 14:30-31). We are
to go and do likewise.

Summary

In order to be successful, a program of Biblical charity must
have focus. It cannot simply set out to "help the poor." If it does,
it will inevitably flounder and fail. Instead, it must identify local

needs, pinpoint target groups, and establish precise priorities. To accomplish these things, the charity outreach must learn to stop, look, and listen to its surrounding community.

The place to begin the observation process is with demographics. Demographics, the science of vital statistics, encompasses the gathering, sorting, and evaluation of data so that informed projections can be made. By tapping the information pools of local Churches, community service organizations, schools, law enforcement agencies, and the business sector, a charity outreach can accurately appraise the unique needs, resources, and circumstances of its immediate environment.

But, even when all the charts and graphs have been drawn; even when all the phases and trends have been plotted; even when all the data and statistics have been gathered; and even when the usefulness of demographics has been exhausted, the task of observation is not over. The most helpful information about the needs of the poor will come from the poor themselves. Thus, it is essential that personal relationships be established and nurtured with the people who will supposedly benefit from the charity outreach.

Knowing the needs of a community and knowing the needs of the poor can mean the difference between a powerful and influential charity ministry and a flustered folly. Stop, look, and listen.

Like a mighty army, moves the Church of God,
Brothers, we are treading
    where the saints have trod.
We are not divided, all one body we,
One in hope and doctrine, one in charity.
Onward, Christian soldiers,
    marching as to war,
With the cross of Jesus going on before.

                              Sabine Baring-Gould

Blest be the tie that binds
Our hearts in Christian love!
The charity of kindred souls

                              John Fawcett

Forward through the ages, in unbroken lines
Move the faithful spirits,
    at the call divine:
Gifts of differing measure,
    hearts of one accord,
Manifold the service, one the sure reward.
Not alone we conquer, not alone we fall;
In each loss or triumph, lose or triumph all,
Bound by God's far purpose,
    in one living whole,
Move we on together, to the shining goal.

                              Frederick Hosmer

TEN

COOPERATION: POOLING RESOURCES

In Harlem, Harv Oostdyk mobilized dozens of Churches from a variety of theological and denominational backgrounds not only to help the poor and bring the Gospel to the ghetto, but to begin to map out Scriptural strategies and tactics for the elimination of systemic poverty altogether. Oostdyk's STEP Foundation was able to translate vision into cooperative action. And the impact on Harlem has been nothing short of phenomenal.[1]

How did he do it? How was he able to coordinate so many divergent forces into a cohesive and comprehensive team? How was he able to enlist ministry teams, task forces, think-tanks, and friendship committees from Churches already overloaded and understaffed?

In Houston, Jeff Wallace recently spearheaded a campaign to gather food for the needy during the winter months. Garnering support from businesses, community service groups, Churches, and even local government leaders, Wallace's HELP Services program was able to raise over three and a half tons of groceries in less than two months. He was instrumental in bringing together various interests that had never before cooperated with one another. And he did it with no office, no staff, no budget, and no experience.

But how was he able to stir the positive interest of the media and gain favor with the magistrates? How was he able to coordinate Baptists, Methodists, Catholics, Presbyterians, charismatics, and Nazarenes, as well as a number of unbelievers, into a viable and unified force of compassionate concern?

As you may well have suspected, both Oostdyk and Wallace share a number of critical attributes in their approach to motivat-

ing and coordinating others for the work of Biblical charity. Both
are unswervingly committed to the full authority of Scripture.
Both recognize the necessity of grounding charity in the work
ethic. Both believe that it is the responsibility of Churches to equip
families for compassionate action, to enlist private enterprise in
the endeavor, and to engage in systematic demographic research.
But, in addition to this, both are organized. Very organized.

Don't let anyone fool you. Their successes cannot be quickly
and easily duplicated. Their methods cannot be mindlessly imi-
tated. But a number of important lessons can be learned by giving heed to their models. Like Oostdyk and Wallace, we can get
ourselves organized. We can plan. We can mediate, motivate,
and mobilize. We can establish priorities, set goals, and formulate tactics. We can organize for Biblical charity.

The Local Church Task Force

The first step in organizing Biblical charity is to establish a
local Church task force.

The Church at Antioch was a young congregation on the edge
of a vast pagan frontier (Acts 11:19-23). But, it was a stronghold
of faithfulness and zeal (Acts 11:24-26). So, when the disciples
there learned of a great famine in Judea, they quickly responded
with sacrificial compassion and charity (Acts 11:27-29). Knowing
that their relief efforts had to be organized in order to be efficient, they established a task force to oversee the collections, and
then to deliver and distribute them appropriately (Acts 11:30).

Many, many years later, on the edge of quite another frontier, circuit-riding Calvinistic Methodist preachers,[2] under the
auspices of a group called the Antiochian League, encouraged
their small congregations to similarly organize.[3] Wherever possible, they would select three or four of the Ohio farmers to form
a relief task force. That way, whenever flooding, poor harvests,
or sickness struck the community, the Church could immediately respond. It would be ready for any calamity. It would know
who was responsible for what. It would be organized.

In our own day, the Antiochian approach to local Church organization and mobilization would significantly increase our
effectiveness in dispensing Scriptural aid to the needy. By applying the task force model of the early Church and the American

frontiersmen to our own Biblical charity projects, we would, in short order, be able to mount a viable challenge to the federal welfare system.

Once a group of believers expresses an interest in living out the full implications of authentic Word-and-deed Christianity, call them together for a brief, informal meeting. Call them together with the specific intention of establishing a local Church task force. At that time, lay out several options for future involvement: a weekly home Bible study, a new Sunday School class, a biweekly coffee/strategy session, or whatever. But, by all means, make it clear that the task force, in whatever form it might eventually take, would bear the brunt of the responsibility for the Church's Biblical charity ministry.

This responsibility would include the following:

First, the task force would be responsible to initiate a comprehensive demographic operation. It is the task force that must discover and identify local needs. It must do the calling, expedite the surveys, and ask the questions. Certainly, no one else in the Church is going to do it. The task force is composed of the most committed, the most motivated, and the most active members of a congregation. If the information you need is going to be gathered at all, then the task force must do the gathering.

Second, the task force would be responsible to keep the rest of the Church members informed. When you have sorted through all the data and can clearly identify needs in the community, then let the Church know. Motivate the members. Stir them to pathos. Educate them. Invite them to attend a special presentation where the basics of Biblical charity are outlined. Offer a series of weekend training sessions where the principles of Scripture and the lessons of history are applied to local conditions and crises. A long-term, comprehensive program of Biblical charity cannot hope to get off the ground until the task force rallies the support of the rest of the Church.

Third, the task force would be responsible to map out strategies and tactics for the rest of the Church to follow. The task force is composed of the Biblical charity pioneers in any given Body. Thus, they must give form and leadership to the benevolent outreaches of the Church. Specific proposals from the task force should be periodically presented to the pastor, the elders, or the deacons. Goals, agendas, and priorities should be developed. Cost projections, man-hour requirements, and facility needs also must be calculated. Make certain that all the bases are covered. There is no reason in the world why privation should be perpetuated in our communities just because we weren't prepared or organized enough and, thus, were bureaucratically stymied.

Fourth, the task force would be responsible for mobilizing families for compassionate action. It is not enough simply to inform and train families in the congregation. It is not enough to lay out an intricate mosaic of plans, strategies, tactics, and priorities. At the bottom line, implementation is the name of the game. When emergencies arise, the task force must be able to spring into action, and to stimulate others to do likewise. Ultimately, it really doesn't matter that we know all the arguments against federal welfare and all the basics of Biblical charity if we cannot translate that knowledge into action. The task force makes certain that a Church's Good Samaritan faith does not lay latent like some protokinetic mass. The task force activates phone banks, mobilizes workers, locates surplus beds, routs out extra food, and generally takes care of details.

Fifth, the task force would be responsible to develop cooperative relationships with private businesses. Contacts with grocery stores, print shops, community associations, banks, etc., should be nurtured so that their vast resources can be coordinated effectively. Community relations are essential. Why not have various task force members set up meetings with the owners and managers of each of the businesses so that the program of Biblical charity can be fully explained and support elicited? Or, perhaps, community meetings could be held with personal invitations hand-delivered to each person. However you do it, make certain that the task force never becomes ingrown and stagnant. The work of Biblical charity must be pushed outward in ever-widening circles.

Sixth, the task force would be responsible for nurturing positive contacts with the media. One person on the task force should probably be appointed to handle all press relations, keeping in mind that it could very well turn into a very busy, very time-consuming job. Most community newspapers welcome press releases, publicity photos, and informative letters to the editor.

Use them. Radio talk shows provide an excellent platform for Christians to call attention to issues. And they are surprisingly easy to engage. Television is a bit more difficult, but even here, an alert task force and media representative can open up wonderful opportunities. One caution, though: don't become a nuisance. Let things fall into place and trust God to give you favor. If you do the work of charity with zeal and verve, the media will take notice. And the word will spread.

The Community Coalition

Once a task force has activated a local Church and a functioning model of compassion has been implemented, other Churches will begin to exercise interest in the program or, at the very least, the concept. When that starts to happen, it's time to take the next big step in organizing for Biblical charity: establishing a community association or coalition. The purpose of this association is to pool resources and to network efficiently, so that the scope of Biblical charity can expand beyond the bounds of any single Church. It is to coordinate activities, share ideas, minimize overlap, and maximize compassion. Composed of members of the task force of several Churches, the association benefits from the shared strengths of a number of unique charity outreaches. Even so, bigger doesn't always mean better. As Harv Oostdyk has said, "Don't try to organize more than four to seven Churches. If you try to organize a lot of Churches, you are often limited to your lowest common objection. Let a small handful of Churches demonstrate success, and you will find many others following the initial attempt."[4] So, start small.

But don't start unambitiously. The community coalition can be a powerful tool to feed the hungry, shelter the homeless, and clothe the naked. By bringing the weight of several different Churches to bear on poverty, a number of important, but otherwise impossible, tasks are accomplished.

A community coalition of sorts was brought together in Jerusalem to sort through some sticky theological questions and to give directions to the ever-expanding mission of the first-century Church (Acts 15:1-6). The Jerusalem Council convened with the most anointed minds in Christendom in attendance: Paul, Barnabas, Jude, Silas, Simeon, and James. Together they gave impetus to evangelism, suasion to ethics, and impulse to charity (Acts 15:15-21). Together, they launched a program of worldwide Christian cooperation and accountability.

By pooling our resources, coordinating our thinking, and focusing our aid through community coalitions, not only can we facilitate dynamic structures of justice and mercy, but we can once again unleash a Great Commission force such as has not been witnessed for a long, long time.

First, the community coalition enables individual Churches to share the charity burden. If one outreach program is over-loaded, the other can step in and shoulder some of the load for a while. If one outreach program has access to free dental care and another to cheap housing and still another to large stores of food commodities, then sharing back and forth only makes sense. Obviously, the members of the coalition will need to be in close communication with one another so that new developments, surpluses, or shortfalls can be closely monitored. The essential element here is selfless sharing. If each of the task forces and each of the Churches involved is genuinely concerned for the poor, and seriously committed to the ethical mandate to exercise compassion, then petty rivalries and denominational differences will be happily dispatched. The coalition will work harmoniously, sharing responsibility, splitting expenses, and pooling resources. Different ventures will require different levels of commitment and coordination, but a community coalition that is organized along loose, informal lines, and nothing more, is certainly good enough to start with. A more complex organization, with committees, officers, budgets, etc., may be necessary later, but in the beginning, small is beautiful; informal is best.

Second, the community coalition makes possible joint projects that would be beyond the realm of feasibility for any of the Churches acting alone. For instance, the coalition could rent warehouse space and begin a food bank. Canned goods, staples, and other nonperishables could be collected from all over the community, and then stored at the one central location. Distribution would be simpler, faster, and more efficient. Gaps could be closed, care made more uniform, and costs reduced.

Another joint project, made possible by the coordinated efforts of a coalition, would be an emergency shelter. Instead of each

Church or task force stretching itself to the limits, staffing, funding, and supervising separate sheltering ministries, why not channel all that time, energy, and money into a mutual project? An already existing shelter can be updated, renovated, adapted, and then run cooperatively by the coalition. Or, if the need demands it, a new shelter could be built. But, either way, no one Church is forced to bear the full brunt of such a work alone.

Computer networking is still another joint project that the community coalition could facilitate. By tapping into a common data base, each charity outreach can have instant access to a tremendous amount of invaluable information. Cross-referencing client information can help minimize fraud. Common mailing lists can help mobilize work crews during emergencies. Referral lists, commodity sources, and information pools can help expedite case loads. With hardware and software prices dropping dramatically and modern technologies improving at an equally dramatic rate, computer networking makes sense, even for the smallest and most informal charity associations.

Referrals

Even after a local Church has organized a task force to oversee the work of charity, and then, several like-minded Churches have united their various task forces into a community coalition, there are still some situations too complex and too monolithic to deal with adequately on a local level. Outside referrals still will have to be made. For this reason, each charity outreach needs to compile a notebook that lists community agencies, social service programs, United Way groups, doctors, lawyers, public health clinics, and rehabilitative services. A number of agencies in every community perform special services: care for battered women, drug and alcohol recovery clinics, veterans retraining programs, care for the elderly, homes for abused children, crisis pregnancy centers, etc. Each charity outreach ought not only to know what help is available to the needy, but how to procure it. Are there waiting lists for any of the programs? What about costs? Are there prerequisites, conditions, and qualifications? Find out and notate your referral list accordingly. Include admitting procedures, names, addresses, phone numbers, office hours, and any other bits of information you can discover. That way, when a needy family shows up at your door, you can know precisely how and where help can be found. Even if the local task force or the community coalition is unable to satisfy a need, supplicants won't be turned away cold.

James Harrold for many years served faithfully as the research secretary for London's great Victorian preacher, Charles Haddon Spurgeon. Among the many tasks that consumed his furiously paced fourteen-hour days, Harrold was responsible to channel all requests for aid to appropriate charities. Since Spurgeon had seen to the establishment of an astounding sixty-six different organizations, that was no mean feat. In 1886, he compiled a notebook that referenced and cross-referenced each of those organizations, along with several hundred of the other English evangelical charities. Though that notebook required a diligent and single-minded devotion over a period of three and a half months, the project proved itself well worth the effort. Writing in 1916, a full thirty years after the notebook was first prepared, J. L. G. Harringdon commented, "England's great war effort would be nigh unto impossible were it not for the persistent labors of the Christian charities. But these works of commendable compassion would be all too inaccessible were it not for the now outdated, yet ever indispensable, Spurgeonic publication of J. W. Harrold."[5]

It is quite unlikely that our referral lists will remain serviceable as long as Harrold's did. But they will prove to be no less indispensable.

Precautions

There is one problem with being so organized. It is a problem that both Harv Oostdyk and Jeff Wallace have readily admitted to: the impersonalization of compassion. Church task forces, community coalitions, and referral lists can so institutionalize and centralize the apparatus of care that private charity falls into the same traps and commits the same errors as the welfare bureaucracy. "We need to be organized," said Wallace, "but somehow, some way, we've got to continue to love, to work one-on-one, to build real relationships, and to really, really care. Otherwise we'll never see the poor established in industry, independence, thrift, and self-respect."

According to economist Gary North, "The tactical problem facing Christians is this: how can we gain the benefits of a centralized . . . organization, yet avoid the concomitant bureaucratization?"[6] How can we, in other words, maintain that essential balance between the one and the many?

Although there are no easy answers to this dilemma, there are several specific bureaucratic vices that we can guard against and, thus, better maintain the one and the many sensibility.

First, beware of caring by committee. We are a covenant people[7] and we are called to work in unison for justice and mercy, but individual needs require individual attention. This is why, even though cooperation and organization facilitate a broader range for projects of compassion, families remain the primary agents of Biblical charity. For all their benefits, task forces, community coalitions, and referral lists can never replace the warmth of the human touch.

Second, beware of passing the buck. Referral lists are meant to be used as a tool for more effective care, not as a cop-out. We must never give in to the temptation to give the "other guy" all the tough cases. Spurgeon once commented that most Christian charity wound up being "a shuttling of A to B to C to D wherein he was informed there was no help to be found."[8] We must constantly be on guard against this tendency.

Third, beware of specialization to exclusion. There is a shelter in Memphis that accepts only "black men from ages of forty-five to sixty-five who suffer from alcoholic debilitation and homelessness." Another shelter in Lincoln limits its aid to "battered women, with children, between the ages of twenty-five and forty." One halfway house in Spokane stipulates, "Trucking industry personnel and Vietnam War veterans with serious chemical dependencies." Obviously, any outreach to the poor or afflicted needs to have a narrow focus so that effective care and counsel can be provided. But the trend toward overspecialization has fragmented the social service coverage in the United States into an abominably complex jigsaw puzzle. "It has almost gotten to the point," says George Getschow of *The Wall Street Journal*, "that you have to be poor *plus something* to get help from a private charity: poor plus addicted to drugs, or poor plus mentally ill, or poor plus a member of the pipefitters' union."[9] Specialization is fine as

long as it does not work to the exclusion of those we have been
called to help.

Task forces, community coalitions, and referral lists are invaluable aids to implementing Biblical charity. But we must
keep them in perspective. We must be organized, but never so
organized that we lose the sensitivity, the accountability, and the
individuality so central to authentic Christianity.

Summary

Organization is essential. If our charity outreaches are to be
truly effective in relieving poverty, we must plan. We must
mediate, motivate, and mobilize. We must establish priorities,
set goals, formulate tactics, coordinate resources, and build net-
works of cooperation.

The first step in organizing for Biblical charity is to establish a local Church task force. This core group, committed to
living out the full implications of the Good Samaritan faith,
would be responsible for initiating a demographic operation; for
educating, motivating, and training the congregation to fulfill its
Scriptural obligations; for mapping out strategies, tactics, goals
and agendas; and for mobilizing families, coordinating businesses, and informing the media. In short, the local Church task
force would spearhead the full implementation of Word-and-
deed compassion.

The next step in organizing for Biblical charity is the formation of a community coalition. Once a Church has established a
task force, and a functioning model of compassion has been implemented, other interested Churches and organizations can be
coordinated to share the burdens of charity, extending the societal
impact far beyond what any single Church could accomplish.
Joint projects, like food banks, emergency shelters, social service
centers, and computer networks, could then be effectual.

Finally, in organizing for Biblical charity, provision will need
to be made for those uniquely complex cases where special facilities or resources are required. A system or network of referrals
will enable each ministry to focus on its own peculiar area of expertise without fear that needs will go unmet.

Of course, there is always the risk that, with organization,
impersonalization will reduce our compassion to a cold bureau-

cratic donation. So, although haphazardness is to be avoided at all costs, we must be no less wary of over-organization.

Charity must be organized in order to be effective. But it must be personal in order to be Biblical.

A job is crucial psychologically, over and above the paycheck.

Alvin Toffler

The man who has a job, has a chance.

Elbert Hubbard

" 'Tis the voice of the sluggard";
   I heard him complain,
"You have waked me too soon,
   I must slumber again."

Isaac Watts

Idleness is a living man's tomb.

Latin proverb

Every successful ethnic group in our history rose up by working harder than other classes in low-paid jobs, with a vanguard of men in entrepreneurial roles. But the current poor, so it is supposed, can leap-frog drudgery by education and credentials, or be led as a group from poverty, perhaps by welfare mothers trained for government jobs.

George Gilder

To youth I have but three words of counsel: work, work and work.

Bismark

JOBS: THE
BOOTSTRAP ETHIC

The Charity Organization Society was England's leading private charity agency in the late nineteenth century. It operated on the Biblical principle of aid to foster self-help. According to Charles Loch Mowat, the historian of the society, it "embodied an idea of charity which claimed to reconcile the divisions in society, to remove poverty, and to produce a happy, self-reliant community. It believed that the most serious aspect of poverty was the degradation of the character of the poor man or woman. Indiscriminate charity only made things worse; it demoralized. True charity demanded friendship, thought, the sort of help that would restore a man's self-respect and his ability to support himself and his family. True charity demanded gainful employ."[1]

The Society aimed to implement to the fullest extent possible the bootstrap ethic so predominant in Scripture. Again, according to Mowat, it sought: "First, to place in gainful employ those able to work; Second, to occupy, with industry within the Society, all those incapable of placement; And, third, to acquire the means with which to supply the other incapacitated needy with the necessities of life."[2]

Spurgeon, who was a public advocate and avid supporter of the society, heralded it as "a charity to which the curse of idleness is subjected to the rule of the under-magistrate of earthly society: work."[3]

This is the appropriate aim of Biblical charity: to rid the impoverished of "the curse of idleness" and to rebuild self-reliance and productivity. More than anything else, the poor need jobs. So, Biblical charity seeks to explore the markets, equip the applicants, and expand the opportunities so that full employment can be secured for all but the totally infirm.

Considering the current shape of American industry, however, that may not be a particularly easy task.

Structural Changes in the Economy

Since the early sixties, the progressive decline in basic industries such as steel, automobiles, textiles, rubber, oil, and consumer electronics has been a prominent feature of the U.S. economic ecology. Although the number of jobs created year by year continues to grow, most of those jobs are in the low-wage service sector. High-paying jobs in heavy industry are rapidly disappearing.

The United States' share of world trade declined sixteen percent from 1960 to 1970.[4] It declined another twenty-three percent during the seventies,[5] and it declined still another eighteen percent during the eighties.[6] Meanwhile, every other industrialized nation except Britain maintained or increased its share. Although short-term problems such as the volatility in the stock market, huge federal deficits and fluctuating energy costs have been significant, several structural factors have contributed to the wave of layoffs and permanent plant closings in basic U.S. industries as well.

First, in many industries such as steel, rubber, and automobiles, skyrocketing labor costs and a lack of effective domestic competition have pushed prices ever upward. In fact, many such industries, steel in particular, have priced themselves out of the world, and even the domestic, market.

Second, the industries have often failed to invest in more efficient manufacturing methods. For example, even in the face of stiff Japanese competition in the late sixties, and after the imposition in 1969 of "voluntary" restrictions on steel imports, U.S. steel industry capital expenditures through 1984 remained below 1968 levels.[7] Meanwhile, Japanese steel producers were increasing capital investment by more than twenty-three percent per year.[8]

Part of the problem has been that management, held hostage by labor, has been unable to modernize. Jurisdictional battles between trade unions during times of slow or no growth have led to uninformed resistance to changes designed to improve productivity, and thus to lower unnecessarily high construction costs. But then, part of the problem has simply been poor management. Those in the higher echelons have plainly not been responsive enough to the changing climate of the world market.

Third, the protectionist policies of the federal government have contributed to industrial decline by failing to tie subsidies, tax allowances, and trade barriers to enforceable commitments by industry to upgrade facilities, and improve efficiency and productivity.

Most subsidies to declining industries have been based on emotional appeals by industry and labor to save jobs. However, most of the firms have only perpetuated or, in some cases, intensified the downward spiral of layoffs and plant closures.

Ironically, the import controls, tax breaks, and regulatory relief measures that the government has instituted, at industry's behest, have actually pushed countries like Japan and West Germany more quickly into higher technology products and into higher cost consumer items. For example, setting import limits on Japanese subcompact automobiles has encouraged Japanese manufacturers to enter the van, truck, and luxury car markets. Similarly, restrictions on low-cost textile imports are encouraging Hong Kong manufacturers to begin competing in the high-fashion field.

Use of import restrictions to bail out poorly managed businesses has the direct effect of artificially raising U.S. prices, which can harm otherwise competitive businesses by increasing their costs for parts. Steel quotas, for example, can be blamed for higher manufacturing costs for U.S. automobile makers and shipbuilders, which have inordinately increased the costs of their products in comparison with foreign manufacturers.

Fourth, an increasing shift of investment capital away from the United States has contributed to the decline of the national industrial base. Between 1950 and 1980, direct foreign investment by U.S. businesses increased sixteen hundred percent, from twelve billion dollars to one hundred billion dollars.[9] Over the same period, gross domestic private investment increased less than half as quickly, from fifty-four billion dollars to just over four hundred billion dollars.[10] The translation into practical terms is easy enough to make. U.S. capital is broadening the job base overseas, thus expanding the global marketplace, while, at the same time, the job base at home is forced to grow much less rapidly or, in some cases, to actually shrink.

Fifth, U.S. industries fall well behind Japanese and Korean firms in recognizing the value and need for large-scale retraining of the work force. Understanding that the key to future competitiveness lies in increasing the skill and flexibility of labor, these high-tech pioneers are simply outclassing businesses here with massive reeducational programs.

Sixth, though futurists like John Naisbitt have predicted widespread labor shortages in the decade ahead,[11] there is a dramatic "mismatch between where the jobs are and where the workers are. In the Washington, D.C., area, for instance, unemployment rates in the suburbs fluctuate between two percent and four percent, while unemployment rates in Washington are close to nine percent. While many city residents could fill suburban jobs, neither transportation systems nor information networks serve to get people to where the jobs are."[12] And similar situations exist in cities all across the nation.

What all this means is that good paying jobs are tougher to find than ever before. And worse, even after workers find jobs, security is nonexistent. If Biblical charity's immediate and primary goal is to find jobs for the unemployed and the destitute, then we really have our work cut out for us.

Finding Jobs

Finding jobs — jobs adequate to support whole families — may not be an easy task. But then, neither is it an impossible task. There are jobs to be had out there in the marketplace. Despite industrial constriction and business decline, there remains a healthy expansion of job opportunities. If we can just find them and match them to the deserving poor in our midst, then the work of Biblical charity will have gone a long way toward eliminating the blight of poverty in the United States. There are any number of ways that this can be effectually accomplished.

For instance, a job referral service can be initiated that will seek out employment opportunities for the poor. Simply appropriate a bulletin board at the Church where job notices can be posted. The jobs can be collected at random. See a help-wanted sign at the grocery store? Just call the information into the Church office. Know a friend of a friend of a friend who's hiring warehouse help? Quick, post it on the job board. Anywhere, anytime, jobs come to your attention, post them on the board. The deserving poor will work. We simply need to facilitate them a bit.

The job board will need to be updated on a regular basis so that each posting remains current. Also, for administrative ease, each notice should be standardized. To accomplish both of those objectives easily, simply mock up a blank form and photocopy several dozen copies. The form should have spaces for the job description, pay scale, skills required, personnel contact, job site, address, phone number, and date. Make certain that each job notice has all the information filled in before posting. That will not only eliminate clerical hassle, but will also save a great deal of time and effort on the part of the applicants.

Keep the job board in an open area that has free and easy access, and then utilize it continually in your counseling and helping ministries.

If the job board remains a bit sparse, peruse the want ads in the local paper and check with the employment commission, the Chamber of Commerce, or the Jaycees. It's amazing what just a little initiative can do.

In the Houston suburb of Humble, a job board was begun by HELP Services during the worst part of 1982's economic constriction. Not only was there never a time when the board was lacking for jobs, but as word spread in the community, extra space had to be added twice. The local hospital, the city's maintenance department, and several large businesses all committed to notify HELP immediately anytime job openings occurred. A local Christian radio station set up a temporary labor pool so that homeowners in need of minor repairs or maintenance could contact the HELP office, thus facilitating market growth and entrepreneurial activity. In less than five months, at a time when all leading economic indicators pointed to unrelenting stagflation and decline, HELP was able to place over four hundred poor applicants in permanent jobs, and another three hundred fifty in temporary situations. Now, those figures pale in significance when compared to the massive unemployment rates of the same period. But, on the other hand, if every Bible-believing Church in America had a charity outreach and each of those charity outreaches was as aggressive as HELP was in discovering and even creating job opportunities, then the poverty crisis would at last become a manageable situation.

In Chicago, a jobs program for the poor was established by Jesus People, USA (JPUSA), a small, inner-city Christian community. From the early seventies onward, the program expanded by leaps and bounds so that not only were job referrals made, but several small businesses were begun. Gathering together a crew of skilled and unskilled laborers, they began to seek out small projects: remodeling, painting, auto repair, roofing, small appliance repair, carpentry, and landscaping. They put the willing to work. They did whatever was necessary to implement Scriptural compassion by stopping the cycle of welfare dependence and unemployment.

Thomas MacKay, the famed nineteenth-century English *laissez-faire* advocate, declared that true charity "consists in a recreation and development of the arts of independence and industry." He called, "not for more philanthropy, but rather for more respect for the dignity of human life, and more faith in its ability."[13] It is to our shame that movements like the libertarians and the Mormons and the Unificationists have understood and applied this much better on the whole than we have. Evangelical organizations like HELP and JPUSA are few and far between, while the Mormons, for example, have a comprehensive nationwide employment and relief program that is a model of efficiency and effectiveness.

In 1767, George Rogers Wooldridge wrote in a petition to the king of England: "The direst need among the private destitute is work. Neither the Crown's philanthropy nor the Church's charity can so readily ease their plight as can full employ. Besides separating malingerers from the just, work establishes the people in the holy duty of industry."[14]

Similarly in our day, Dr. E. V. Hill, pastor of the Mt. Zion Missionary Baptist Church in Watts, has said, "The prime objective of the compassionate Church is not merely to pacify the poor with preaching programs and pastry provisions, but to promote productivity."[15]

This is the essence of Biblical charity: helping the poor to help themselves. So, even at a time when the economy is constrained, outreaches that aim tangibly to translate poverty into productivity must allow job placement to take precedence over everything else.

Reeducation

Unfortunately, many of the poor have been so debilitated for so long by the lulling effects of welfare that they are actually unable to enter the job market. They don't know the proper way to conduct an initial interview. They don't know how to keep a job, even if they are able to get one. They have never had to learn the basic personal disciplines necessary to work with, and for, others. They don't know how to manage their time. And they certainly don't know how to manage their money. After all, they've become totally dependent upon the paternalistic state. They've always been taken care of before, with no need to worry about any of these things. Therefore, if our Biblical charity outreaches are to help them help themselves by eradicating "the curse of idleness," a reeducation program must be undertaken.

Edna Jones was an all-too-typical Fourth Ward ghetto resident when she walked into the offices of HELP in 1983. She had been on welfare all her life. She had five children, ages three, seven, ten, fourteen, and sixteen. Her boyfriend, who had been staying with her off and on for five years, was the father of the youngest child. For the moment, they all lived together in a small, rundown house across the street from Houston's rat- and roach-infested federal housing project. Although she had regularly attended a storefront Pentecostal mission for all her thirty-four years, she had only recently become a Christian; hence, the new outlook that brought her to HELP.

Immediately, the HELP staff went to work on the systemic problems in the Jones family. They recommended that the three-year-old begin attending a new Christian day care center that had recently been established in the Fourth Ward. There, she would receive educational enrichment in preparation for entering formal school in two years. The seven-, ten-, and fourteen-year-old children were found to be far below normal in math and reading skills. Thus, HELP workers enrolled all three in extensive tutorial programs provided by a local Baptist association of Churches. The sixteen-year-old was, essentially, a drop-out. Although officially in the ninth grade, he tested at the fourth grade reading level. Since Mrs. Jones herself had received little formal education, and was also virtually illiterate, both mother and son were enrolled in special adult educational programs that had been started in the community. Both were also placed in part-time job situations developed by the HELP placement service.

HELP workers then began to teach the family basic financial management skills, from budgeting to tithing, from thriftiness to resourcefulness. Before long, the stranglehold that poverty and dependence had exercised for so long began to loosen, and the family's lot improved for the first time ever.

Oscar Jackson, the man who had been living with the family, was placed in a training program reflecting his vocational interests, and, within six months, had gotten an excellent job with an independent building contractor in town. Weeks later, he and Mrs. Jones were married and the whole family went off welfare.

Without the comprehensive care and consistent follow-up provided by HELP's reeducation program, it is highly unlikely that the family would have ever been able to escape the welfare trap. Even the offer of jobs would have been futile. But with training and personal attention, they were afforded the tools necessary for the development of self-reliance and responsibility.

Thus, to do the work of Biblical charity effectively, our outreaches will not only have to provide job opportunities, they will have to provide a comprehensive reeducation program to equip the poor so they can take advantage of those job opportunities.

First, the poor, like all others, must be instructed in the life-transforming tenets of the Gospel of grace (Matthew 28:19-20). They must hear the Good News (Luke 4:18). They must comprehend that their gravest obstacle to a full and abundant life is poverty of the soul (John 10:10). Biblical charity is not rooted in the Social Gospel. It is rooted in the Gospel.[16] So, start with the Gospel. Never be deterred from the evangelistic opportunities that Biblical charity presents (Colossians 4:5).

Second, the poor must be taught Biblical principles of personal finances.[17] Show them what the Bible has to say about the tithe (Malachi 3:8-12), budgeting (Luke 14:28), saving (Proverbs 6:6-11), goals and priorities (Proverbs 1:8-19), cosigning (Proverbs 6:1-5; 11:15), and indebtedness (Romans 13:8), and they will invariably become better stewards and more economically secure. Preventive maintenance is the best maintenance. Even if a family loses its primary source of income, it will not suffer if it has learned to practice Scripturally sound financial habits. It will have room for financial breathing. It will not even need charity. And that is the best kind of charity: teaching the poor how to stand on their own.

Third, the poor must be taught Biblical principles of providence. Their families need to prepare. They need to know that it is supremely advantageous to prepare. Skills like gardening, canning, sewing, and first aid are critical assets in times of economic constriction. Again, it is to our shame that groups like the Mormons have grasped this bit of Scriptural wisdom much better than we have. If a Mormon family loses its income, it needn't make a mad dash to the unemployment office. It has a year's supply of groceries stowed away, along with a parcel full of other essential commodities. There is no need to panic, no need to fret. The family has contingency plans and survival tactics to fall back on. On the other hand, most Christians, and certainly most of the poor in our midst, wake up to a new world every morning. If we fail to plan, we've planned to fail.

Fourth, the poor must be taught Scriptural principles of health and hygiene.[18] The Bible's emphasis on cleanliness (Leviticus 14-15; Numbers 19; Deuteronomy 23), diet (Leviticus 11), and rest (Exodus 20:8-10), makes it clear that our bodies are to be taken care of. Much of the financial disaster that people face today is due to a violation of this emphasis. Again, preventive maintenance is the best maintenance. We've been most charitable when we've taught others how to avoid needing charity.

Fifth, the poor must be taught the godly concepts of industry and craftsmanship. Not only should they learn about the work-ethic, they should learn how to implement it.

According to an old Hebrew proverb, "He who does not teach his son a trade, teaches him to steal." Here we are in modern

America with a society filled to overflowing with such ill-equipped sons. No wonder crime and poverty have reached crisis proportions. Economist Gary North has said, "In the modern economy, few men can teach their sons their trade. Their trade is too specialized and it requires professional training, or trade union approval, or some sort of licensing, or a work permit. In short, salaried men do not work with their sons. Moreover, the old Puritan practice of sending sons to an apprentice, and taking in other men's sons as apprentices has also disappeared, and with the disappearance of apprentices we have also witnessed the disappearance of the old crafts. This has involved a cultural loss to society, but in a time of shrinking division of labor, it may well involve far more than cultural loss."[19]

According to the Scriptural pattern, the small, family business serves several crucial functions. First, family businesses provide every person in the society, even the poor, with a trade. As a primary occupation, that trade converts into capital development for both the family and the community. As a secondary occupation, that trade forms an especially effectual employment insurance. Second, family businesses establish habits of discipline and diligence, crucial to any successful endeavor in the free marketplace. Third, family businesses promote self-motivation and incentive for achievement. Family involvement in enterprise does not create an artificial or makeshift togetherness, but a community, based on shared goals, shared priorities, and shared labor. Fourth, family businesses affirm and confirm the primary economic values of productivity and efficiency. The child in a family business learns more, plans better, works harder, and buys cheaper. The child in a family business is an asset to society. He is prepared for the future. He is creating a legacy. And, last but not least, he is making money!

If we would only teach, equip, and facilitate the poor so that they can begin to establish small, efficient, cost-effective, and labor-intensive family businesses, we would do more for our society's economic outlook than any number of corporate shakedowns, tariff restrictions, union confederations, or governmental regulations. Out of the back room, from a corner of the garage, off the living room floor, or out of the trunk of the car, those tiny, family operations could very well be, in fact, most certainly would be, the most functional and effective structures of charity in our society.

In Wilmington, Clayton Cooper has instituted a program of reeducation that takes each of these elements into account. Working out of the Delaware Community Center, he takes the poor off the streets and helps them find jobs, but only after teaching them everything from basic reading skills to Scriptural principles. "You can't just take a prostitute off the corner and say, 'Listen, God says you can't do this,' and expect to make much headway," says Cooper. "You have to have alternatives. You have to do some reeducating."

Biblical charity is not mere philanthropy. It is doing anything and everything necessary to enable the poor to stand on their own, to provide for their families, and to prepare for the future.

Precautions

Some of the poor that you will run across in your work of compassion are not going to be interested in improving their lot. They are not going to be interested in jobs, or reeducation, or anything of the kind. They will refuse to work and demand a handout. These are the kinds of people you can expect to attract every now and then if you undertake a Biblical charity outreach. These are the kinds of people that Scripture labels "sluggards."

The teaching on sluggards is clear and precise. The Bible says that sluggards waste opportunities (Proverbs 6:9-10), bring poverty upon themselves (Proverbs 10:4), are victims of self-inflicted bondage (Proverbs 12:24), and are unable to accomplish anything in life (Proverbs 15:19). A sluggard is boastful (Proverbs 10:26), lustful (Proverbs 13:4), wasteful (Proverbs 12:27), improvident (Proverbs 20:4), and lazy (Proverbs 24:30-34). He is self-deceived (Proverbs 26:16), neglectful (Ecclesiastes 10:18), unproductive (Matthew 25:26), and impatient (Hebrews 6:12).

So what are you to do with such a person, should he show up at your doorstep? According to Scripture, "If a man will not work, neither let him eat" (2 Thessalonians 3:10).

Does that mean that a sluggard is not to receive any charity whatsoever?

No. He simply receives a different kind of charity.

Charity to the *deserving* poor involves loosening "the bonds of wickedness," undoing "the heavy burden," and letting "the oppressed go free" (Isaiah 58:6). It involves "dividing bread with the hungry, bringing the homeless poor into the house, and covering the naked" (Isaiah 58:7).

Charity to the *sluggardly*, on the other hand, involves admonition and reproof (2 Thessalonians 3:15; Proverbs 13:18). The compassionate and loving response to the sluggard is to warn him. He is to be warned of the consequences of immorality (Proverbs 5:10), of sloth (Proverbs 6:11), of deception (Proverbs 10:3), of negligence (Proverbs 10:4), of selfishness (Proverbs 11:24), of boastfulness (Proverbs 14:23), of slackfulness (Proverbs 19:15), of drunkenness (Proverbs 21:17), of gluttony (Proverbs 23:21), and of thievery (Proberbs 28:22). Charity to the sluggardly does not add to his complacent irresponsibility by making life increasingly easier to abuse through promiscuous entitlement programs. Instead, charity to the sluggardly equips and enables him to move beyond dependency and beyond entitlement.

According to economist Robert Kuttner, "The first premise of the free market is that people get more or less what they deserve. If the state or private charities tamper with that principle of desert, the most efficient producers may well stop working so hard, while those who happen to be inefficient, or even slothful, will be overcompensated. This is why the poor presumably need the spur of their own poverty."[20]

Biblical charity must never mimic the folly of welfare by tampering with "the principle of desert." At this point, it might do us well to remember though that the principle of desert will not, indeed cannot, deny compassionate and merciful relief to the infirmed, the disabled, the elderly, or the dependent young. As Charles Murray has asserted, "There is no such thing as an undeserving five-year-old."[21] Biblical charity is enjoined by Scripture to help the poor help themselves. It is designed to provide them with a hand, not a handout.

Summary

The goal of Biblical charity is to transform poverty into productivity. Thus, finding jobs for the jobless is an ultimate priority.

But finding jobs just isn't as easy as it once was. Structural changes in the economy due to international competition, inefficient manufacturing techniques, protectionist trade policies, and inadequate retraining have produced grave disparities between the types of jobs available and the number of qualified workers seeking employment.

Finding jobs is not, however, an impossible task, for there are jobs to be had. It is up to our charity outreaches to find those jobs and then match them to the deserving poor in our midst. Through a job referral service and a career counseling program, the poor can be reabsorbed into the economy, thus breaking the cycle of deprivation.

Sadly though, because of the debilitating effects of the federal welfare system, which indisputably encourages indolence and sloth, many of the chronically unemployed poor will need more than just a referral and a bit of counseling. They'll need comprehensive reeducation. So, in order to free them from the trap of dependency, our charity outreaches will have to teach them basic principles of regeneration, finances, providence, health and hygiene, and industry. They will not only have to find fit employment for the poor, they will have to fit the poor for employment.

Thus, to help the poor help themselves, Biblical charity will need to find them jobs, train them for jobs, and even create jobs for them. The bootstrap ethic sets Biblical charity apart from mere philanthropy. And that is simply due to the fact that it is designed to provide the poor with a hand, not a handout.

A compassionate heart feels for the emotionally, spiritually, psychologically, and physically sick. And such a heart finds ways to express those feelings. The expression will be practical, tangible, edible.

John Mosqueda

To the work! To the work!
Let the hungry be fed,
To the fountain of life let the weary be led;
In the cross and its banner
    our glory shall be
While we herald the tidings
    that sets the captives free.
Toiling on, toiling on,
Let us hope and trust,
Let us watch and pray
And labor till the Master comes.
To the work! To the work!
We are servants of God.
Let us follow the path
    that our Master has trod;
With the balm of His counsel
    our strength to renew,
Let us do with all our might
    what our hands find to do.

Fanny Crosby

"You sharin' with us, Muley Graves?" Muley fidgeted in embarrassment. "I ain't got no choice in the matter." He stopped on the ungracious sound of his words. "That ain't like I mean it. That ain't . . . I mean . . . ," he stumbled, "What I mean is, if a fella's got somepin' to eat an' another fella's hungry . . . why, the first fella ain't got no choice."

John Steinbeck

T W E L V E

FOOD: LOAVES
AND FISHES

During one episode in John Bunyan's classic, *Pilgrim's Progress*, Christian seems to be hopelessly mired in "the Slough of Despond." No amount of effort seems sufficient to redeem him from such a perilous plight, so Christian resigns himself to a sad, sedentary demise. Suddenly, though, out of nowhere, a fellow pilgrim named Help comes to the rescue. With a single reach of the hand and a hearty tug, Help pulls Christian out of the slough and onto safe ground once again. In short order, both pilgrims are off and on their way, their destination now one trial closer than before.

If for no other reason than for clarity's sake, it is a good thing Bunyan set this scene in the early seventeenth century. Had he written it in contemporary America, the scenario would had to have been substantially more complex. Help would not have been able to just walk right up to the edge of the slough and yank Christian out. Oh, my, no!

Instead, Help would probably have been required to submit an environmental impact statement on pilgrim removal. In triplicate, of course.

Upon receipt of Environmental Protection Agency approval, Help then would have been required to conduct a sectional opinion survey or, perhaps, call for a communitywide referendum, thus securing permission from the citizenry to undertake such a bold course of action.

Next, he would have had to retain a lawyer, to protect him from criminal and/or civil liabilities; a press secretary, to schedule all future media appearances; and a literary agent, to find the best market for this "life story," tentatively entitled *Slough, Great Thou Art.*

Finally, since he was a devout man, he would have had to return to his prayer closet in order to ascertain rightfully "God's will" in the matter.

Meanwhile, of course, Christian would have expired in the slough, thus writing a premature and an entirely unsatisfactory ending to the tale.

Somehow we have complicated even the simplest of human transactions. Deals are no longer sealed with a handshake. They are dependent upon clause after clause of legalese. Marriages are no longer bound by vows. They are consummated by bilateral prenuptial property contracts. Helping is no longer a matter of neighborly concern. It is stipulated, conditioned, and administered by legislation and litigation.

Humanism's grand scheme has backfired and, as a result, our society is less human than ever before.

Biblical charity acts as an immutable humanizing force in the midst of such modern inhumanity. Biblical charity reaches across all barriers and defies all odds to rescue, without any delay, those caught in the sloughs of despond and deprivation. Biblical charity extends a steady, ready hand in times of need.

Now is one of those times. Need grips our land. Job opportunities and reeducation programs offer long-term solutions for that need. But, for the short-term, the hungry need food.

Food for the Hungry

The federal response to hunger has, for years, focused on food giveaway policies. The Food Stamp Program, the School Lunch and Breakfast Programs, the Special Supplemental Food Program for Women, Infants, and Children (WIC), the Summer Food Program, the Child Care Feeding Program, the Elderly Nutrition Program, the Meals-on-Wheels Program, and the FDIC Cheese and Butter Distribution Program were all designed to eradicate the awful menace of hunger in our land. But the paternalistic state's loaves-and-fishes mentality is bankrupting the entire system. And still a hungry horde of federal dependents cries out for more. It is apparent that the federal food programs, as monolithic as they have become, are inadequate. The state has failed. People are hungry.

In response to the hunger crisis, many Christians have called on the government to add still more food relief programs. They have urged legislators to honor the so-called "right to food." They demand that radical wealth redistribution programs be enacted. Or, for lack of any other tactic, they supplement the federal give-away debacle by imitating its extravagance. Loaves and fishes for everyone. Come one, come all.

Biblical charity also focuses on food relief, but from an entirely different perspective. It takes as its model the Scriptural and covenantal reliance on faith, family, and works to help transform poverty into productivity. Instead of trading their dignity for five-pound blocks of cheese, the poor are nurtured and established in hope, truth, and integrity.

The Exchange Program

Short-term emergency food relief is an obvious stepping off point for the development of a functioning model of Biblical charity. For years, Churches have kept food pantries as a regular function of their benevolence programs. Canned goods, staples, and other nonperishables stored in a small room or closet were, thus, always available in case of emergencies.

By wedding the concept of provident labor to the food pantry plan, mere benevolence is translated into a Biblical charity dynamic.

Very simply, instead of the Church's *giving* the food pantry's provisions away, it *exchanges* groceries for work.

Every Church has innumerable tasks that could be undertaken by the able poor in our midst: yard work, painting, trash pick-up, janitorial tasks, envelope stuffing, minor repairs, etc. If by some wild chance there is no work available at the Church, then the poor can be enlisted for public service: litter clean-up, rubbish removal, and park maintenance.

Steven Gloudier runs the food pantry ministry of Grace Community Church in the small, midwestern farming community of Wozinak. "Our Church has always had a strong commitment to the disadvantaged," he said, "but we've not always known how to express Biblically that commitment. Really, until we adopted the model Scriptural exchange of faith, family, and work, we operated more on instinct and sentiment than anything else. As a result, we never really saw any of our efforts make a difference, either in the lives of the poor, or in the community. Now that's all changed. When people need groceries or some other kind of help, we just put them to work for a while. Even when our bitter Minnesota winters keep everyone inside, there is always something that needs to be done: a wall to be painted, a faucet to be repaired, a floor to be mopped, or whatever. I gather a couple of sacks of groceries while the folks are at work on their assigned task. Then, when the job is done, they can go on their way, knowing that they've earned the food. It wasn't a handout."

The Scriptural exchange model for food relief has several distinct advantages over mere benevolence or philanthropy.

First, the exchange and model is simple. There is no red tape. There are no bureaucratic hassles. There are no lines to wait in, forms to fill out, or conditions to satisfy. If an applicant works, he eats. If he refuses, then he returns home empty-handed. There are no ifs, ands, or buts about it.

Second, the exchange model instantly differentiates between the deserving and undeserving poor. Sluggards won't work. The truly needy will. There is no need to run character profiles or social service histories on each of the applicants. If they are willing to work hard to improve their lot, then they are eligible for these initial emergency provisions of Biblical charity.

Third, the exchange model removes the stigma of shame from charity. As Thomas MacKay has observed, "The bitterest element in the distress of the poor arises, not from mere poverty, but from the feeling of dependence which, of necessity, must be an ingredient in every measure of philanthropy. This feeling cannot be removed, but is rather intensified by liberal measures of relief."[1]

Rather than reinforcing helpless dependence, the exchange model encourages independence and self-reliance through industry.

When famine struck ancient Egypt, Joseph, a servant of Pharaoh, initiated an exchange program quite akin to the exchange model. It was a compassionately designed program to save a languishing land from starvation (Genesis 41:36). But instead of being a compulsory federal planning measure (Genesis

41:56), or a philanthropic giveaway scheme (Genesis 47:15-16), the program was a voluntary, free exercise of the entrepreneurial function (Genesis 41:57).

Joseph set up the relief program so that the poor and the hungry could obtain food from Pharaoh's storehouses in exchange for money (Genesis 41:56), livestock (Genesis 47:16), land (Genesis 47:20), or work (Genesis 47:24). He made certain that the program's administration would be marked by simplicity (Genesis 41:55), and that it would remain decentralized, so that local conditions could be taken into account (Genesis 41:48). Incentive and industry were carefully protected and even encouraged so that the poor could, once the famine was over, rebuild their lives and maintain their independence (Genesis 47:26).

There were no handouts in Joseph's plan because handouts cannot make a difference against the onslaught of poverty and hunger. As economist Milton Friedman has said, "The one who is starving today can be fed today. But what of tomorrow when he will begin to starve all over again?"[2] The exchange concept of food relief stops the cycle of hunger by reinforcing principles of responsibility, diligence, and work. The exchange concept of food relief is a future-oriented, rather than a present-oriented, approach to poverty and, thus, it not only meets immediate needs, it paves the way for a brighter tomorrow.

Restocking the Storehouse

Joseph had an almost unlimited supply of food with which to operate his exchange program (Genesis 41:49). Most Church food pantries, on the other hand, are not so abundantly endowed.

So, where are we to acquire the resources with which to function? How can we keep our stores of canned goods, staples, and other nonperishables from being in a state of perpetual exhaustion?

First, families in the Church can supervise the restocking process. As they conscientiously become more and more committed to live out authentic Christianity, active participation in the food pantry's operation will naturally occur. So, why not just suggest that each family buy a few extra items each time they go grocery shopping? Or, perhaps, a periodic restocking party could be held at the Church so that families can donate supplies to the ministry. Or, maybe the families could be divided up so that each one is responsible for a particular food item over the course of a few months. One Church in Baltimore has a food sign-up sheet. Instead of families' donating altar flowers week by week, they can donate food for the pantry. Another Church in San Diego divides its restocking responsibility between Sunday School classes.

With each family in the Church supplying just a few items at a time, a food pantry ministry will have no trouble whatsoever in maintaining adequate levels of nonperishables.

Second, a garden plot can be set aside each summer so that the pantry can be stocked with fresh vegetables. In Pittsburgh, a community garden yielded about thirty-five tons of vegetables for the poor and unemployed. "We could've done better," said garden director Jeff Gerson, "but the weeds finally did us in!" In the last major harvest of the season, about ten thousand pounds of produce was picked by five hundred volunteers. The vegetables were delivered to the Pittsburgh Community Food Bank where they were then distributed to over seven hundred charitable agencies in twenty-two counties, including three hundred Church food pantries in the Pittsburgh area. Allegheny County's Parks Department provided eight acres of land for the garden, Mellon Bank and the Western Pennsylvania Conservancy donated seeds and supplies, and volunteers did the work. "There were a lot of sore backs," said park spokesman Michael Diehl, "and a lot of smiles on the faces of the volunteers."

Most Churches have at least small plots that they could similarly cultivate and, thus, restock their food pantries with nature's best.

Third, grocery stores will very often donate dated or damaged foodstuffs that are edible but unsalable. Dented cans, day-old bread, expired dairy products, or slow-moving stock are yours for the asking at many stores. In Lincoln, Bernie Slavik collects over five hundred loaves of day-old bread each day from a large grocery chain. Needless to say, his Church's food pantry never lacks for bread. In Duluth, Martin Epsilos distributes several hundred cases of canned vegetables each week to three food pantries. "I probably could get more," he says, "but neither my back nor my pick-up could handle it."

If store managers knew that they could depend on the Christian community to distribute their excess and unsalable goods to the poor, we would never again have to worry about restocking our pantries' shelves.

Fourth, youth groups can be enlisted to unleash their seemingly unlimited store of creative fervor on the restocking problem. Through scavenger hunts, mission projects, car washes, bake sales, and service trips, youth groups have, over the years, raised a tremendous amount of money. So, why not channel all that energy and gumption into the Biblical charity outreach?

Instead of wasting their time on "punch-and-cookies fellowships," the youth of our Churches could help solve one of the most persistent problems of our food pantries: restocking the storehouse.

The Brown Bag Project

Although many of the problems of a food pantry can be minimized through careful management and prudent administration, others are not so easily dispatched.

An almost constant inventory procedure must be set into motion so that the pantry does not go through continuous fluctuations in stock. The last thing a poverty ministry needs is its own feast or famine cycle.

...d that, nutritional balance must be maintained some-
...pantry has no soup, no tuna, and no beans, but a thou-
...s of white hominy, then the help offered to the poor is
...to be of much comfort.

...vay to overcome these difficulties is to put together an
...taff of volunteers from the Church who can effectively
...he buying, the distributing, the stocking, and the in-
...g of the entire poverty outreach. They would make
...hat every disbursement would be nutritionally bal-
...s well as take necessary Biblical measures to guard
...aud and abuse. But, then, how many Churches in
...have the personnel, the funds, the time, and the re-
...) put together such a staff? Not many.

...ow we're back at square one. Our only options are either
...he food pantry ministry to stumble along by guess and

by golly, or to come up with a creative alternative to the large, efficient staff that accomplishes essentially the same thing.

The Brown Bag Project is just such an alternative.[3]

The Brown Bag Project solves the problems of stocking, storing, and inventorying. It solves the problem of nutritional balancing and equitable distribution. It even eliminates the need for a large, well-trained staff.

Here's how it works:

Print up several hundred small labels with a list of items necessary for a balanced diet for a family of four over a four- to five-day span. Such a list should need to include at least:

- 4 16-ounce cans of vegetables
- 4 16-ounce cans of meat like tuna or chili
- 4 16-ounce cans of fruit
- 4 10-ounce cans of soup
- 1 package of noodles or macaroni and cheese
- 1 package of dry beans
- 1 package of cereal, either dry or cookable
- 1 package of crackers
- 1 package of powdered milk
- 1 jar of peanut butter
- 1 family-size bar of bath soap

In short, the list should entail one good hefty sack of groceries.

Once these labels have been printed, then the Church youth group can spend a Saturday afternoon pasting them onto large brown bags obtained through the cooperative generosity of a local grocer. Having done that, they can distribute the sacks to each home in the congregation or neighborhood to be subsequently filled with the specified items.

In a way, the *Brown Bag Project* is nothing more than a carefully orchestrated, closely administered food drive. But the headaches that it eliminates from a Church pantry program make it an administrative boon.

The Brown Bag Project can eliminate waste, encourage congregationwide participation, stimulate community interest, and serve the needy in a way that virtually no other ministry could. So why not get your Church in line? Why not start brown-bagging it?

Precautions

Any Church that actively involves its families in an emergency food relief program must exercise extreme caution in avoiding legal liability for its compassion. In our overly litigious society, it is vital that we protect our Churches, our families, and ourselves as best we can.

First, since the Biblical charity food pantry operation is an exchange program—food for work—have each applicant sign a liability release form before putting him to his task. This standard administrative chore will enable the ministry to sidestep legal headaches and heartaches should anyone ever be injured. A very simple waiver will do. Just make certain that it is filled out completely, signed, and dated.

Second, inventory the food stock often, culling out any items that you even suspect may be spoiled. Even though most states protect charities with "Good Faith Donor Laws," there is no sense in flirting with disaster. Keep the food supplies away from extremes of heat and cold, and do not distribute anything you would not want to serve to your own family.

Third, paperwork is the bane of any endeavor, but it is essential, nonetheless. Make certain that you keep excellent records. Know who you have served, where they are from, and where they can be reached. A single standard form on each applicant can be quickly filled out and filed, so that vital information is never far away. Also, keep a record of who has donated what. Note dates, times, amounts, and anything else that you may deem relevant. A systematic accounting of all the ins and outs of the ministry is not only a protection against legal liability, it is an indispensable characteristic of good management.

Through our food pantries, we won't be able to solve completely the problem of hunger in America, but we will be able to effect enough short-term relief that our long-term strategies can begin to make a difference in systemic poverty. Through our food pantries, we can buy the time we need to reconstruct the economy, and encourage the poor in self-reliance and productivity. Through our food pantries, we can pull the poor from the slough of despond and send them on their way once again.

Summary

The hungry need food. Obviously. In response to this need, the federal government has created a plethora of giveaway programs. But its promiscuous loaves-and-fishes mentality is not only bankrupting the entire system, it is entrapping the poor.

The response of Biblical charity to hunger, on the other hand, deliberately mitigates idleness and indigence by adhering to an exchange model found in Scripture: food relief in return for work. The exchange model has several advantages over philanthropic benevolences. First, it is simple — no line, no red tape, and no bureaucratic hassles. Second, it instantly differentiates between the deserving and the undeserving poor. Third, it removes the stigma of shame from charity since it encourages independence and self-reliance.

Upon that base, any Church can initiate an effective food pantry program. And by involving families, Sunday School classes, youth groups, and local businesses, the problems of stocking, inventorying, and distributing food to the needy can be efficiently managed, while keeping costs down to a bare minimum.

There is hunger in the shadow of plenty. And the saddest part of it all is that it need not be so. Biblical charity is a viable alternative.

Why ride a subway all night in New York City? For the same reason that Jesus was born in a stable: There is no room in the inn.

Michael Harrington

In a cave, a lowly stable,
    Christ our Lord was born;
No room was to be had, no inn to be found
As angelic splendor lavished
    on homelessness that morn.

Charles McQuade

A shade by day, defense by night
A shelter in the time of storm.
No fears alarm, no foes afright,
A shelter in the time of storm.
The raging storms may round us beat
A shelter in the time of storm.
We'll never leave our safe retreat
A shelter in the time of storm.

Vernon J. Charlesworth

Lord, may Thy Church, with mother's care
Selflessly, her refuge share,
And grant as mornings grow to eves
Passioned haven to scattered sheaves.

Howell Hopkins

We blithely sing of "bringing in the sheaves," yet shirk the duty of bringing in. How can this be? If we are to have the sheaves, then we must have the gumption to actually bring them in.

Andrew Murray

SHELTER: NO ROOM IN THE INN

Eviction. It's not a pretty sight.

A helter-skelter of chairs, tables, clothes, dishes, and toys heaped irreverently on a sidewalk as an angry landlord and distraught constables confront a former tenant, even angrier and more distraught than they: this is eviction. And, sadly, though not a pretty sight, it is an all too common sight.

According to a recent congressional study of homelessness, evictions have increased a hundredfold over the last five years. Even the recovery-enhanced decade of the eighties has seen a twenty-eight percent jump in the number of tenant expulsions.[1]

Theresa Walden, a regional manager for Harold Farb Properties, the nation's largest apartment developer, reported, "In the past, most of our evictions have involved irresponsible tenants. They were either loud or destructive or chronically late with rent payments. But the recent spate of evictions has involved families that have always been responsible before; they've just fallen on hard times—unemployed or what have you. We try to work with them as long as we can, but after a while, well . . ."

The National Conference of Mayors estimates that of the nearly two million homeless poor in the United States, only about five hundred thousand are "chronically, permanently unemployed and homeless." The rest are merely "facing temporary economic setbacks . . . due to eviction, family strife, or other unexpected factors."[2]

Walt Koselgrave has personally faced temporary economic setbacks several times. "The first time I got laid off, I didn't think things would get too bad. But since I took my room by the week, I was havin' to sleep in my car. That's not too safe here in Brooklyn, so I tried stayin' with friends for a while. That wears thin pretty fast, though. So I was back on the street again. Thing is, when you've got nowhere to wash up and stuff, it's tough to go on job interviews. When I finally got on at Macy's, things started looking up, but then after the Christmas rush, they let me go. Now I don't know what I'm gonna do. Guess it's back to the street."

Jeanie Wilson was a victim of physical abuse in her own home. "Bill used to come home drunk every Friday night," she said, "and no matter how careful the kids and I would be, he'd end up hitting on us. After a while, I just couldn't take it anymore. We got an apartment and moved out." Unfortunately, the various deposits, the first month's rent, and day care costs quickly depleted Jeanie's meager savings. When she lost her job a month later, she applied for federal assistance and even visited a few local charities, but little help was available and none was forthcoming. "Everyone was real nice, real sympathetic. But I'm going to need more than sympathy. If I get evicted, I've got no place to go. I can't subject the kids to further abuse by going back to Bill, but then, I can't subject them to the street either."

When a tornado ripped through the trailer park where Jack and Lisa Smythe lived, they lost everything they owned. "I'd been laid off for almost thirteen months," said Jack, "but, you know, until this happened, we had things pretty well under control. We'd saved over the years, so we had a nest egg. I started a small repair business. Everything was fine . . . until this." Of course, the Smythes collected on insurance and federal disaster benefits. "Even with all that, we barely had enough to pay off all our bills. We set aside some for a couple of month's rent at this apartment complex, but when that runs out, I don't know what we'll do. Pray a lot, I guess."

The Federal Solution

The federal government has responded to the plight of the displaced poor like Walt Koselgrave, Jeanie Wilson, and the Smythes. But its response has been an unqualified disaster. Its housing projects, urban renewal initiatives, and public shelters have wreaked more havoc in the lives of the poor than homelessness would have of its own accord.

The dream of a federal solution to the sheltering crisis died in St. Louis on July 15, 1972, at 3:32 p.m. — or thereabouts — when the infamous Pruitt-Igoe housing project was given the final *coup de grâce* by dynamite. Previously, it had been vandalized, mutilated, and defaced by its inhabitants and, although millions of tax dollars were pumped back into the project, trying to keep it alive by fixing the broken elevators, repairing smashed windows, repainting, etc., it was finally put out of its misery.

Pruitt-Igoe was constructed according to the most progressive ideals of the federal social planners. Its elegant fourteen stories represented the best that they had to offer. But their best was just not good enough.

Architect and social critic Charles Jencks has said, "without a doubt, the ruins should be kept, the remains should have a preservation order slapped on them so that we keep alive the memory of this failure in planning and architecture."[3] Like the artificial ruin constructed on the estate of eighteenth-century eccentric Elton Waidswelth to provide him with "instructive reminders of former vanities and glories," we should learn to value and protect our former disaster. As Oscar Wilde said, "Experience is the name we give to our mistakes,"[4] and there is a certain health in leaving them judiciously scattered around the landscape as continued lessons.

Perhaps with Pruitt-Igoe thus left as a spur to our memories, we can turn from the federal government to the Christian community for viable solutions to the sheltering crisis. Perhaps with lessons from the project's disastrous demise still fresh in our minds, we can begin to see Biblical charity as the only practical answer to the plight of the temporarily displaced.

The Biblical Solution

Our obligation to the homeless and displaced poor is indisputable. We are "to love those who are aliens" (Deuteronomy 10:19). According to the Old Testament definition, the alien was anyone passing through another's land. The stranger, or sojourner, was a resident alien living in the foreign land, as opposed to traveling through. Both found themselves at a real disadvantage. Being homeless, they were often unable to provide for themselves in a landed agricultural society. They were in danger of being abused, manipulated, and exploited by the natives of a region who knew the language, customs, and civil structure better than they did. For all intents and purposes, the displaced alien was weak and powerless, dependent on others for refuge and provision.

God's people are especially qualified to provide refuge and to express love to the alien, because they have historically found themselves in similar circumstances of vulnerability: ". . . aliens and strangers in the world" (Hebrews 11:13).

It was in this context then that God gave His people—aliens themselves—specific commands regarding everyday treatment of the displaced (Exodus 22:21; 23:9; Leviticus 19:9-10). Since God Himself loves the alien, giving him refuge (Deuteronomy 10:18), God's people are to follow suit. God's people are the solution to the sheltering crisis.

But how? If the federal government, with its resources and all its expertise, has failed to care adequately for the displaced, how can the people of God expect to succeed? How can Christians possibly meet the needs of the homeless poor like Walt Koselgrave, Jeanie Wilson, and the Smythes?

Open Hearts, Open Homes

The first thing that Christians can do to care for the displaced is to begin to practice what David and Ruth Rupprecht call "radical hospitality."[5] Open your home to the homeless. Shelter the dispossessed in the life-giving environs of your family. Almost any middle-class family in America can find room somewhere for temporarily housing the displaced. Of course, time limits, house rules, and accountability structures must be clearly and precisely laid out in order to protect privacy and sanity, but when all is understood, hospitality is a beautiful expression of Biblical charity.

In recent years, Christians have been reminded again and again of their calling to basic hospitality. *Open Heart, Open Home* by Karen Mains,[6] *Be My Guest* by Virginia Hall,[7] *The Way Home* by Mary Pride,[8] and the book by the Rupprechts, *Radical Hospitality*, have all spotlighted our duty as believers to use our homes for others. But their emphasis is but a reiteration of a foundational New Testament theme. Paul told the believers in Rome,

"Share with God's people who are in need. Practice hospitality" (Romans 12:13). Peter charged his readers to "offer hospitality to one another without grumbling" (1 Peter 4:9). And John assented, saying, "We ought therefore to show hospitality" (3 John 8).

Interestingly, the Scriptural definition of hospitality is much broader than the modern one. Hospitality is not just having a few friends over for lunch after Church, or a couple of buddies sitting around the living room, munching on popcorn and watching Monday Night Football. Scriptural hospitality involves much more. Christ's own words are instructive in this: "When you give a luncheon or dinner, do not invite your friends, your brothers or relatives, or your rich neighbors; if you do, they may invite you back and so you will be repaid. But when you give a banquet, invite the poor, the crippled, the lame, the blind, and you will be blessed. Although they cannot repay you, you will be repaid at the resurrection of the righteous" (Luke 14:12-14).

In short, genuine hospitality involves, as author Mary Pride has so aptly pointed out, "inviting poor, blind, lame, and otherwise needy believers to our feasts, not just those who are already our bosom pals."[9] Biblical charity cuts to the heart of the sheltering crisis by honoring the Scriptural mandate to show hospitality. For "God sets the lonely in families" (Psalm 68:6).

Shelly Mulligan moved into the Michaelson household when she was just entering the second trimester of an unplanned pregnancy. "The counselor at the Crisis Pregnancy Center was so incredibly compassionate," she said. "I went in hoping for an abortion. Of course, after I'd seen the slide presentation, there was just no way. But the counselor not only explained to me what the Bible has to say about the sanctity of human life, she also shared with me the Good News of the love and forgiveness of Christ. I went on my way, a new creation bearing a new creation. Two miracles at once!" Later, when Shelly was kicked out of her home by her parents, she contacted the Crisis Pregnancy Center once again. "I don't really know what I was expecting, but I certainly wasn't expecting to be invited into a home. I couldn't believe it! That people could really care that much for someone they hardly even knew! If I'd had any doubts about Christianity before, they were all resolved when the Michaelsons took me in."

That's Biblical charity.

A second tactic that may be effective for short-term emergency housing is the larger community shelter. Various federal and local shelters, most notably in New York City and Philadelphia, evidence the pitfalls in this type of approach to the problem of homelessness. Even so, a privately financed, carefully administered shelter can stand in the gap during times of extreme economic or natural cataclysm. A Church gym, fellowship hall, educational building, or even a sanctuary can be transformed into a haven of hope with just a few cots and blankets.

During the coldest weeks of the winter, innumerable Churches all across the nation exercise this charity option. In Sioux Falls, Pastor Darrel Omarta reported that his Church's sheltering ministry "gave us more opportunity to witness for Christ and really live for Christ than we normally have all year. But, besides fulfilling our duty to minister to the disadvantaged, the shelter occasioned an exceptional opportunity for *us* to grow in strength and maturity as a Church and as individual believers."

That's Biblical charity.

But even though hospitality and community sheltering are both Biblical and effectual for temporary displacements and emergencies, they do not offer permanent solutions to the problem of homelessness. Besides, both hospitality and sheltering present Christians with a whole host of problems: safety, security, privacy, responsibility, accountability, and liability.

So, what other alternatives are there?

Creative Lease Agreements

Over the past several years a number of alternative solutions to the low-income housing crisis have been proposed: rent control legislation,[10] sweat equity construction,[11] rehabilitated youth hostels,[12] reverse gentrification,[13] tenant-controlled projects,[14] voucher systems,[15] enterprise zone inducements,[16] and rural cooperatives.[17]

But perhaps the best alternative involves creative lease arrangements with apartment complexes. This tactic is one that deals with the problem of shelter over the long term. Landlords can be approached by Churches involved in Biblical charity, and a deal can be negotiated whereby tenants exchange work for all deposits and the first few months' rent. Families with no money, no job, and no hope can suddenly find themselves gainfully employed — at least part-time — and adequately housed. The landlord, on the other hand, has hungry, willing crews of workers to upgrade the maintenance of the property, as well as a high occupancy rate and insurance for the future, when a soft rental market might otherwise drive him to the brink of bankruptcy.

Sharon Parks owns and manages over one hundred apartment units in her Houston suburb of Humble. Because of a slumping real estate market, her occupancy rate has been running at a miserably low forty-one percent for the last few years. So, when a representative of HELP Services came to her office recently to discuss some creative and mutually beneficial leasing options, she was quite interested. "Oh, sure, I was leery at first," she said. "But then I thought, 'What have I got to lose?' With the market as soft as it was, I was almost willing to try anything." Three displaced families with whom HELP had been working were placed in apartments under a three-month conditional lease. In exchange for security deposit, move-in costs, utility hook-up, and the first month's rent, each family was to have specific tasks assigned around the complex: light maintenance, vacancy clean-up, painting, and minor repairs. "I was amazed at how well the arrangement worked. One of the families didn't last, but the other two not only stayed on, they've become significant assets to our apartment community. And the excellent publicity that we've gotten has pushed our occupancy rates well over seventy percent. I'd do it again in a second."

There are several reasons why this approach to sheltering the needy is so effective:

First, creative leases follow the exchange model in principle and in practice. The poor actually provide for themselves. We merely facilitate their industry and independence. They are thus equipped and enabled to earn their own way. A creative lease does not give the poor family a handout, but a hand.

Second, creative leases do not constitute a drain on the economy. They, in fact, enhance the economic outlook of a community by innovatively pooling resources, bartering services, and encouraging productivity.

Third, creative leases are flexible, decentralized, and defined according to local conditions. Thus, they can be custom-tailored to meet unique circumstances without bearing undue long-term liabilities.

Precautions

Besides bringing in the sheaves, any Biblical charity outreach is bound to bring in its share of thieves as well. There is nothing you can do to avoid that. But there are several things you can do to minimize their effect of the ministry.

First, take every precaution to protect the families involved in the ministry from harm. Never leave them vulnerable. Never leave them in the lurch. Never leave them to their own devices. "Guard the flock" (Acts 20:28). All applicants for aid should be thoroughly screened. They should be apprised of the conditions and responsibilities that they'll be expected to uphold. And don't make exceptions. If a person, no matter how deprived, refuses to abide by the Scriptural principles laid out by the ministry, they simply are not eligible for aid. No amount of whining or crying or moaning or groaning should sway you from this firm conviction. For safety's sake, stick with the rules.

Second, keep scrupulous records. Get everything in writing. Fill out each application completely. Sign all leases and keep duplicate copies. Operate on a professional basis. If ever you are forced to appear in court — and in this litigious society you never can tell when you'll wind up facing a judge — make certain that you can fully support your integrity. If you utilize computer records, make absolutely certain that you make back-up disks. Never leave yourself open to false accusations.

Third, make certain that none of your charitable activities provokes dependence. All charity should be temporary. Make that stipulation at the outset. Biblical charity is never to be a gravy train for sluggards and "professional bums." Develop each program in such a way that it naturally "weans" applicants from relief. The purpose of our efforts is not to transfer the poor from one dole to another, it is to translate poverty into productivity. We must offer efficient, inexpensive, decentralized, and genuinely compassionate care to the disadvantaged, all the while guarding against ingratitude, sloth, negligence, and irresponsibility.

Summary

Homelessness is a serious problem in America. As many as two million people bed down each night in some back alley, abandoned warehouse, or quiet public park.[18]

Again, the federal response is sorely inadequate at best, ominously destructive at worst.

But unless and until Christians provide Biblical alternatives, the poor will have to continue to contend with either the alleys and warehouses or the Pruitt-Igoes. There are no other options.

By meeting the needs of the "aliens" and "sojourners" in our midst, by opening our homes to the homeless, or by operating short-term community Church shelters, the vicious cycle of indolence and irresponsibility can be effectively broken. Or, even better, by working out long-term, creative lease arrangements with local landlords, the homeless can be given a fresh start and a new hope.

And that really and truly is Biblical charity.

PART FIVE

THE FUTURE

From the coast of Africa,
To the plains of America
There's a hungering. There's a hungering.
From the barrios in east L.A.,
To the mountain range in Kilauea,
There's a hungering. There's a hungering.

But the hunger never will be filled
By Hands Across America.
What they need in Ethiopia
Is a taste of Latter Rain.

From the streets of London town,
To the jungle nights in Vietnam,
There's a hungering. There's a hungering.
And I'd even guess on Easy Street,
Where they always have enough to eat,
There's a hungering. There's a hungering.

Dennis Welch (1986)

"Defeat" must not grace the tongue of God's chosen. "Retreat" is no course of action for His own. We must ever march onward. That is our duty and our destiny.

Athanasius

At two o'clock in the morning,
    if you open your window and listen
You will hear the feet of the Wind
    that is going to call the Sun.
And the trees in the shadow rustle,
    and the trees in the moonlight glisten.
And though it is deep, dark night,
    you feel that the night is done.

Rudyard Kipling

Far and near the fields are teeming
With the waves of ripened grain;
Far and near their gold is gleaming
Over the sunny slopes and plain.
Lord of the Harvest, send forth reapers!
Hear us, Lord, to Thee we cry;
Send them now the sheaves to gather
Ere the poverished swoon and die.
Send them forth with morn's first beaming.
Send them in the noontides glare;
With the sun's lost rays are gleaming,
Bid them gather everywhere.

John O. Thompson

FOURTEEN

OBEDIENCE: GO WITH WHAT YOU'VE GOT

In 1821, Dr. John Rippon, pastor of the New Park Street Chapel in Southwark, London, began a ministry to the homeless poor. A complex of almshouses was erected on a property adjacent to the Church and the monumental task of rehabilitation was begun. Rippon wrote, "Christian compassion is driven by a holy and zealous compulsion when sight be caught of deprived distress. Talk not of mild and gentle acts, of soft provisions and hesitant walk. Christian compassion knows only boldness and sacrifice. Lest we strike the Judas bargain and go the way of the goats, let us invite the strangers in. Let us shelter the aliens beneath a covering of charity and Christlikeness."[1]

When Charles Haddon Spurgeon succeeded Rippon to the pastorate of New Park Street Chapel in 1854, the work with the poor continued unabated. When the Church moved to larger facilities in 1861, it was apparent to Spurgeon that the almshouses, too, would need to be moved into larger and more up-to-date facilities. Therefore, he launched the construction of a new building for them. According to press reports at the time, "no greater effort has ever been expended on behalf of the city's destitute."[2]

The new structure consisted of seventeen small homes which, in the manner of the times, were joined together in an unbroken row. There, in home-style fashion, the poor were not only sheltered, but also provided with food, clothing, and other necessities. In succeeding years, a school, an orphanage, and a hospital were added, each an expression of that holy and zealous compulsion: Christian compassion.

Both Rippon and Spurgeon looked upon their work of sheltering the homeless as part and parcel with the rest of their ministry. It was inseparable from their other labors: preaching, writing, praying, and evangelizing. It was inseparable, in fact, from their faith in Christ.

Once a doubter accosted Spurgeon on a London thoroughfare and challenged the authenticity of his faith. Spurgeon answered the man by pointing out the failure of the secularists in mounting practical and consistent programs to help the needy thousands of the city. In contrast, he pointed to the multitudinous works of compassion that had sprung from faith in Christ: Whitefield's mission, Mueller's orphanage, Bernardo's shelter. He then closed the conversation by paraphrasing the victorious cry of Elijah, boisterously asserting, "The God who answereth by orphanages, LET HIM BE GOD!"[3]

Authentic Faith

In the Gospel of Matthew, Jesus describes a scene that may help us to understand the compulsion of Rippon and Spurgeon to wed faith and deeds so sacrificially. The scene is not a comfortable one for us to imagine. It seems to cut across the grain of all we have come to hold near and dear. It pictures a far different test of faithfulness than we might have proposed. But then, after all, it is His prerogative, for it is His judgment:

> When the Son of Man comes in His glory, and all the angels with Him, He will sit on His throne in heavenly glory. All the nations will be gathered before Him, and He will separate the people one from another as a shepherd separates the sheep from the goats. He will put the sheep on His right and the goats on His left.

> Then the King will say to those on his right, "Come you who are blessed by my Father; take your inheritance, the Kingdom prepared for you since the creation of the world. For I was hungry and you gave Me something to eat, I was thirsty and you gave Me something to drink, I was a stranger and you invited Me in, I needed clothes and you clothed Me, I was sick and you looked after Me, I was in prison and you came to visit Me."

> Then the righteous will answer Him, "Lord, when did we see You hungry and feed You, or thirsty and give You something to drink? When did we see You a stranger and invite You in, or

needing clothes and clothe You? When did we see You sick or in prison and go visit You?"

The King will reply, "I tell you the truth, whatever you did for one of the least of these brothers of mine, you did for Me."

Then He will say to those on His left, "Depart from Me, you who are cursed, into the eternal fire prepared for the devil and his angels. For I was hungry and you gave Me nothing to eat, I was thirsty and you gave Me nothing to drink, I was a stranger and you did not invite Me in, I needed clothes and you did not clothe Me, I was sick and in prison and you did not look after Me."

They also will answer, "Lord, when did we see You hungry or thirsty or a stranger or needing clothes or sick or in prison, and did not help You?"

He will reply, "I tell you the truth, whatever you did not do for one of the least of these, you did not do for Me."

Then they will go away to eternal punishment, but the righteous to eternal life (Matthew 25:31-46).

Authentic Christianity can be tested in accord with deeds — specifically, deeds of kindness to the poor and disadvantaged. Clearly, "Religion that God our Father accepts as pure and faultless is this: to look after orphans and widows in their distress and to keep oneself from being polluted by the world" (James 1:27).

Understanding this, Pastors Rippon and Spurgeon and a whole host of faithful believers throughout the ages labored arduously on behalf of the deprived. They united Word and deed. Theirs was an authentic faith.

But what of us? What of our faith? How will we fare "when the Son of Man comes in His glory?"

Incentives and Initiatives

The primary incentive for Christians to develop functional outreaches of Biblical charity, then, is ethical. God commands, so we obey. We *must* obey or "go the way of the goats."

We don't offer charity simply because there is a need. We don't offer charity simply because it is gratifying. We don't offer charity simply because we feel guilty. We offer charity because the Law of God has much to say about our social responsibilities. We offer charity because that is the way of authentic Christianity.

Notice that the ethical duty to live out the full implications of the faith is not conditioned on the resources we may or may not have at hand. It is an unconditional duty. Rich or poor, powerful or weak, every Christian is called to exercise compassion. We are not to allow constraints of time, money or influence to deter us from our high calling. We are to go with what we've got — even if what we've got is minimal to the extreme. Like our Macedonian forebears, we are to "give according to our ability and even beyond our ability" (2 Corinthians 8:3).

Notice, too, that the ethical duty to offer Biblical charity to the broken and afflicted is not conditioned on the talents, skills, or gifts we may or may not have. According to Scripture, every Christian has been accorded one or more supernatural spiritual gifts (1 Corinthians 12:7; 1 Peter 4:10). And each of the gifts — be it teaching, helps, wisdom, evangelism, or any of the others — can be marshaled to the support of a ministry of compassion. Again, we are to go with what we've got. We must let nothing stand in our way.

Fulfilling Our Commission

Those of us willing to walk in accord with the ethics of authentic faith have been given a mandate: Win the world for Jesus Christ. Leave no stone unturned. Leave no institution untouched. Leave no endeavor undone.

The strategy for accomplishing this monumental task of worldwide conquest is clearly stated in Scripture: "For though we live in the world, we do not wage war as the world does. The weapons we fight with are not the weapons of the world. On the contrary, they have divine power to demolish strongholds. We demolish arguments and every pretension that sets itself up against the knowledge of God, and we take captive every thought to make it obedient to Christ" (2 Corinthians 10:3-5).

As theologian David Chilton has observed, according to this Scripture, "the army of Christ is invincible: we are not fighting in mere human power, but with weapons that are 'mighty in God' (Ephesians 6:10-18), divinely powerful, more than adequate to accomplish the job. With these weapons at our disposal, we are able to destroy everything that the enemy raises up in opposition to the Lord Jesus Christ. We are taking *every thought* captive to the obedience of Christ: Christ is to be acknowledged as Lord everywhere, in every sphere of human activity. We are to think God's thoughts after Him: at every point, following His authoritative Word, the Law book of the Kingdom. . . . The goal of our warfare is total victory, complete dominion for the Kingdom of Christ. We will not settle for anything less than the entire world."[4]

Our commission demands that we bring the Gospel of grace to men and nations, making disciples and "teaching them to obey *everything*" that Christ has commanded (Matthew 28:19-20).

Thus, our commission has not been fulfilled, nay, it has yet to be undertaken, if we do not bring the message and the practice of charity first to the Church, and then beyond to "the uttermost parts of the earth" (Acts 1:8).

> Though I speak with the tongues of men and of angels, and have not charity, I am become as sounding brass, or a tinkling symbol. And though I have the gift of prophecy, and understand all mysteries, and all knowledge; and though I have all faith, so that I could remove mountains, and have not charity, I am nothing. And though I bestow all my goods to feed the poor, and though I give my body to be burned, and have not charity, it profiteth me nothing. Charity suffereth long, and is kind; charity envieth not; charity vaunteth not itself, is not puffed up, doth not behave itself unseemly, seeketh not her own, is not easily provoked, thinketh no evil; rejoiceth not in iniquity, but rejoiceth in the truth; beareth all things, believeth all things, hopeth all things, endureth all things. Charity never faileth (1 Corinthians 13:1-8, KJV).

The Kingdom of God shall advance slowly but surely His dominion, which is an everlasting dominion, and which shall not pass away, will be seen by every eye, beheld by every man.

Basil the Great

Ours is the call to be broken bread and poured out wine. Only then can we confidently sing of sheaves brought into the barns of plenty.

Oswald Chambers

As the westering sun stoops
     to drink from the sea
So the Finger of God descends,
     destroying my complacency.
The whispering tides bear their tales
     to the sand;
The swell of Your Sovereignty
     contains my spirit's command.
The winter wind patterns pavanes
     as it harps through the trees,
The Breath of God blows,
     compelling my minstrelsy.

Kemper Crabb

The typical American Christian is an economic conservative with a guilty conscience. This is because he hears so much conflicting information about his Christian responsibilities in this area, he doesn't know what to do.

John Eidsmoe

FIFTEEN

SLOWLY BUT SURELY: BACK TO THE BRIDGE

There were fourteen of us standing along the riverbank. We'd all been there before, one year earlier, making our first acquaintance under the most grievous of circumstances. The old rusty girders of the bridge loomed large overhead, but the memories each of us harbored of that fateful day loomed even larger.

Elsie Weltzberg was silently sobbing. Henry Blass stared, unblinking, across the softly rippled surface of the water. And Johnny Porston's family — what was left of it — huddled uncomfortably round about one another as I began to read from Scripture, dedicating the sludge of the woe-begotten spot as "a memorial to the people of God forever" (Joshua 4:7). Our memorial was not as significant as the twelve stones, one for each of Israel's tribes, that Joshua had stacked on the Jordan's west bank some three thousand years earlier, but it was certainly no less dramatic in the minds of our motley group. Like Joshua, we had defied the odds, overcome debilitating difficulties, and bypassed legions of naysayers in order to possess the promise of God. We, too, had crossed over from the howling wilderness to the land of hope. We, too, had been stranded, only to be tested and tried on the almost unending sands of uncertainty, despair, and privation. And we, too, had, by the sheer grace of God, prevailed. "It's pretty amazing when you really think about it," said Elsie, "how far we've all come in a year."

I agreed.

When Johnny Porston lept suicidally from his high perch on that bridge, Elsie, Henry, and the others were rootless, homeless, jobless, hopeless sojourners in the land. I was the naively inexperienced pastor of an idealistic and energetic, but equally inexperienced, congregation.

One year later, together, we had gone a long, long way in our journey from poverty to productivity. Elsie was working regularly now, for the first time in more than sixteen years, as a waitress in a sandwich shop. "I don't suppose I'm on the road to riches," she would often remark, "but, at least, I'm on the road out of the gutter."

Henry had just recently started his own trash-hauling business and was looking forward to the day when he could leave his job as a convenience store clerk to devote his full attentions to the new enterprise.

The others were all well fed, clothed, housed, and gainfully employed as well. And, as for me, I too could give testimony that the Scriptural path from paucity to prosperity was sure, secure, and tenable, even if not without its parlous parts.

Starting from Scratch

With little more than a few sacks of groceries stashed in a back-room pantry, our Church's fledgling outreach to the poor was hardly prepared to tackle the complex web of problems that had exiled Elsie, Henry, and the others from America's mainstream, and that had driven Johnny to such extreme desperation. Our rented facilities were already woefully inadequate. Our finances were stretched to the limit. And our available resources, experienced counsel, and community support amounted to just about nil.

But we didn't let that stop us. Taking seriously Scripture's charity mandate, we determined to forge ahead.

"I'd been run through every wringer welfare's ever devised," Elsie later said, "and I'd never made a lick of improvement in all the years I'd been on the dole. In fact, I was worse off than ever before. Cheap wine and a life of wandering from one handout to the next were all I'd come to know. So, I was pretty skeptical, as you can well imagine."

Elsie wasn't the only one who was skeptical. After all, how could we possibly expect to succeed when the governmental system had failed so miserably, despite its vast resources, unparalleled expertise, and unnumbered years of trial-and-error experience? But, then, we had to try. So, we did.

Most of our work was conducted over the phone at first. We called Churches, social service agencies, libraries, government offices, YMCAs, and anyone or anything else we could think of calling. We combed the city to see what services were currently available elsewhere, and, perhaps, to coordinate our efforts with theirs. We also called store owners, landlords, doctors, dentists, Jaycees, lawyers, bankers, journalists, and deejays in an attempt to find jobs, solicit help, and/or spread the word. We contacted realtors, city council members, and Sunday Schools. We conducted radio interviews, wrote newspaper articles and editorials, and made cameo appearances on television.

It wasn't long before jobs came pouring in: babysitting, carpentry, retail sales, warehouse stocking, fast food services, plumbing, inventory control, odd jobs, and small appliance repair. Coordinating our efforts with other local Churches and agencies was also accomplished naturally, through word of mouth. Sheltering homes opened up. Manufactured commodities and seconds were made available. Services were offered, professional and personal.

Ambitious Reckoning

We had never intended simply to provide alternatives to welfare. We wanted ultimately to supplant the governmental system with the Biblical pattern. And that was what was beginning to occur. Even if only in seed form.

But more, we had wanted first and foremost to demonstrate our fidelity to the Lord Jesus Christ by unadorned obedience to the dictates of Scripture. We had wanted to expand the work of the Kingdom through evangelistic, sacrificial, and compassionate ministry. We had wanted to contribute, in whatever way we could, to the reclamation of American culture along godly lines. Quite a set of ambitions! Those ambitions are almost immeasurable against data, statistics, and circumstances.

But, as the fourteen of us walked away from the ankle-deep mud at the river's edge, I knew that those original ambitions, though by no means fully satisfied, were slowly, surely being fulfilled. I had only to look into the faces of Elsie, Henry, and the others to know.

APPENDIX A

A SOCIAL GOSPEL?

Around the turn of the century, a new theology grew to prominence among Liberal Protestants in Europe and America. It was dubbed the *Social Gospel* movement.

Essentially, *Social Gospel* advocates promoted a message of "salvation by works."[1] They argued that true spirituality consisted of good deeds in the realm of politics, economics, and social justice. Very much like the modern-day proponents of *Liberation Theology*, they reduced the Good News of Jesus Christ to a revolutionary ideology.[2]

By suggesting that authentic Christianity will inevitably concern itself with the plight of the poor, it may seem to some that I have accepted, at least in part, the tenets of this aberrant theology. Nothing could be further from the truth, however.

"Salvation by works" or "salvation by Law" is the most ancient of all heresies. It is indeed, "another Gospel" (Galatians 1:6). It is a "different Gospel" (Galatians 1:7). It is a "contrary Gospel" (Galatians 1:9). It is a Gospel repudiated throughout both the Old and New Testaments: Abraham condemned it (Genesis 15:6; Romans 4:3; Galatians 3:6); Moses condemned it (Deuteronomy 27:26); David condemned it (Psalm 32:1-2; Psalm 51:1-17); Isaiah condemned it (Isaiah 1:10-18); Jeremiah condemned it (Jeremiah 4:1-9); Amos condemned it (Amos 5:1-17); Habakkuk condemned it (Habakkuk 2:4); Paul condemned it (Romans 9:32; Galatians 3:10; Ephesians 2:9); and Peter condemned it (2 Peter 1:3-4; 2:1-22).

"Salvation by works" is heretical in every way imaginable. It abolishes the significance of the cross (Galatians 5:11). It makes light of Christ's sacrifice (Galatians 2:21). It nullifies the work of the Holy Spirit (Galatians 3:3-5). It abrogates the necessity of grace (Romans 4:4). "Faith is made void and the promise is

199

nullified" (Romans 4:14) because it makes man and man's ability the measure of all things (Matthew 15:6-9). Thus, the *Social Gospel* is nothing more than another form of *Humanistic Paganism.*[3]

Salvation according to the Bible is a work of sovereign grace. There is absolutely nothing we can do to merit God's favor: "He saved us, not on the basis of deeds which we have done in righteousness, but according to His mercy, by the washing of regeneration and renewing by the Holy Spirit, whom He poured out upon us richly through Jesus Christ our Savior, that being justified by His grace we might be made heirs according to the hope of eternal life" (Titus 3:5-7).

So, where do works fit in? The Apostle Paul tells us that though we are saved "by grace through faith" (Ephesians 2:8), "not as a *result* of works" (Ephesians 2:9), we are "created in Christ Jesus *for* good works" (Ephesians 2:10).

In other words, good works are something we do *because* we have been justified, not in order *to be* justified. Concern and care for the poor is an *effect* of salvation, not the *cause* of salvation. It is a way of *life*, not a way of *salvation.* And therein lies all the difference.

This then is the faith "which was once for all delivered to the saints" (Jude 3). This is the faith that orthodox believers have held to throughout the centuries — from the Patristic Age, through the Protestant Reformation, and to the present day:

Ignatius of Antioch (14-107). "Carnal people cannot act spiritually, or spiritual people carnally, just as faith cannot act like unbelief, or unbelief like faith. . . . Those who profess to be Christ's will be recognized by their actions. . . . They will give and be given graciously unto the poor just as the Lord gave and was given unto them."[4]

Clement of Rome (34-100). "Let us not merely call Him Lord. . . . Let us acknowledge Him by our actions of mercy and charity."[5]

The Didache (110). "Every prophet who teaches the truth but fails to practice what he preaches is a false prophet. . . . Ministry to the afflicted is but a mark of faith. Yet the absence of that mark is evidence of an absence of that faith."[6]

Basil of Caesarea (330-379). "A man who has two coats or two pair of shoes, when his neighbor has none, evidences a lack of grace in his life. . . . The redistribution of wealth is in no wise the point. The revealing of faith is the point."[7]

John Chrysostom (347-407). "The essence of the Gospel is not concern for the poor but it certainly provokes that concern. In fact without that concern, the essence of the Gospel surely has not been grasped."[8]

Ambrose of Milan (339-397). "Faith is the begetter of a good will and of good actions to the least of these."[9]

Jan Hus (1369-1415). "Doubt must be cast on fruitless lives. Profession must be followed by deeds of charity, otherwise that profession is false."[10]

Martin Luther (1483-1546). "Where there are no good works, there is no faith. If works and love do not blossom forth, it is not genuine faith, the Gospel has not yet gained a foothold, and Christ is not yet rightly known."[11]

The Augsburg Confession (1530). "It is necessary to do good works; not that we may trust that we deserve grace by them, but because it is the will of God that we should do them."[12]

The Belgic Confession (1561). "It is impossible that the holy faith can be unfruitful in man."[13]

The Heidleberg Catechism (1563). "It is impossible that those who are unplanted into Christ by true faith, should not bring forth fruits of mercy and graciousness."[14]

The Westminster Confession (1646). "Good works, done in obedience to God's commandments, are the fruits and evidences of a true and lively faith: and by them believers manifest their thankfulness, strengthen their assurance, edify their brethren, adorn the profession of the Gospel, stop the mouths of the adversaries, and glorify God whose workmanship they are, created in Christ Jesus thereunto; that, having their fruit unto holiness, they may have the end, eternal life."[15]

Matthew Henry (1662-1714). "Man may as soon take pleasure in a dead body, void of soul, or sense, or action, as God takes pleasure in a dead faith, where there are not works."[16]

Jonathan Edwards (1703-1758). "That religion which God requires, and will accept, does not consist in weak, dull, lifeless wishes, raising us but a little above a state of indifference. God, in His Word, greatly insists upon it, that we be in good earnest, fervent in spirit, and our hearts vigorously engaged in mercies."[17]

On and on the testimony of faith through the ages affirms a Gospel evidenced by social concerns but condemning a *Social Gospel* dependent upon those concerns.

APPENDIX B

THE VILLARS STATEMENT ON RELIEF AND DEVELOPMENT

In the spring of 1987, a group of forty evangelical Christians from around the world gathered in Villars, Switzerland, to examine the topic of "Biblical Mandates for Relief and Development." For five days, we engaged in intense discussion, debate, and private reflection, our energies focused by a number of prepared study papers. As a result of our consultation, the following list of concerns was enumerated. If effective relief and development — or in other words, Biblical charity — is to be carried out in any measure, then these concerns most certainly will have to be addressed.[1]

A World in Need

The extent of hunger and deprivation around the world is a reality haunting modern times. Confronted with disaster, disease, and chronic poverty, relief and development agencies have provided massive material assistance. Yet for all the resources expended, hunger and deprivation appear to be increasing. The sad reality is that so much effort has produced little in long-term results.

This reality calls us as Christians to reassess the work of relief and development in light of God's Holy Word. It is our conclusion that the consistent application of Biblical teaching will require a reorientation of relief and development practices, and that this may involve a change in our understanding of human need and in strategies to relieve suffering.

"Relief and development" is an expression that recognizes two Biblical principles. Relief refers to the insistence in both Testaments that the people of God must help the hungry and oppressed. Development stems from the Biblical vision of a people exercising their proper stewardship of God's gifts—of societies that are productive, healthy, and governed justly. Together relief and development envision substantial improvement in economic and human well-being.

We acknowledge our own sinfulness and fallibility, and we recognize that other committed Christians may not agree with all our convictions. Nevertheless, we are compelled by God's Word and by the reality of human suffering to share our convictions with Christians and others. We do not claim to have spoken the final word. Thus we offer the following conclusions of the Villars consultation for research, dialogue, and open debate among all who claim Christ as Lord.

Issues of Concern

With this as our goal, we raise our concerns, over the following issues:

- The failure to operate from a distinctively Biblical perspective in both methods and goals.

- The tendency to focus on meeting material needs without sufficient emphasis on spiritual needs.

- The attempt to synthesize Marxist categories and Christian concepts, to equate economic liberation with salvation, and to use the Marxist critique, without recognizing the basic conflict between these views and the Biblical perspective.

- The emphasis on redistribution of wealth as the answer to poverty and deprivation without recognizing the value of incentive, opportunity, creativity, and economic and political freedom.

- The attraction to centrally controlled economies and coercive solutions despite the failures of such economies and their consistent violation of the rights of the poor.

- A disproportionate emphasis on changing structures without recognizing the frequency with which this only exchanges one oppressive structure for another.

- The danger of Utopian and ideologic entrapment, whether from the left or the right.

- Neglecting to denounce oppression when it comes from one end or the other of the political spectrum.

- Focusing on external causes of poverty in exploitation and oppression without confronting those internal causes that are rooted in patterns of belief and behavior within a given culture.

- The need to make conversion and discipleship essential components of Christian relief and development work, and to carry these out in conjunction with the local Church.

- The need to apply the teaching of the Bible as a whole in the areas of personal life, family, and work, but equally in the shaping of the culture and social life.

- The need to reaffirm the Biblical support for the family as the basic social and economic unit and its right to own and control property, and to stand against any ideology that would diminish the family's proper role in any of these areas.

- The need to oppose a false understanding of poverty which makes poverty itself a virtue, or that sanctifies those who are poor on the basis of their poverty.

Biblical Perspective

In response to these issues, we draw attention to the following Biblical teaching and its implications for relief and development:

- God created mankind in His own image, endowing man with freedom, creativity, significance, and moral discernment. Moreover, prior to the Fall man lived in harmony with all of God's creation, free from pain, suffering, and death.

- The devastating reality of sin and evil (hunger, oppression, deprivation, disease, death, and separation from God) is the result of man's rebellion against God, which began at the Fall and continues through history.

- The causes of hunger and deprivation, therefore, are spiritual as well as material and can only be dealt with adequately insofar as the spiritual dimension is taken into account.

- Man's rebellion against God affects every aspect of human existence. The Fall resulted in God's curse on creation and in destructive patterns of thought, culture, and relationships, which keep men and women in bondage to poverty and deprivation.

- The work of Christian relief and development, therefore, must involve spiritual transformation, setting people free from destructive attitudes, beliefs, values, and patterns of culture. The proclamation of the Gospel and the making of disciples, then, is an unavoidable dimension of relief and development work — not only for eternal salvation, but also for the transformation of culture and economic life.

- When people were held in bondage to hunger and deprivation by unjust social structures, the Bible consistently denounced those who perpetuated such oppression and demanded obedience to God's law. The Biblical emphasis, then, is not on "sinful structures" but rather on sinful human choices that perpetuate suffering and injustice.

- God's ultimate answer for suffering and deprivation is the gift of His only Son, Jesus Christ, who broke the power of sin and death by His own death and resurrection. The decisive victory was won on the cross in the atoning death of Christ for all who would believe Him. The final victory will be accomplished when Christ returns in power and glory to reign with His people. Until that time all who claim Jesus as their Lord are called to care for those in need as the Holy Spirit enables them to share the only message of the true hope for a broken world.

The Villars Statement was signed by the following consultation participants:

David M. Adams
Trans World Radio
Hilversum, Netherlands

Michael Cromartie
Ethics and Public Policy Center
Washington, D.C.

Howard F. Ahmanson
Fieldstead & Company
Irvine, Calif.

Lane T. Dennis
Good News Publishers/
Crossway Books
Westchester, Ill.

Roberta Green Ahmanson
Fieldstead & Company
Irvine, Calif.

Theodore Baehr
Good News Communications
Atlanta, GA

Clarence Bass
Bethel Theological Seminary
St. Paul, Minn.

Charles Bennett
Food for the Hungry
Geneva, Switzerland

Pierre Berthoud
Faculte Libre de Theologie
Reformee
Aix-en-Provence, France

Spencer Bower
Christian Service Fellowship
Minneapolis, Minn.

Otto de Bruijne
Association of Evangelicals in
Africa and Madagascar
Nairobi, Kenya

Phillip Butler
InterDev
Seattle, Wash.

David Chilton
Church of the Redeemer
Placerville, Calif.

Gene Dewey
United Nations
Geneva, Switzerland

Homer E. Dowdy
International Institute for Relief
and Development
Versoix, Switzerland

George Grant
Christian Worldview Institute
Fort Worth, Tex.

Carrie Hawkins
Herbert Hawkins, Inc.
Pasadena, Calif.

Preston Hawkins
Herbert Hawkins, Inc.
Pasadena, Calif.

Evon Hedley
World Vision
Monrovia, Calif.

Alan Jensen
Biblical Institute for Leadership
Development, International
Ames, Iowa

Henry Jones
Spiritual Overseers Service
Irvine, Calif.

Patricia D. Lipscomb
Fieldstead & Company
Irvine, Calif.

Ranald Macaulay
L'Abri Fellowship
Huemox, Switzerland

Ronald H. Nash
Western Kentucky University
Bowling Green, Ky.

Vishal Mangalwadi
Traci Community and ACRA
New Delhi, India

Brian P. Newman
Hunger News Bureau
Versoix, Switzerland

Rob Martin
Fieldstead & Company
Irvine, Calif.

Marvin Olasky
University of Texas
Austin, Tex.

Don McNally
University of Toronto
Hamilton, Ontario

Marvin Padgett
Logos Bookstore
Nashville, Tenn.

Udo W. Middlemann
International Institute for
Relief and Development
Versoix, Switzerland

Clark Pinnock
McMaster Divinity College
Toronto, Canada

Darrow L. Miller
Food for the Hungry
Scottsdale, Ariz.

Herbert Schlossberg
Fieldstead & Company
Minneapolis, Minn.

Gareth B. Miller
Farms International
New York, N.Y.

Allen R. Seeland
AGW Group, International
Glen Ellyn, Ill.

Ken Myers
Berea Publications
Philadelphia, Pa.

Susumu Uda
Kyoritsu Christian Institute for
Theological Studies and Mission
Tokyo, Japan

Tetsunao Yamamori
Food for the Hungry
Scottsdale, Ariz.

END NOTES

Introduction

1. *Seeds*, December 1984.
2. *New York City Tribune*, 2 Jan. 1986.
3. *USA Today*, 31 July 1987.
4. *Eternity*, May 1988.
5. *USA Today*, 31 July 1987.
6. *Insight*, 27 June 1988.
7. I have, for instance, written several other specialized texts on the subject and have several more in the works including *The Dispossessed: Homelessness in America* (Westchester, Ill.: Crossway Books, 1986), and *In the Shadow of Plenty: Biblical Principles of Welfare & Poverty* (Fort Worth, Tex.: Dominion Press, 1986).
8. I have written a manual—though it can in no way be considered to be comprehensive—designed to help churches launch their charity outreaches: *To the Work: A Step-by-Step Guide for Biblical Charity Ministries* (Tyler, Tex.: Institute for Christian Economics, 1988).
9. P. T. Bauer, *Dissent on Development* (Cambridge, Mass.: Harvard University Press, 1976).
10. Stuart Butler, *Enterprise Zones: Reviving the Inner Cities* (New York: Universe Books, 1981).
11. Anna Kontratas and Stuart Butler, *Out of the Poverty Trap: A Conservative Strategy for Welfare Reform* (New York: Free Press, 1987).
12. Charles Murray, *Losing Ground: American Social Policy 1950-1980* (New York: Basic Books, 1984).
13. Lawrence Mead, *Beyond Entitlement: The Social Obligations of Citizenship* (New York: Free Press, 1986).
14. John Jefferson Davis, *Your Wealth in God's World* (Phillipsburg, N.J.: Presbyterian and Reformed Publishing Co., 1984).
15. George Gilder, *Wealth and Poverty* (New York: Basic Books, 1981).
16. Ronald Nash, *Poverty and Wealth: The Christian Debate Over Capitalism* (Westchester, Ill: Crossway Books, 1986).
17. Walter Williams, *The State Against Blacks* (New York: McGraw-Hill, 1982).
18. Michael Novak, *The Spirit of Democratic Capitalism* (New York: Simon & Schuster, 1982).
19. Henry Hazlitt, *Man vs. the Welfare State* (New York: University Press of America, 1983).
20. Warren T. Brookes, *Economy in Mind* (New York: Universe Books, 1982).
21. Gary North, *Inherit the Earth: Biblical Principles of Economics* (Fort Worth, Tex.: Dominion Press, 1987).
22. Herbert Schlossberg, *Idols for Destruction* (Nashville, Tenn.: Thomas Nelson Publishers, 1983).

23. Thomas Sowell, *Knowledge and Decisions* (New York: Basic Books, 1980).
24. David Chilton, *Productive Christians in an Age of Guilt-Manipulators*, 3rd ed., (Tyler, Tex.: Institute for Christian Economics, 1985).
25. Sun Tzu, *The Art of War* (San Francisco: Zhou Kai Books, 1964), p. 17.
26. Cornelius Van Til, *The Defense of the Faith* (Phillipsburg, N.J.: Presbyterian and Reformed Publishing Co., 1967), p. 8.

Chapter 1 — A Cry for Help: The Bridge

1. *Washington Post*, 3 Feb. 1981.
2. *Detroit Free Press*, 27 July 1982.
3. *Wall Street Journal*, 11 Jan. 1983.
4. *USA Today*, 12 Jan. 1984.
5. *New York Times*, 9 Nov. 1984.
6. *USA Today*, 31 July 1987.
7. *Consumer Reports*, June 1987.
8. *Newsweek*, 2 Jan. 1984.
9. *Houston Chronicle*, 30 Nov. 1982.
10. *USA Today*, 10 Jan. 1983.

Chapter 2 — Poverty: In the Shadow of Plenty

1. Sadly, this is just as true today as when I first penned these words in 1985 on page 3 of my book, *In the Shadow of Plenty: Biblical Principles of Welfare and Poverty*, co-published the next year by Thomas Nelson Publishers in Nashville, Tenn., and Dominion Press in Fort Worth, Tex.
2. Ibid.
3. Ibid.
4. Ibid.
5. Ibid.
6. See my discussion of the farm crisis in *The Dispossessed: Homelessness in America*, published by Crossway Books in Westchester, Ill., during the United Nations' International Year of Shelter for the Homeless: 1987.
7. Grant, *In the Shadow of Plenty*, p.3.
8. Grant, *The Dispossessed*, pp. 110-23.
9. Obviously, unhealthy and self-depreciating economic policies and trends *add* to the problem of systemic poverty — witness the collapse of personal health, wealth, and well-being in the socialistic economics of Europe, Africa, and Asia — but the point here is that a *permanent* underclass has now developed that remains essentially unaffected by the government's various political and economic machinations.
10. James D. Squires, ed., *The American Millstone: An Examination of the Nation's Permanent Underclass* (Chicago, Ill.: Contemporary Books, 1986), p. 12.
11. Ibid.
12. Grant, *In the Shadow of Plenty*, p. 3.
13. Stuart Butler and Anna Kontratas, *Out of the Poverty Trap* (New York: Free Press, 1987), p. 47.
14. Nancy Amidei, et al, *Hunger in the Eighties: A Primer* (Washington, D.C.: Food Research and Action Center, 1987), p. 46.
15. *Washington Post*, 12 Jan. 1984.

16. Amidei, pp. 62-66, 73.

17. These figures have been derived from various reports from service providers and advocacy groups. They are in some cases undoubtedly inflated. I fully realize that ideological coordination of the various groups can aggravate even the naturally expected "evangelistic estimates." Even so, to quibble over exact figures is to miss the point: there *are* hungry and homeless people out there. In *The Dispossessed*, I attempt a scientifically sane approach to analyzing the conflicting data, but for our purposes here, a simple acceptance that deprivation exists at a scandalously high level is sufficient.

18. *Children's Defense Budget* (Washington, D.C.: Children's Defense Fund, 1985), p. 40.

19. Julia Wittleson, *The Termination of Poverty* (Boston: Holy Cross Press, 1983) p. 19; and Ruth Sidel, *Woman and Children Last: The Plight of Poor Women in Affluent America* (New York: Penguin Press, 1986), pp. 15-20.

20. Ken Auletta *The Underclass* (New York: Vintage Books, 1983) p. 68.

21. Ibid., pp. 68-69.

22. Kim Hopper and Jill Hamberg, *The Making of America's Homeless: From Skid Row to New Poor* (New York: Community Service Society of New York, 1984), p. 24.

23. Auletta, p. 69.

24. Lenore J. Weitzman, *The Divorce Revolution: The Unexpected Social and Economic Consequences for Women and Children in America* (New York: Free Press, 1985).

25. Auletta, p. 69.

26. George Grant, *Grand Illusions: The Legacy of Planned Parenthood* (Brentwood, Tenn.: Wolgemuth & Hyatt, 1988).

27. Mary Pride, *The Way Home: Beyond Feminism, Back to Reality* (Westchester, Ill: Crossway Books, 1985).

28. *American Demographics*, May 1986.

29. Ibid.

30. Ibid.

31. Herton Ford, *Belly Up in the Midwest* (Lincoln, Neb.: American Farm Bureau Press, 1983), p. 14.

32. *Insight*, 28 April 1986.

33. *Houston Chronicle*, 18 May 1986.

34. *The New American*, 5 May 1986.

35. Carlton Forbes, *Forgiving Souls: Paying the Way for Our Own Enemies* (Salt Lake City: Freedom Reigns Books, 1985).

36. Grant, *The Dispossessed*, pp. 130-31.

37. Ibid., pp. 127-28.

38. Ibid., pp. 130-31.

39. Ibid., pp. 128-30.

40. David Chilton, *Power in the Blood: A Christian Response to AIDS* (Brentwood, Tenn.: Wolgemuth & Hyatt, 1987), pp. 5-6.

41. Ibid., p.6.

42. Gene Antonio, *The AIDS Cover-up* (San Francisco: Ignatius Press, 1986), p. 133.

43. *Sacramento Union*, 20 Jan. 1987.

44. Chilton, p. 22.

45. Walter Barlow, *AIDS Information Institute Report, 1987* (Los Angeles: AIDS Information Institute, 1988), p. 61.

46. Ibid., p. 63.

47. This imagery was first presented in broadcast form in November 1982, on the daily syndicated program "The Christian Worldview." It was later reproduced by permission in a number of different media, including pamphlets for Humble

Evangelicals to Limit Poverty (HELP), Operation Blessing, Southern Foods Co-Op, and articles for the *Humble Echo, The Houston Post, The Columbia Citizen-Journal,* and *Newsweek.*

48. Mary Ellen Hombs and Mitch Snyder, *Homelessness in America: A Forced March to Nowhere* (Washington, D.C.: Community for Creative Non-violence, 1982), pp. 75-8.
49. *Newsweek,* 2 Jan. 1984.
50. *Houston Chronicle,* 2 June 1983.
51. *Newsweek,* 2 Jan. 1984.
52. *Wall Street Journal,* 12 Nov. 1982.
53. Ibid.
54. *Houston Chronicle,* 2 June 1983.
55. *Houston Post,* 26 June 1983.
56. *USA Today,* 1983, quoted in Humble Evangelicals to Limit Poverty newsletter, November 1983.
57. Source: Community for Creative Non-violence.
58. Source: Community Service Society of New York.
59. Source: Community for Creative Non-violence.
60. Source: Coalition on Temporary Shelters.
61. *New York Magazine,* 21 Feb. 1983.
62. *USA Today,* 1983, quoted in Humble Evangelicals to Limit Poverty newsletter, November 1983.
63. *Wall Street Journal,* 12 Nov. 1982.
64. Source: Humble Evangelicals to Limit Poverty.
65. *Dallas Times-Herald,* 13 July 1982.
66. *Newsweek,* 21 Dec. 1982.
67. *Wall Street Journal,* 7 March 1983.
68. This concept was first introduced by Michael Harrington in his book *The Other America* (New York: Vintage Press, 1962). When it was first released, the book shook the Kennedy administration to the core and formed the basis for the development of the "war on poverty" in the years to come.
69. Bread for the World, Background Paper #63.
70. *USA Today,* 18 March 1983.
71. Source: Community Service Society of New York.

Chapter 3 — Welfare: The War on the Poor

1. For an excellent overview of this important policy statement and its historical and political background, see Stuart Butler and Anna Kondratas, *Out of the Poverty Trap: A Conservative Strategy for Welfare Reform* (New York: Free Press, 1987).
2. Milton and Rose Friedman, *Free to Choose* (New York: Harcourt, Brace, Javanovich, 1979), p. 87.
3. Ibid.
4. Ibid.
5. Ibid.
6. Ibid.
7. Ibid.
8. J. Peter Grace, *Burning Money* (New York: Macmillan, 1984), p. 108.
9. Friedman, p. 87.
10. Charles Murray, *Losing Ground* (New York: Basic Books, 1984), p. 48.

11. Ibid.
12. Ibid.
13. Ibid.
14. Ibid.
15. George Grant, *In the Shadow of Plenty: Biblical Principles of Welfare and Poverty* (Fort Worth, Tex.: Dominion Press, 1986), p.121.
16. Ibid.
17. Ibid.
18. J. Robert Dumouchel, *Government Assistance Almanac 1988* (Washington, D.C.: Regnery Gateway, 1988).
19. Butler and Kondratas, pp. 1-7.
20. Ibid., p. 16; and Karl de Schweinitz *England's Road to Social Security* (Philadelphia: University of Pennsylvania Press, 1943).
21. Ibid.
22. See George Grant, *The Dispossessed: Homelessness in America* (Westchester, Ill.: Crossway Books, 1986.
23. "The Poor Law Commission for the Poor Law Reform of 1934," quoted by Mark Blaug in "The Myth of the Old Poor Law and the Making of the New," *Journal of Economic History*, (June 1963), p. 152.
24. William Wilkins, *The Unknown FDR: Zen Politics at the Outset* (New York: The York Press, 1967), p. 85.
25. Albert Donaldson, *American History in Review* (Tulsa, Okla.: Christian Truth Publishers, 1971), p. 426.
26. Murray, p. 22.
27. Blaugh, p. 153.
28. Ibid., p. 154.
29. Thomas Algier, *The American Legacy* (Chicago: Heritage Publishing Co., 1959), p. 13.
30. Thomas MacKay, *Methods of Social Reform* (London: John Murray, 1896), p. 13.
31. Hardy L. Kalwaski, *Poor Richard and the American Ethic* (Boston: Commons Press, 1874), p. 317.
32. *New York Times*, 20 April 1967. Quoted in Donaldson.
33. See Ronald J. Sider, *Rich Christians in an Age of Hunger: A Biblical Study* (Downers Grove, Ill.: Inter-Varsity Press, 1984).
34. See Fred Block, et al., *The Mean Season: The Attack on the Welfare State* (New York: Pantheon Books, 1987).
35. See Jonathan Kozol, *Rachel and Her Children: Homeless Families in America* (New York: Crown Publishers, 1988).
36. Michael Harrington, *The New American Poverty* (New York: Holt, Rinehart, and Winston, 1984).
37. Murray, p. 8.
38. Ibid., by extrapolation from Murray's figures.
39. Grace, p. 108.
40. *Newsweek*, 27 Dec. 1982.
41. Charles Murray, *Budget Priorities and Trends in the Federal Effort to Combat Juvenile Delinquency* (Washington, D.C.: Government Printing Office, 1976).
42. George Gilder, *Visible Man: A True Story of Post-racist America* (New York: Basic Books, 1978).
43. Thomas Sowell, *The Economics and Politics of Race* (New York: William Morrow and Co., 1983).
44. Murray Rothbard, *For a New Liberty* (New York: Macmillan, 1973).
45. See George Grant, *In the Shadow of Plenty: Biblical Principles of Welfare and Poverty* (Fort Worth: Dominion Press, 1986).

46. See Marvin Olasky ed. *Freedom, Justice, and Hope: Toward a Strategy for the Poor and the Oppressed* (Westchester, Ill.: Crossway Books, 1988).

47. See E. Calvin Beisner, *Prosperity and Poverty: The Compassionate Use of Resources in a World of Scarcity* (Westchester, Ill.: Crossway Books, 1988).

48. George Gilder, *Wealth and Poverty* (New York: Basic Books, 1981).

49. Ibid.

50. See George Gilder, *Men and Marriage* (Kenner, La.: Pelican Press, 1987).

51. See George Grant, *Grand Illusions: The Legacy of Planned Parenthood* (Brentwood, Tenn.: Wolgemuth & Hyatt, 1988).

52. See Lawrence Mead, *Beyond Entitlement: The Social Obligations of Citizenship* (New York: Free Press, 1986).

53. See Henry Hazlitt, *Man vs. the Welfare State* (New York: University Press of America, 1983).

54. Grace, p. 105.

55. See Jack Kemp, *An American Renaissance* (New York: Harper & Row, 1979).

56. Grace, p. 112.

57. Ibid.

58. See Barbara Jordan and Elspeth Rostow, *The Great Society: A Twenty Year Critique* (Austin: LBJ Library and School of Public Affairs, 1986).

59. Walter E. Williams, *The State Against Blacks* (New York: McGraw-Hill, 1982).

60. Thomas Sowell, *Civil Rights: Rhetoric or Reality?* (New York: William Morrow and Co., 1984).

61. See Barry Bluestone and Bennett Harrison, *The Deindustrialization of America* (New York: Basic Books, 1982).

62. *Social Services Handbook and Survey* (Houston: HELP Services, 1984).

63. Grace, pp. 113-14.

64. See Grant, *Grand Illusions*, pp. 63-86.

65. See Johathan Kozol, *Illiterate America* (New York: Anchor Press/Doubleday, 1985).

66. See Grant, *The Dispossessed*, pp. 111-24.

67. Butler and Kondratas, pp. 37-38.

68. Ibid., pp. 142-47.

69. Ibid., pp. 226-43.

70. Rothbard, p. 184.

71. Quoted in Yale Brozen, "Welfare Without the Welfare State," *The Freeman*, December 1966, p. 47.

72. Rothbard, p. 184.

73. I say "substantially" simply because it is clear enough that the Bible does not *forbid* state-sponsored efforts to care for the needy in emergency situations (Genesis 41:33-55). Even so, in our current situation, a time of governmental abstinence would not be a corrective overreaction, especially considering the utter neglect of the *primary* Biblical programs of Biblical compassion that welfare has wrought.

Chapter 4—Authentic Christianity: Word and Deed

1. See George Grant, *In the Shadow of Plenty: Biblical Principles of Welfare and Poverty* (Fort Worth, Tex.: Dominion Press, 1986).

2. See George Grant, *The Dispossessed: Homelessness in America* (Westchester, Ill.: Crossway Books, 1986).

3. See David Chilton, *Power in the Blood: A Christian Response to AIDS* (Brentwood, Tenn.: Wolgemuth & Hyatt, 1988).

4. Ulrich Teitelbaum, *Dissenting Voices: A Punctuated Legacy of Protest in the Christian Era* (New York: Yolem Press, 1971), p. 364.
5. J. W. Harrold, *The Diaconate* (London: Gospel Seed Publications, 1926), p. 88.
6. Ibid., p. 92.
7. John Calvin, John T. McNeill, trans., *Institutes of the Christian Religion* (Philadelphia: Westminster Press, 1960), p. 1097.
8. Ibid., p. 1098.

Chapter 5 — Biblical Charity: Faith, Family, and Work

1. J. R. Andrews, *George Whitefield, A Light Rising in Obscurity* (London: Morgan and Chase, 1930), p. 19.
2. C. H. Spurgeon, *Metropolitan Tabernacle Pulpit, Volume 23* (London: Morgan and Chase, 1930). p. 19.
3. Nathaniel Samuelson, *The Puritan Divines: Collected Sermons, Vol. 6* (London: Merrick and Sons, 1902), p. 91.
4. Spurgeon, p. 349.
5. See George Grant, *Grand Illusions: The Legacy of Planned Parenthood* (Brentwood, Tenn.: Wolgemuth & Hyatt, 1988).
6. See George Grant, *The Changing of the Guard* (Fort Worth, Tex.: Dominion Press, 1987).
7. See George Grant, *In the Shadow of Plenty: Biblical Principles of Welfare and Poverty* (Fort Worth, Tex.: Dominion Press, 1986).
8. See Robert G. Clouse, ed., *Wealth and Poverty: Four Christian Views* (Downers Grove, Ill.: Inter-Varsity Press, 1984).
9. Arthur Simon, *Bread for the World* (Grand Rapids, Mich.: Wm. B. Eerdmans, 1975).
10. Ruth Sidel, *Women and Children Last* (New York: Penguin Books, 1986).
11. R. L. Dabney, *A Defense of Virginia and the South* (Harrisonburg, Va.: Sprinkle Publications, 1977), pp. 5-6.
12. Gary North, *Unconditional Surrender: God's Program for Victory* (Fort Worth, Tex.: Dominion Press, 1988), p. 137.
13. George Gilder, *Wealth and Poverty* (New York: Basic Books, 1981), p. 74.
14. Ibid.
15. Max Weber, *The Protestant Ethic and the Spirit of Capitalism* (New York: Charles Scribner's Sons, 1958).
16. Len A. Walt, *Puritan Thought and Capitalism* (London: Gospel Press, Ltd., 1958), p. 127.
17. Claud L. Fevre, *L'Ecriture de Thrasymachos* (Paris: Parbleu Libraire-Editeur, 1963), p. 92.
18. Gilder, p. 74.
19. *U.S. News and World Report*, 17 March 1986.
20. Ibid.
21. Sergius Makyros, *Social Thought in the Eastern Church Traditions* (New York: Pan-Orthodox Publishing Concern, 1962), p. 19.
22. Michael Novak, *The Spirit of Democratic Capitalism* (New York: Simon & Schuster, 1982).
23. Hugh Latimer, *Sermons Before King Edward VI* (Philadelphia: North Valley Publishers, 1897), p. 184.
24. Richard Steele, *The Tradesman's Calling* (Hartford, Conn.: Mills Printers, 1903), pp. 14-15.

25. Martin Luther, *The Estate of Marriage* (St. Louis: Lutheran Educational Foundation Press, 1969), p. 84.

26. Hyksos Pappas, *Cotton Mather: An Immigrant's Patron* (New York: Athena Book Printer, 1926), p. 67.

27. William Tyndale, *Parable of the Wicked Mannon* (Toronto: Knox and Knox, 1961), p. 140.

28. John Calvin, trans. T. H. L. Parker, *Calvin's New Testament Commentaries* (Grand Rapids, Mich.: William B. Eerdmans, 1972), p. 88.

29. Benjamin Tatar, *Luther and the Work Ethic of Protestantism* (Glasgow: St. Anthony's Press, 1949), p. 34.

30. James B. Jordan, letter to the author, 11 November 1984.

31. Langdon Lowe, *The Work of God in the South* (London: Murray Stockbrough, and Wilson, 1896), p. 38.

32. David Chilton, *Productive Christians in an Age of Guilt-Manipulators,* 2nd. ed. (Tyler, Tex.: Institute for Christian Economics, 1981), pp. 65-66.

33. Herbert Schlossberg, *Idols for Destruction* (Nashville, Tenn.: Thomas Nelson, 1983), pp. 314-15.

34. John Naisbitt, *Megatrends* (New York: Warner Books, 1982), p. 153.

35. R. J. Rushdoony, *The Institutes of Biblical Law* (Phillipsburg, N.J.: Presbyterian and Reformed Publishing Co., 1973), p. 249.

36. Chilton, p. 85.

37. See Grant, *Grand Illusions*, pp. 87-104.

38. Schlossberg, p. 314.

39. Gary DeMar, *God and Government: Issues in Biblical Perspective, Vol. 2* (Atlanta, Ga.: American Vision Press, 1984), p. 212.

Chapter 6—Faith: Developing a Mission

1. Alvin Toffler, *Future Shock* (New York: Bantam, 1971), p. 158.

2. E. F. Schumacher, *Small Is Beautiful: Economics as if People Mattered* (New York: Harper & Row, 1975), p. 82.

3. James Sire, *How to Read Slowly* (Downers Grove, Ill.: Inter-Varsity Press, 1978), pp. 14-15.

4. Cornelius Van Til, *The Defense of the Faith* (Phillipsburg, N.J.: Presbyterian and Reformed Publishing Co., 1976), p. 8.

5. Franky Schaeffer, *Addicted to Mediocrity* (Westchester, Ill.: Crossway Books, 1981).

6. Elton Trueblood, quoted in D. Bruce Lockerbie, *The Timeless Moment* (Westchester, Ill.: Crossway Books, 1980), p. 63.

7. Note: James B. Jordan, *Through New Eyes: Developing a Biblical View of the World* (Brentwood, Tenn.: Wolgemuth & Hyatt, 1988).

8. See for example, Alexander Schmemann *For the Life of the World* (Crestwood, N.Y.: St. Vladimir's Seminary Press, 1973); and David Chilton, *The Days of Vengeance: An Exposition of the Book of Revelation* (Fort Worth, Tex.: Dominion Press, 1987).

9. James B. Jordan, letter to the author, 11 November 1984.

10. For a speakers' bureau, contact: The Christian Worldview Institute, P.O. Box 185066, Fort Worth, TX 76181.

11. A comprehensive manual for the charity work of deacons is: George Grant, *To The Work: An Operations Manual for Biblical Charity Ministries* (Tyler, Tex.: Institute for Christian Economics, 1988).

12. *Wall Street Journal*, 3 Jan. 1985.
13. Francis A. Schaeffer, *A Christian Manifesto* (Westchester, Ill.: Crossway Books, 1981), p. 17.

Chapter 7—Family: Charity Begins at Home

1. *Kansas City Times*, 6 Aug. 1983.
2. Ellen Baxter and Kim Hopper, *Homeless Adults on the Streets of New York City* (New York: Community Service Society, 1981).
3. Ellen Baxter, "Geel, Belguim: A Radical Model for the Integration of Deviancy," in *The Community Imperative* (Philadelphia: Community Care Organization, 1980), p. 67.
4. Gary North, *Unconditional Surrender: God's Program for Victory* (Tyler, Tex.: Geneva Press, 1981), p. 96.
5. Mary Pride, *The Way Home* (Westchester, Ill.: Crossway Books, 1985), p. 185.
6. *American Opinion Magazine*, January 1985.
7. *The Utah Register*, November 1980.
8. *American Opinion Magazine*, January 1985.
9. *The Utah Register*, November 1980.
10. Richard Halverson, *How I Changed My Thinking About the Church* (Grand Rapids, Mich.: Zondervan Publishing House, 1972), pp. 73-74.
11. Frank Tillapaugh, *The Church Unleashed* (Ventura, Calif.: Regal Books, 1982), p. 18.
12. R. J. Rushdoony, *The One and the Many* (Fairfax, Va.: Thoburn Press, 1978).

Chapter 8—Work: Facilitating Private Initiative

1. See J. William Jones, *Christ in the Camp: Religion in the Confederate Army* (Harrisburg, Va.: Sprinkle Publications, 1986).
2. Langdon Lowe, *The Work of God in the South* (London: Murray, Stockbrough, and Wilson, 1896), pp. 241-42.
3. Ibid., pp. 264-69.
4. Ibid., p. 114.

Chapter 9—Who and What: Identifying Needs

1. R. J. Rushdoony, *Politics of Guilt and Pity* (Fairfax, Va.: Thoburn Press, 1978).
2. Gary North, "Bread and Butter Evangelism," in *The Journal of Christian Reconstruction*, Symposium on Evangelism, Vol. VIII, No. 2 (Winter, 1981).
3. Robert Thompson, *Unemployed* (Downers Grove, Ill.: Inter-Varsity Press, 1983), p. 5.
4. In 1986, I too lived on the streets of New York City with the homeless. The results of that experience are recorded in my book *The Dispossessed: Homelessness in America* (Westchester, Ill.: Crossway Books, 1986).

Chapter 10—Cooperation: Pooling Resources

1. Harv Oostdyk, *Step One: The Gospel and the Ghetto* (Basking Ridge, N.J.: Sonlife International, 1983).

2. Yes, there is such a thing as a "Calvinistic Methodist." In fact, it was the un-swerving Calvinist, George Whitefield, who actually founded the Methodist movement. It wasn't until much later that the Arminian Wesley brothers became involved in the work. See Arnold Dallimore, *George Whitefield: A Biography* (Westchester, Ill.: Crossway Books, 1979).
3. William Stranton, *The Antiochian League* (Des Moines, Iowa: The Methodist Common Fund, 1939).
4. Oostdyk, P. 253.
5. J. L. G. Harringdon, *The Social Service Charities* (Manchester, U.K.: Ehrhardt Books, 1916), p. 3.
6. Gary North, *Backward, Christian Soldiers?* (Tyler, Tex.: Institute for Christian Economics, 1984), p. 182.
7. See Rousas John Rushdoony, *The One and the Many* (Fairfax, Va.: Thoburn Press, [1971] 1978), p. 129ff.
8. Eric Hayden, *Letting the Lion Loose* (Glasgow, U.K.: Forsyth Middleton and Co., Ltd., 1984), p. 52.
9. George Getschow, interview with author, 23 June 1983.

Chapter 11—Jobs: The Bootstrap Ethic

1. Charles Loch Mowat, *The Charity Organization Society, 1869-1913* (London: Methuen and Co., 1961), p. 35.
2. Ibid.
3. Charles Haddon Spurgeon, quoted by Joshua Wheelright, *Societies of Care* (New York: Wilson and Wilson Publishers, 1962), p. 107.
4. *Wall Street Journal*, 19 Jan. 1983.
5. Ibid.
6. *Statistical Abstract*, February 1988.
7. *Tulsa World*, 4 Aug. 1983.
8. Ibid.
9. Jonathan Stratten, *Foreign Trade: A History of Capitalism's Demise from 1947-1980* (Pasadena, Tex.: Jacinto Press, 1982), p. 36.
10. Ibid.
11. John Naisbitt, *The Years Ahead* (Washington, D.C.: Amacom, 1984), p.6.
12. Ibid., p. 9.
13. Thomas MacKay, *Methods of Social Reform* (London: John Murray, 1896), p. 13.
14. George Rogers Wooldridge, *Collected Works* (Dublin, U.K.: McCarthy and Ian, 1919), p. 13.
15. Bolton Averson, *Homiletical Excellence and Literary Vision* (Kansas City, Kan.: Nazarene Schools Press, 1979), p. 42.
16. See Appendix A.
17. See Jack Strauss, *Financial Freedom* (Brentwood, Tenn.: Wolgemuth & Hyatt, 1988).
18. See Dale and Kathy Martin, *Living Well* (Brentwood, Tenn.: Wolgemuth & Hyatt, 1988).
19. Gary North, *Government by Emergency* (Fort Worth, Tex.: American Bureau of Economic Research, 1983), p. 256.
20. Robert Kuttner, *Economic Illusion: False Choices Between Prosperity and Social Justice* (Boston: Houghton Mifflin Co., 1984), p. 13.
21. Charles Murray, *Losing Ground* (New York: Basic Books, 1984), p. 61.

Chapter 12 — Food: Loaves and Fishes

1. Thomas MacKay, *Methods of Social Reform* (London: John Murray, 1896), pp. 259-60.
2. *Houston Post*, 18 Oct. 1984.
3. *The Brown Bag Project* was originally developed in early 1982 by the staff workers at HELP Services in Houston. The concept was later fine-tuned by Biblical charity volunteers in Colorado Springs. See Bernard Thompson, *Good Samaritan Faith* (Ventura, Calif.: Regal Books, 1984) pp.109-14.

Chapter 13 — Shelter: No Room in the Inn

1. Lawrence Barreara, *The Housing Depletion Crisis* (New York: The Community Social Service Society, 1988) p. 47.
2. Ibid.
3. Charles Jencks, *Post-modern Architecture* (New York: Rizzoli, 1983), p. 62.
4. Oscar Wilde, *Collected Vignettes* (New York: Oldenberg and Sons, 1981), p. 204.
5. David and Ruth Rupprecht, *Radical Hospitality* (Phillipsburg, N.J.: Presbyterian and Reformed Publishing Co., 1983), p. 13.
6. Karen Burton Mains, *Open Heart, Open Home* (Elgin, Ill.: David C. Cook Publishing Co., 1981).
7. Virginia Hall, *Be My Guest* (Old Tappan, N.J.: Fleming H. Revell Co., 1981).
8. Mary Pride, *The Way Home* (Westchester, Ill.: Crossway Books, 1985).
9. Ibid., p. 188.
10. This alternative is discussed in some detail — and with technical analysis in my book, *The Dispossessed: Homelessness in America* (Westchester, Ill.: Crossway Books, 1986) pp. 97-110.
11. Ibid.; and Millard Fuller, *No More Shacks* (Waco, Tex.: Word Books, 1986).
12. Ibid.; and Anthony Campolo, *Ideas for Social Action* (Grand Rapids, Mich.: Zondervan, 1983).
13. Ibid., and Johnathan Kozol, *Rachel and Her Children* (New York: Crown Books, 1988).
14. Ibid.; and Stuart Butler and Anna Kondratas, *Out of the Poverty Trap* (New York: Free Press, 1987).
15. Ibid.
16. Ibid.
17. Ibid.; and Michael B. Katz, *In the Shadow of the Poorhouse: A Social History of Welfare in America* (New York: Basic Books, 1986).
18. The numbers of homeless are hotly contested by social policy experts. For an analysis of their game of percentage point Ping-Pong see my book *The Dispossessed*, pp. 28-33.

Chapter 14 — Obedience: Go with What You've Got

1. John Rippon, *The Early Sermons of Rev. John Rippon at Park Street* (Southwark, U.K.: Sword of Life Books, 1958), p. 471.
2. Raymond T. McNally, *Baptist Life in 19th-century England* (Memphis, Tenn.: The Baptist Historical Society, 1963), p. 56.
3. Arnold Dallimore, *Spurgeon* (Chicago: Moody Press, 1984), p. 130.

4. David Chilton, *Paradise Restored* (Fort Worth, Tex.: Dominion Press, 1985), pp. 213-14.

Appendix A — A Social Gospel?

1. Walter Rauschenbusch, *A Theology for the Social Gospel* (New York: Harper Brothers, 1917).
2. Ronald H. Nash, ed., *Liberation Theology* (Milford, Mich.: Mott Media, 1984).
3. Francis A. Schaeffer, *A Christian Manifesto* (Westchester, Ill.: Crossway Books, 1981).
4. Ibid., p. 64.
5. Eusebius Bobrinskoi, *Social Thought in the Early Church: Alms, Healing, and Dominion* (New York: Slavic International Press, 1949), p. 62.
6. Ibid., p. 79.
7. Ibid., p. 84.
8. Ibid., p. 91.
9. Ibid., p. 85.
10. Hardin Blanchard, *The Forerunner of the Reformation: An Analysis of the Hussite Movement* (London: Lollard Publication Board, 1927), p. 136.
11. John Dillenberger, ed., *Martin Luther* (New York: Doubleday, 1961), p. 18.
12. Philip Schaff, ed., *Creeds of Christendom* (Grand Rapids, Mich.: Baker Book House, 1977), pp. 3:24-25.
13. Ibid., pp. 3:410-413.
14. *Heidleberg Catechism* (Toronto: Reformed Educational Board Press, 1962), p. 78.
15. *The Confession of Faith of the Presbyterian Church in the United States* (Richmond, Va., John Knox Press, 1942), pp. 95-96.
16. Matthew Henry, *Commentary on the Whole Bible* (Old Tappan, N.J.: Fleming H. Revell, 1969), p. 981.
17. Edward Hickman, ed., *The Works of Jonathan Edwards* (Edinburgh: Banner of Truth, 1979), p. 237.

Appendix B — The Villars Statement on Relief and Development

1. For additional copies of this statement in brochure form or for response and expressions of concern contact: The Villars Committee on Relief and Development, Office of Communications, P.O. Box 26010, Philadelphia, PA 19128.

ABOUT THE AUTHOR

A pastor for more than a decade, George Grant is now the director of the Christian Worldview Institute, an educational outreach and service ministry. His work with the poor has been profiled in *The Wall Street Journal*, ABC's "Nightline," CBN's "700 Club," the *Christian Herald*, *Moody Monthly*, the *Houston Post*, the *Dallas Times-Herald*, the *Columbus Citizen-Journal*, the *Houston Chronicle*, Mutual Radio, and numerous other national media outlets.

Mr. Grant is a popular speaker and the author of several books on social issues and theology:

In the Shadow of Plenty: Biblical Principles of Welfare & Poverty

The Dispossessed: Homelessness in America

The Changing of the Guard: Biblical Principles of Political Action

A Christian Response to Dungeons & Dragons (with Peter Leithart)

Grand Illusions: The Legacy of Planned Parenthood

To the Work: A Step-by-Step Guide for Biblical Charity Ministries

For information regarding booking George Grant for speaking engagements or to be placed on his newsletter mailing list, please contact:

The Christian Worldview Institute
P. O. Box 185066
Fort Worth, TX 76181

COLOPHON

The typeface for the text of this book is *Baskerville*. Its creator, John Baskerville (1706-1775), broke with tradition to reflect in his type the rounder, yet more sharply cut lettering of eighteenth-century stone inscriptions and copy books. The type foreshadows modern design in such novel characteristics as the increase in contrast between thick and thin strokes and the shifting of stress from the diagonal to the vertical strokes. Realizing that this new style of letter would be most effective if cleanly printed on smooth paper with genuinely black ink, he built his own presses, developed a method of hot-pressing the printed sheet to a smooth, glossy finish, and experimented with special inks. However, Baskerville did not enter into general commercial use in England until 1923.

Copy editing by Nancye Willis
Cover design by Kent Puckett Associates, Atlanta, Georgia
Typography by Thoburn Press, Tyler, Texas
Printed and bound by Maple-Vail Book Manufacturing Group
Manchester, Pennsylvania
Cover Printing by Weber Graphics, Chicago, Illinois